Emerging-Economy State and International Policy Studies

This is the first series to highlight research into the processes and impacts of the state building and economic development of developing countries in the non-Western World that have recently come to influence global economy and governance. It offers a broad and interactive forum for discussions about the challenges of these countries and the responses of other countries to their rise. The term 'emerging-economy state,' a part of the series title, or its shorthand 'emerging states,' is intended to promote dialogues between economists who have discussed policy problems faced by 'emerging-market economies' and scholars in political science and international relations who have discussed 'modern state formation.' Many emerging states are still in the middle-income status and not immune from the risk of falling into the middle-income trap. The manner of their external engagement is different from that of the high-income countries. Their rise has increased the uncertainty surrounding the world. To reduce the uncertainty, good understanding of their purpose of politics and state capacity as well as their economies and societies would be required. Although the emerging states are far from homogenous, viewing them as a type of countries would force us into understand better the similarity and differences among the emerging states and those between them and the high-income countries, which would in turn to help countries to ensure peace and prosperity. The series welcomes policy studies of empirical, historical, or theoretical nature from a micro, macro, or global point of view. It accepts, but does not call for, interdisciplinary studies. Instead, it aims to promote transdisciplinary dialogues among a variety of disciplines, including but not limited to area studies, economics, history, international relations, and political science. Relevant topics include emerging states' economic policies, social policies, and politics, their external engagement, ensuing policy reactions of other countries, ensuing social changes in different parts of the world, and cooperation between the emerging states and other countries to achieve the Sustainable Development Goals (SDGs). The series welcomes both monographs and edited volumes that are accessible to academics and interested general readers.

Satoru Kumagai · Masashi Nakamura

Economic Development Strategies

Insights from Malaysia on Overcoming the 'Middle-Income Trap'

Springer

Satoru Kumagai
Institute of Developing Economies, Japan
External Trade Organization (IDE-JETRO)
Chiba, Japan

Masashi Nakamura
Institute of Developing Economies, Japan
External Trade Organization (IDE-JETRO)
Chiba, Japan

ISSN 2524-5023 ISSN 2524-5031 (electronic)
Emerging-Economy State and International Policy Studies
ISBN 978-981-95-6898-7 ISBN 978-981-95-6899-4 (eBook)
https://doi.org/10.1007/978-981-95-6899-4

This Springer imprint is published by the registered company Springer Nature Singapore Pte Ltd.
The registered company address is: 152 Beach Road, #21-01/04 Gateway East, Singapore 189721, Singapore

Preface

This book aims to provide a comprehensive overview of Malaysia's political and economic transformations over the past half-century and to derive insights for escaping the "middle-income trap." It is the outcome of a research project conducted by the Institute of Developing Economies, Japan External Trade Organization (IDE-JETRO) from 2019 to 2021, entitled "Background and Prospects of Political Change in Malaysia." The discrepancy between the original research project title and the book's content reflects the dramatic political upheavals that occurred in Malaysia during the research period. While the rapid political developments forced us to make significant changes to our research plan, we believe this ultimately worked in our favor, providing us with an opportunity to examine Malaysia's long-term political economy comprehensively. This research was also supported by a Grant-in-Aid for Scientific Research from the Japan Society for the Promotion of Science (JSPS) ("Democratization from Competitive Authoritarianism: Political Economy of Malaysia's Change of Government," Grant Number 19K01466).

The authors were able to write this book, thanks to the accumulated research by our predecessors at the Institute of Developing Economies. We owe a great deal to the accumulated research spanning the past 50 years, including the Yearbook of Asian Affairs and various Malaysian studies conducted over the years. Furthermore, through a JSPS project "Elucidating Interaction Patterns between Politics and Economics in Emerging Countries" (Grant Number 15K21728), conducted primarily at the National Graduate Institute for Policy Studies, we had the opportunity to compare Malaysia with other developing countries. We would like to express our sincere gratitude to all those who participated in these research projects and have been engaged in Malaysian studies and research in developing countries.

Moreover, since we began conducting field research at the Institute of Developing Economies in the 1990s, we could not have developed our "firsthand understanding" of Malaysia without the cooperation of hundreds of companies, government agencies, and researchers who accommodated our visits and interviews. Kumagai is particularly grateful to Dr. Zakaria Abdul Rashid (who was executive director at that time) and all the staff at the Malaysian Institute of Economic Research (MIER), who accepted him as a visiting researcher and treated him exceptionally well.

We would also like to express our sincere thanks to Ms. Mai Fujita (Regional Studies Center, IDE-JETRO) for reviewing the manuscript draft and providing many valuable comments, Mr. Yasuhiro Katsu (Research Dissemination Advisor, IDE-JETRO) for his advice on making the book more accessible from the planning stage, and Ms. Juno Kawakami, Editor at Springer Japan, for undertaking the publication of this book.

It would be our greatest pleasure if this book serves not only as a comprehensive guide to Malaysia's political economy but also as a reference for policymakers in developing countries when considering their development strategies, and continues to be read for years to come.

Chiba, Japan

Satoru Kumagai
Masashi Nakamura

Contents

About the Authors

Satoru Kumagai is a Senior Researcher at the Development Studies Center of the Institute of Developing Economies, Japan External Trade Organization (IDE-JETRO). He holds an MSc in Global Market Economics from the London School of Economics and Political Science and a Master's degree in Media and Governance from Keio University. His research focuses on economic development and regional integration in Asia, with particular attention to strategies for overcoming the middle-income trap.

Masashi Nakamura is the Director-General of the Area Studies Center at the Institute of Developing Economies, Japan External Trade Organization (IDE-JETRO). He earned his Ph.D. from the University of Tokyo and holds a Master's degree in International Studies from Tokyo University of Foreign Studies. Dr. Nakamura's research centers on comparative development strategies and the political economy of Asia, with a particular focus on Malaysia.

Chapter 1
The Theory of the Middle-Income Trap and Malaysia

1.1 Aims of This Book

Since the early 2010s, the term "middle-income trap" has frequently appeared in newspapers and other media. As China and some ASEAN countries are currently in the middle-income stage, the "middle-income trap" has become a popular concept for analyzing economic development in East Asia.

Although the phrase "middle-income trap" may seem easy to understand, it is actually quite complex. The standard explanation—that middle-income countries cannot compete with high-income countries in terms of technology or with low-income countries in terms of wages, leading to a decline in international competitiveness and stagnant economic growth—seems intuitive and convincing. However, the definition of "middle-income countries" and the extent to which a "trap" refers to economic stagnation are not universally agreed upon.

This book aims to reveal the true nature of the "middle-income trap" from economic, political, and institutional perspectives. By focusing on Malaysia, a characteristic middle-income country, and analyzing it in depth, we will explore this phenomenon while examining other middle-income countries worldwide.

According to the World Bank's four income categories, Malaysia is classified as an "upper-middle-income" country as of 2021. Having been in this category for nearly 30 years since 1992, Malaysia is considered to be caught in the "middle-income trap" (Fig. 1.1). However, Malaysia has been enjoying stable economic growth and is projected to become a high-income country by the end of the 2020s. Nevertheless, the World Bank's threshold for high-income countries rises annually, and Malaysia has not been able to keep pace for decades, leading to the perception that it is "trapped."

In middle-income trap studies, Northeast Asia's high-growth economies, such as Japan, South Korea, and Taiwan, are often cited as examples of economies that successfully avoided the trap. However, these "elite" East Asian economies have unique backgrounds from a global perspective. Other countries that became high-income economies in the late twentieth century and beyond also have particular

S. Kumagai and M. Nakamura, *Economic Development Strategies*, Emerging-Economy State and International Policy Studies, https://doi.org/10.1007/978-981-95-6899-4_1

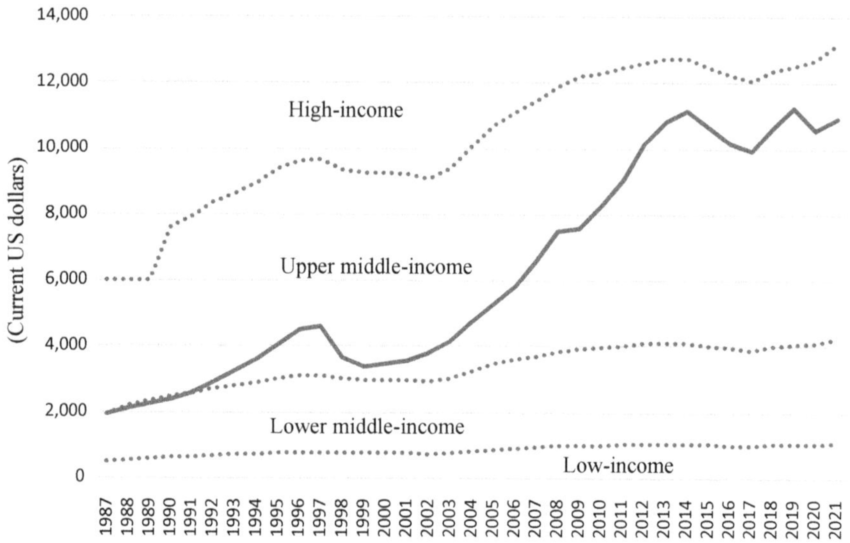

Fig. 1.1 Changes in Malaysia's per capita income level (1987–2021). *Source* Created by the authors based on World Development Indicators (WDI)

circumstances. Singapore and Hong Kong are city-states with small populations and no rural areas, while the high-income Middle Eastern countries are all oil-producing nations. The countries of Eastern Europe have historically been developed regions. In this context, Malaysia is likely to become the first "ordinary" country to join the ranks of high-income countries.

This book analyzes Malaysia's trajectory from a perspective different from conventional studies on the middle-income trap, focusing on how it manages to escape the trap. Until the mid-2010s, research on this topic was rather simplistic, identifying trapped countries and highlighting their deficiencies compared to those that escaped. Since the late 2010s, however, studies have argued that most countries know what they need to do to achieve economic growth, but the real problem is that they cannot implement the necessary measures.

Following this new line of research, this book examines Malaysia's moderate but steady economic growth. By analyzing the problems faced by Malaysia at each stage of its development and how the government has responded to them from both political and economic perspectives, it offers insights into the true nature of the middle-income trap and provides hints on how to escape it.

1.2 What is the Middle-Income Trap?

First, let us review the definition of the key phrase "middle-income trap." The middle-income trap refers to a situation in which a low-income country has developed to the middle-income stage through economic growth, but for some reason, the economic growth rate declines, and the country is unable to enter the high-income country stage. The reason why the economic growth rate declines in the middle-income stage is often explained as "middle-income countries are inferior to high-income countries in terms of technology and inferior to low-income countries in terms of low labor costs, and thus lose international competitiveness."

The middle-income trap may seem like a simple concept when described as above. However, there is no fixed definition of either "middle-income" country (indicating moderate income level) or "trap" (meaning severe economic stagnation). Consequently, researchers have developed their own definitions of the middle-income trap when combining these terms. The situation in the late 2000s, when the research began, was that each researcher had their own definition of the middle-income trap. Early studies on the middle-income trap first focused on defining middle-income countries and the nature of the trap, then identifying which countries were caught in it. For example, according to Felipe's definition by the Asian Development Bank, 35 countries in the world were in the middle-income trap as of 2010, and in Asia, Malaysia, the Philippines, and Sri Lanka were considered to be in the trap.[1]

Felipe's definition of the middle-income trap is as follows. First, he defines countries with a per capita income level of less than US$2000 in purchasing power parity (PPP) as of 1990 as low-income countries, between US$2000 and US$7250 as lower-middle-income countries, between US$7250 and US$10,750 as upper-middle-income countries, and above that as high-income countries. This is his classification and differs from the World Bank's classification. Based on the median value of economic growth data for 124 countries from 1950 to 2010, he then defined countries that took longer than usual to move up one income level to a higher income category as falling into the "middle-income trap" (Fig. 1.2).

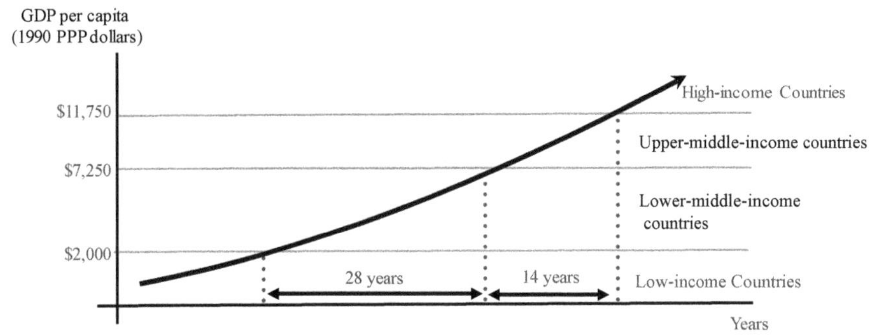

Fig. 1.2 Definition of the middle income trap. *Source* Created by the authors based on Felipe et al. (2012)

Specifically, a lower-middle-income country is in a middle-income trap if it has taken more than 28 years to transition to an upper-middle-income country (an annual average of less than 4.7% in terms of per capita income growth). An upper-middle-income country is in a middle-income trap if it has taken more than 14 years to transition to a high-income country (less than 3.5% of the same).

What happens if we apply Felipe's definition to Malaysia? Malaysia's entry into the lower-middle-income group was in 1969, and its entry into the upper-middle-income group was in 1996. The time required for Malaysia to move from a lower-middle-income country to an upper-middle-income country is 27 years, barely less than the "trap" limit of 28 years, thus avoiding the lower-middle-income trap. However, Malaysia had remained an upper-middle-income country for 15 years as of 2010, when Felipe's study was conducted, and this had already exceeded the 14-year limit for transitioning to a high-income country, so Malaysia is considered to be in the middle-income trap.[2]

1.3 Does the Middle-Income Trap Really Exist?

Here, we will consider the basic premise of this book, "Does the middle-income trap really exist in the first place?" In fact, there is considerable controversy over whether middle-income countries are particularly prone to the "trap" compared to high-income or low-income countries. To confirm this with data, we set a rather strict definition of "trap" as "no growth at all or rather a decline in per capita income compared to 10 years ago" and organized the data (Fig. 1.3). The meaning of the numbers is the average of the percentage of the period 1960–2000 in which the countries in each category were in the "trap."

The data shows that the probability of falling into the "trap" decreases as one moves up the income ladder. Low-income countries are six times more likely to fall

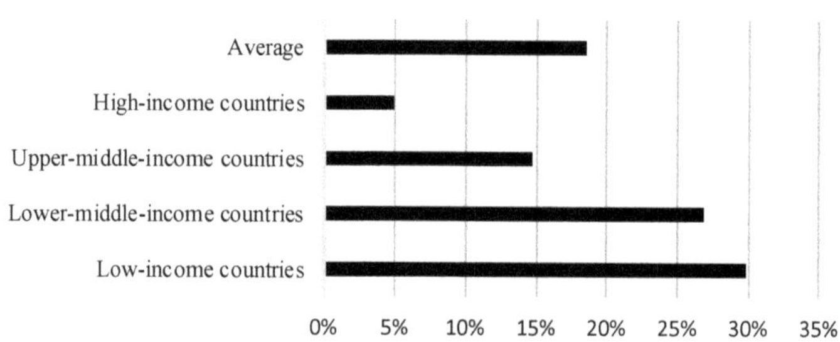

Fig. 1.3 Proportion of time spent in "Trap" by income level (1960–2000). *Source* Created by the author based on Kumagai (2015) Table 1

into the trap than high-income countries. As for middle-income countries, lower-middle-income countries are twice as likely to fall into the trap as upper-middle-income countries. Thus, middle-income countries are indeed more likely to fall into the trap than high-income countries, but they are better off than low-income countries.

Can we conclude from this data that the middle-income trap does not exist? Low-income countries are the most likely to fall into the trap. However, lower-middle-income countries are almost as likely to fall into the trap as low-income countries, and upper-middle-income countries are three times more likely to fall into the trap than high-income countries. Therefore, while a "trap" no doubt exists for low-income countries,[3] the evidence clearly supports the existence of a "trap" for middle-income countries as well. It is difficult for a country to start out as a low-income country, continue its economic growth, and become a high-income country because there are traps everywhere in between.

In fact, data shows that it is not easy for low-income and middle-income countries to grow steadily and become high-income countries. South Korea and Taiwan are the only two cases in the world that have successfully transitioned from low-income to high-income status in recent decades. Similarly, there are only three cases in Asia (Japan, Hong Kong, and Singapore) that started as lower-middle-income countries and entered high-income status. Globally, only European countries (mainly in Eastern Europe) and Saudi Arabia have achieved the same. Japan is the only country other than Europe with a sizable population and achieving high-income status through industrialization.

In other words, even if a low-income country has successfully entered the middle-income stage, it is not safe to say that it has escaped a "trap" that will bring economic growth to a halt. The "trap" of stagnant economic growth awaits even at the middle-income stage. Of the countries that have passed through numerous traps to reach high-income status since 1950, only Japan, South Korea, and Taiwan remain, except for historically advanced European countries, city-states with special conditions, and oil-producing countries.

When considering such a tough road to becoming a high-income country, it is significant that governments and international organizations of East Asian countries that have entered the middle-income stages on the path of economic growth in the past decade have discussed measures for further economic development using the middle-income trap as a common framework for analysis.

1.4 The Middle-Income Trap and the "Convergence" of Growth Rates

In fact, the possibility of a decline in the rate of economic growth as economic development progresses has been pointed out since the 1950s, long before the middle-income trap argument attracted attention. This is because a phenomenon called "convergence" of the economic growth rate was predicted based on the Solow-type economic growth model, which is a representative mathematical model of economic growth. The following is a simple explanation. First, assume that capital (e.g., machinery) and labor are needed to produce something. There is no doubt that to increase production, we need to increase machinery and labor. If we increase machinery and labor "in balance," we can indefinitely increase output.

Now, let us consider "per capita" production. Let us consider the process of cutting a loaf of bread into six slices and packing them into bags. If one worker performing this process manually is given a machine that automatically cuts the bread into six slices, the hourly production rate will dramatically increase. Then, if two machines are given to the same worker, the output will not double, but it will still increase, because one worker will have to operate two machines simultaneously. Then how about a third machine? If we consider the fourth machine and beyond, we will see that the rate of increase in production declines as the number of machines per worker increases. This is called the law of diminishing returns: once capital has increased to a certain point, output per worker will not increase at all.

The same can be said for national economic growth. Low-income countries are analogous to the workers who do not own a single machine. By investing in capital goods, high production growth can be expected. An increase in per capita income in a country is roughly equivalent to an increase in the number of machines owned by workers. On the other hand, just as giving additional machines to already well-equipped workers yields diminishing returns, further capital investment by middle-income countries is unlikely to lead to rapid economic growth, and the growth rate is likely to decline gradually.

If economic growth rates are higher in lower-income countries, then after a long period of time, low-income countries will catch up with high-income countries, and the income levels of the world's countries will converge to the same level. Various empirical studies have been conducted to determine whether this "convergence hypothesis" actually holds. The empirical studies to date have shown no convergence for all countries in the world. Still, income levels tend to converge for groups of countries with similar conditions, such as states in the United States, prefectures in Japan, and European countries.

The economic growth trajectories of East Asian countries show that the economic growth rate always declines as the income level rises, even in high-growth countries. Figure 1.4 plots the relationship between per capita income and average growth rate by decade for Northeast Asian, Southeast Asian, and South American countries from the 1970s to the 2000s. In Northeast Asian and Southeast Asian countries, the economic growth rate tends to decline as the income level rises (moving to the right on the horizontal axis). In Malaysia, the growth rate of per capita income also seems to decline gradually on average as the income level rises. For Latin American countries, there is a period of negative per capita income growth at the middle-income level of $5000 to $10,000 per capita, which appears to be a typical middle-income trap (in Southeast Asia, a similar trend is seen in the Philippines at lower income levels).

Thus, if we follow the traditional Solow economic growth model, the growth rate will decline as economic growth proceeds due to the law of diminishing returns, and

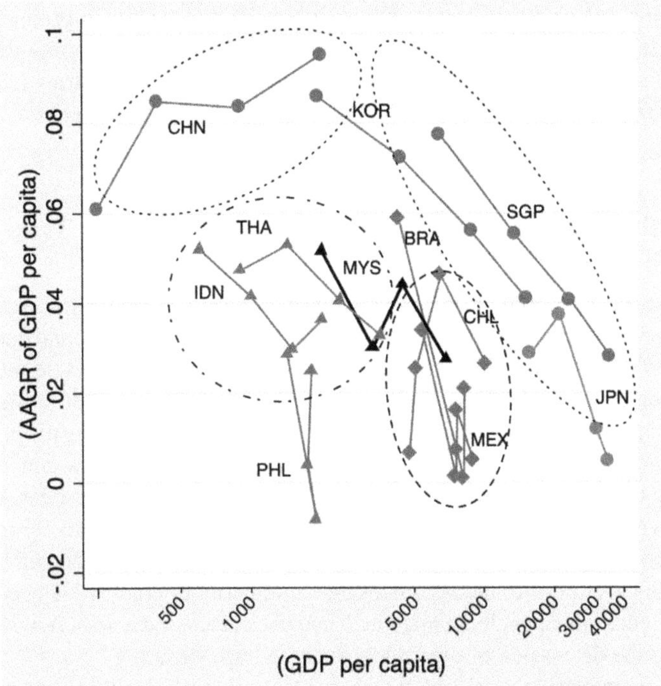

Fig. 1.4 The relationship between 10-year average income levels and per capita income growth rates (1970s–2000s). *Source* Calculated by the author from World Development Indicators (WDI), based on Todo (2015), Fig. 5.2

per capita income growth will stop at some point. How, then, can income continue to increase? In the Solow model, the answer is found in "technological progress." Even if the number of machines per worker does not change, economic growth can continue through technological progress (i.e., improvement in efficiency).

Economic growth that is neither derived from an increase in labor nor from an increase in capital is called the Solow residual, or total factor productivity (TFP). In fact, various studies have shown that between 30% and 50% of the economic growth in developed countries is due to this growth in TFP.[4]

In the 1990s, in "Myth of Asia's Miracle," Paul Krugman, who later won the Nobel Prize in Economics, warned that the rapid economic growth of East Asian countries was a "factor-input driven" rapid growth, in which massive amounts of labor and capital were invested and that it would slow down sooner or later. The middle-income trap arguments share his view.

Even if a low-income country can overcome the "poverty trap" by creating the conditions for economic development and achieving middle-income status through sustained economic growth, it will face diminishing returns as long as it continues to pursue factor input-driven growth that increases capital and labor inputs. Its economic growth rate will eventually decline. Few countries are able to compensate for this decline in the rate of economic growth with sustained increases in productivity and quickly reach the stage of high-income countries. The middle-income trap can be considered as the decline in the economic growth rate when countries fail to make the "shift" from factor input-driven growth to productivity-driven growth.

1.5 Institutions as the Cause of the Middle-Income Trap

Early studies of the middle-income trap focused on identifying countries that fall into the trap, comparing them with countries that do not fall into the trap, and determining what is missing. The characteristics of countries that fall into the middle-income trap are often identified as low-quality human capital, lack of advanced infrastructure, lack of access to financial systems, and high income inequality among the population.

In addition, studies have shown that what a country produces and exports is related to whether or not it falls into the middle-income trap. It has been noted that countries with more sophisticated and diversified exports are less likely to fall into the middle-income trap than countries that rely on a small number of low-grade exports. This is similar to the argument that "industrial upgrading" is necessary for sustainable economic development, which had been discussed in East Asian countries long before the discussion of the middle-income trap began.

Industrial upgrading refers to the shift of a country's leading industries from those that use large amounts of labor (labor-intensive industries) or natural resources (resource-intensive industries) to more sophisticated, capital- and technology-intensive ones.[5]

As mentioned above, the middle-income trap is a situation in which middle-income countries lose in international competition with low-income countries in terms of costs but cannot compete with high-income countries in international competition for technology and capital. This is, in other words, exactly the failure of industrial upgrading.

The factors identified in previous studies as contributing to the failure of industrial upgrading in middle-income countries are intuitively easy to understand. They include insufficient education and lagging human resource development; lack of local firms, especially small and medium-sized firms, in terms of both quality and quantity; inability to break away from dependence on imported components in the manufacturing industry; insufficient R&D efforts; and inadequate development of institutional infrastructure such as financial systems and physical infrastructure such as roads, ports, and electric power.

What is puzzling is why governments in middle-income countries are unable to address the issues, given that these impediments to economic development and industrial upgrading have been clearly identified through academic studies and accumulated experience. The more fundamental cause of the middle-income trap may, in fact, lie not so much in the lack of infrastructure, human resources, or SMEs but in the lack of government capacity to formulate and implement policies or in the absence of incentives for governments to implement industrial upgrading policies.

Recent studies of traps in middle-income countries have investigated this institutional and political issue more thoroughly than earlier studies. For example, studies have shown that countries with high-quality economic institutions relative to their income levels tend to grow faster initially. Still, as their economies grow, their growth tends to stagnate because the required higher-quality economic institutions cannot keep up with the pace of economic development.

1.6 Traps and Politics in Middle-Income Countries

The measures needed to step up from a middle-income country to a high-income country are more difficult to implement than those required to move from a low-income country to a middle-income country. This is because a shift from factor input-driven growth to productivity-driven growth involves the development of human resources and R&D capacity, which in turn requires considerable long-term investment and coordination among various stakeholders.

A wide range of institutions are necessary for industrial upgrading, including schools, vocational training schools, R&D promotion institutions, industry-academia collaboration organizations, and legal systems for protecting intellectual property rights. Since the development and improvement of these systems is very costly, a strong political entity is needed to promote the creation of such systems. This is why broad "upgrading coalitions" oriented toward expanding institutions are said to be most useful for middle-income countries to achieve high-income status.[6] The middle-income trap is not only an economic problem but also a political one.

Middle-income countries often experience serious social divisions during the development stage from low-income countries, which later become factors that impede the formation of "upgrading coalitions." Income inequality, the informal economy, and reliance on foreign direct investment (FDI) generated in the process of economic growth create fissures between the haves and have-nots, formal and informal workers, and foreign and local firms.[7] For example, the content of job training required by regular employees, who are guaranteed long-term employment, differs from that required by informal employees, whose jobs change after a few years. Even if local firms want social investment to improve their R&D capacity, foreign firms that conduct R&D mainly in their home country may not want to bear the cost of such investment. The elite in a disparate society will try to protect their vested interests even if the society's overall level of welfare declines. The more serious these divisions are, the more difficult it will be to create upgrading coalitions.

In addition to social cleavages, authoritarian political institutions also tend to form at the stage of development from low-income countries and are considered a factor that hinders the step up from middle-income to high-income countries.

Regarding the relationship between political institutions and economic development, some argue that democratic political institutions foster inclusive economic institutions, leading to technological innovation and productivity-driven growth.[8]

However, there is also a prevailing notion that premature expansion of political participation can lead to instability within the political system, consequently impeding the formulation and implementation of policies essential for economic development and growth. A study examining the relationship between civil liberties and economic growth in 146 countries between 1990 and 2010, found that low-income countries with lower levels of civil liberties tended to record higher growth rates relative to the level of GDP per capita.[9] However, this relationship reversed after the $8000 level, and countries with higher civil liberties tended to grow faster at higher income levels. It seems that restrictions on civil liberties may contribute to factor-intensive growth strategies but tend to impede productivity growth and innovative capacity development. If so, middle-income countries that have grown under authoritarian political institutions may find these institutions a hindrance to their aspirations to become high-income countries. The balance between economic and political development seems to be one of the factors that distinguish countries that fall into the middle-income trap from those that escape it.

1.7 The Middle-Income Trap and Malaysia

Malaysia is currently classified as an upper-middle-income country, but according to the World Bank, it is expected to become a high-income country by the end of the 2020s. Although it is often pointed out that Malaysia has fallen into the middle-income trap because it has remained an upper-middle-income country for a long period of time, tracing the trajectory of its economic growth shows that Malaysia has continued to achieve "moderate" economic growth over a long period (Fig. 1.5).

In the past 50 years, Malaysia's annual economic growth rate has been negative only four times. In each case, the country was caught up in the significant turbulence of the global economy and did not experience internally driven economic collapse. In all cases, positive growth was recorded in the year following negative growth, and the country never recorded 2 consecutive years of negative growth. Despite the impact of the 1997/98 Asian Financial Crisis and the 2008/09 Global Financial Crisis, Malaysia's average economic growth rate from 1990 to 2015 remained high at 5.9%. In the 5 years leading up to the COVID-19 pandemic (2014–2019), as Malaysia's per capita income approached $10,000, the average economic growth rate was a commendable 4.8%.

In other words, Malaysia is often categorized as a country falling into the middle-income trap. Although it is not an "elite country" in terms of economic growth with a series of double-digit economic growth rates, it is a unique country that has slowly continued its economic development and finally reached the point of becoming a high-income country. If Malaysia continues at this rate, it will likely become the first non-European country to achieve high-income status through industrialization among the "ordinary countries"—that is, after the "elite countries" such as Japan, South Korea, and Taiwan, and the "city-states" such as Singapore and Hong Kong.

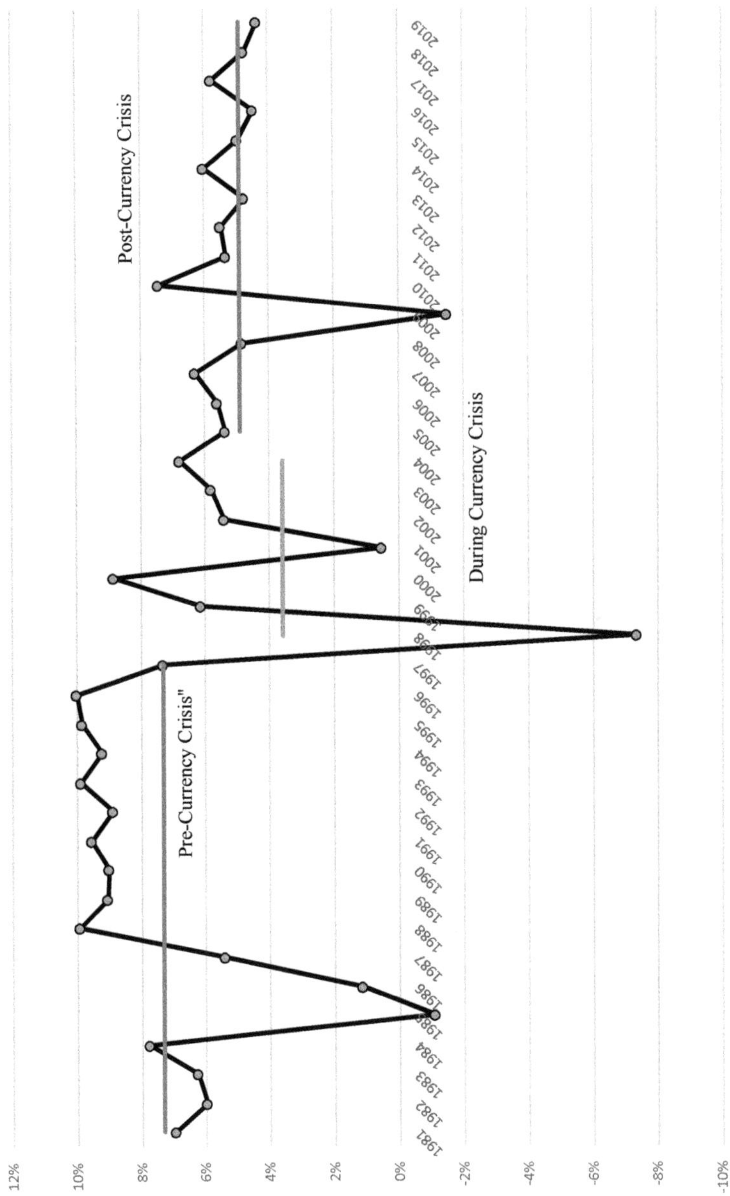

Fig. 1.5 Malaysia's real economic growth rate (1981–2019). *Source* Compiled by the author from World Development Indicators (WDI) and other sources

The Northeast Asian "elite" countries of Japan, South Korea, and Taiwan occupy a unique position in the world in terms of their remarkable cultural homogeneity. According to a study that indexed the cultural diversity of each country on a scale of 0–1 based on the number of major languages, percentage of speakers, and lexical similarity between languages, the average value for 188 countries/regions worldwide was 0.3521, while Japan and Korea were significantly lower, at 0.0119 (180th) and 0.0020 (182nd), respectively.[10] Taiwan is also low at 0.2487 (110th).

Previous studies have indicated that ethnic diversity tends to impede economic growth.[11] When the average value of the above cultural diversity index is calculated for each income level category, a pattern emerges: countries with lower income levels tend to show higher cultural diversity (Fig. 1.6). One of the factors that contribute to this relationship is the cost of cultural diversity in building and operating institutions. For example, in a multilingual society, the language used in public education is a major point of contention. While multilingual education increases educational costs due to the need for language-specific teachers and textbooks, education in a single language may not be sufficiently effective for children whose mother tongue is another language.

Malaysia's cultural diversity index is 0.5877 (42nd), considerably higher than the world average. Nevertheless, even within East Asia, Indonesia (0.6473) and the Philippines (0.5894) have higher values than Malaysia, while Thailand (0.4958) and Myanmar (0.4889) are also higher than the world average. Japan and Korea are outliers, while Malaysia is "normal" by global standards. Many countries face the challenge of coordinating their interests for institution building and improvement under cultural diversity.

In Malaysia, there are significant cultural differences, occupational and residential differences, and income disparities among ethnic groups. The general election of 1969 triggered an outpouring of dissatisfaction among the Malay masses, which led to

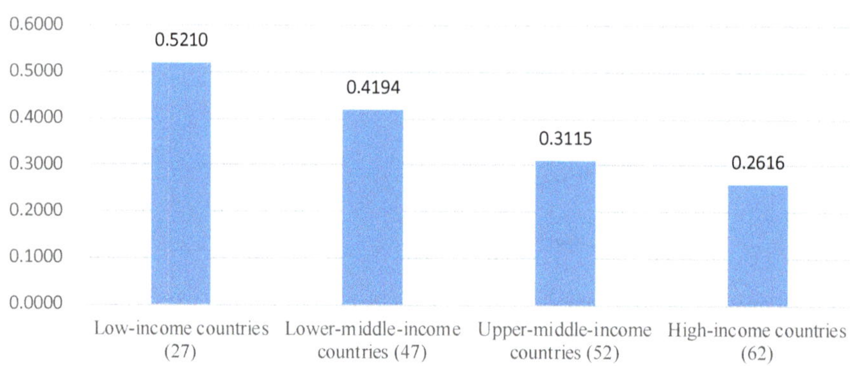

Fig. 1.6 Cultural diversity by income level (average values). *Note* Numbers in parentheses indicate the number of countries. Income categories are as of 2020. *Source* Created by the author based on Gören (2013, pp. 19–23) and WDI

serious riots. The initial New Economic Policy emphasized agricultural support and rural development, which, as discussed later, was also an effective growth strategy.

In the 1980s, however, the government was forced to reconsider its development strategy as the budget deficit ballooned and the international market for primary commodities deteriorated, leading to a recession. While the predominantly Chinese political parties called for a review of the government's support measures for the indigenous people, collectively known as "Bumiputeras," Malay politicians pressed the government to strengthen its support measures. When economic policy becomes a zero-sum game between ethnic groups, any measure favoring one group inevitably alienates the other. The government, caught between a rock and a hard place, sought to resolve the situation by expanding the economic pie. The government tried to create a win-win situation by linking the easing of Bumiputera support measures to economic recovery and the acceleration of growth.

The deregulation of foreign investment in export-oriented manufacturing industries that was implemented as part of this strategy served as a catalyst for Japanese companies to enter the country. In 1991, Prime Minister Mahathir announced his "Vision 2020", which set a goal for Malaysia to become a fully developed country by 2020, clearly prioritizing economic growth. Malaysia subsequently enjoyed a period of rapid growth and successfully managed to narrow inter-ethnic gaps while scaling back excessive inequality correction measures.

Thus, Malaysia has succeeded, at least so far, in both correcting the disparities and achieving economic growth while facing the problem of economic disparities among ethnic groups, a challenge that is typical of multi-ethnic developing countries.

Previous studies on the middle-income trap have often sought to learn from Japan, South Korea, and Taiwan, which have avoided falling into this trap. These studies have focused on their high educational standards, research and development efforts, and supporting institutions and industrial policies. However, for most of the world's countries that lack the exceptional characteristics of these Asian tigers, implementing such policies is inherently difficult, which is precisely why the middle-income trap has become a significant issue. In this regard, Malaysia, an ordinary country, has been continuing its moderate but steady economic growth and is striving to join the ranks of high-income nations. Perhaps we can derive more realistic lessons from Malaysia's experience.

1.8 Structure of This book

This book examines the theoretical mechanisms of economic development in developing countries through the lens of Malaysia's development trajectory. Figure 1.7 summarizes the "engines" that drive economic growth and the factors that impede economic growth for each stage of a country's economic development process, from the low-income country stage (bottom) to the high-income country stage (top). The left side of the figure shows supply-side factors, and the right side shows demand-side factors.

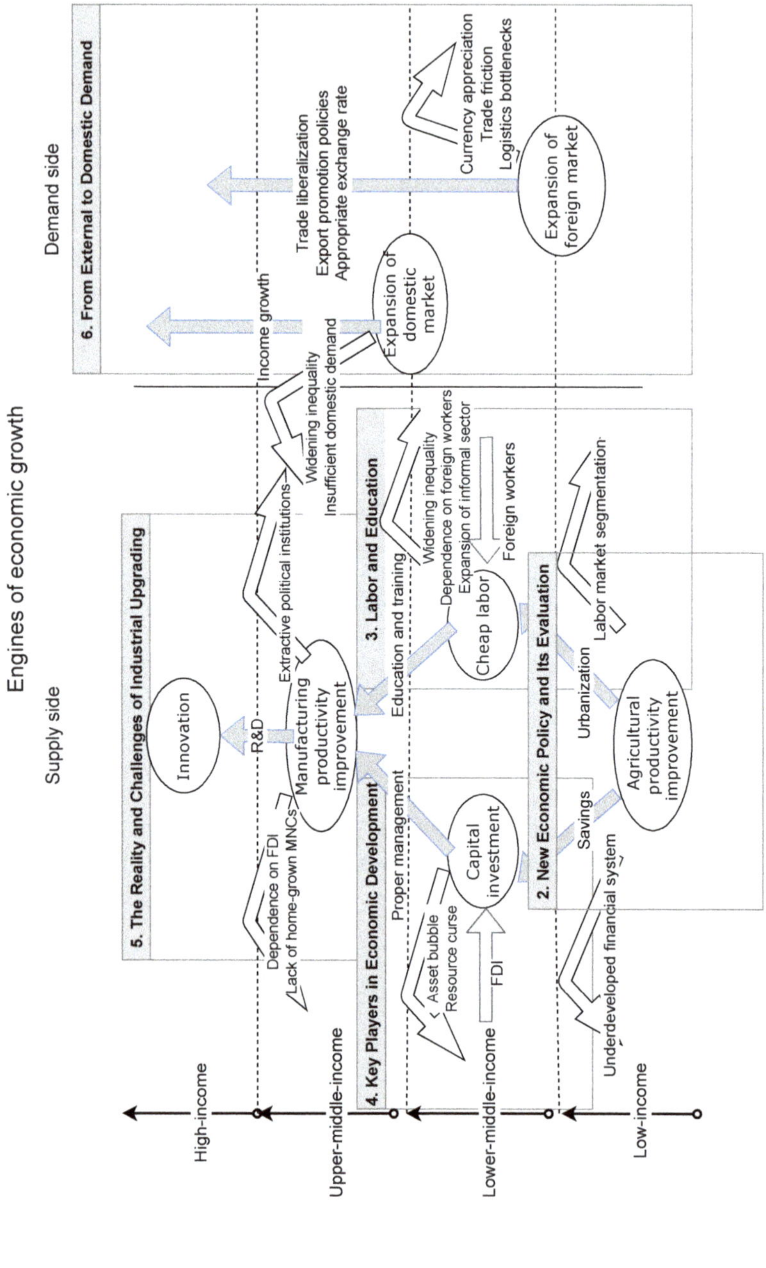

Fig. 1.7 Structure of this book. *Source* Authors

First, for low-income countries to initiate economic development, it is necessary to improve the productivity of the agricultural sector, which accounts for the majority share of the economy in many low-income countries. At the same time, the labor force freed from the agricultural sector and the surplus of products generated in the agricultural sector are invested as capital in the commercial and industrial sectors, thereby promoting economic development from low-income countries to lower-middle-income countries. Continuous economic development cannot be expected if the financial system that links rural surpluses to investment in the urban commercial and industrial sectors is underdeveloped or if the urban and rural labor markets are deeply divided. The first chapter of this book provides an overview of the economic situation in newly independent Malaysia. It shows that the "New Economic Policy" implemented in Malaysia since 1971, which promoted both rural development and urbanization, has been the driving force behind Malaysia's subsequent economic development.

Economic development in lower-middle-income countries proceeds through a quantitative expansion of capital and labor inputs. During this period, the commercial and industrial sectors expand mainly in urban areas, supported primarily by the inflow of cheap labor from rural areas. Thus, industrialization proceeds inextricably linked to urbanization. When the labor supply from rural areas is insufficient, some countries may introduce foreign workers. For a lower-middle-income country to become an upper-middle-income country, it is necessary to educate and train its workers and increase their productivity. However, income inequality, the expansion of informal labor, and dependence on foreign workers hinder education and training for workers. Chapter 3 discusses the role played by the influx of Malay workers from rural areas in the urbanization and industrialization of Malaysia from the 1970s to the 1990s and analyzes the impact of the influx of foreign workers, the transition of economic disparity, and the development of the education system.

In addition to the surplus generated in domestic rural areas, foreign direct investment plays a significant role in the economic development of lower-middle-income countries in many countries. As for the "enterprises" that are responsible for economic development as the substance of "capital," local private enterprises are often insufficiently developed in developing countries, and in many cases, foreign-owned enterprises and state-owned enterprises play a major role. To advance to the stage of upper-middle-income countries, each company must improve its productivity through appropriate management. On the other hand, when a developing country has abundant natural resources, industrial upgrading may be delayed because firms in different industries actively enter and invest in natural resource-related industries, attracted by high profit margins when resource prices soar. Furthermore, if capital flows excessively into real estate investment and a bubble occurs, it will hinder economic development in the long run. Chapter 4 analyzes the roles of domestic private firms, government-affiliated firms, and foreign-affiliated firms in economic development in Malaysia, how policies toward foreign and government-affiliated firms changed from the 1970s to the mid-2000s, and what the political background was to these changes.

For upper-middle-income countries to become high-income countries, it is essential for them to upgrade their industries, and in particular, for companies to focus on research and development (R&D). It is not easy for developing countries that depend on multinational corporations to upgrade their industries, and the challenge is how they can take on a high value-added portion of the global value chain (GVC) controlled by multinational corporations. In addition, an extractive political system is an obstacle to firms conducting R&D in developing countries. Innovation is stifled when free R&D is suppressed, or R&D results are restricted from reaching the market. Chapter 5 analyzes Malaysia's industrial upgrading using trade data and discusses the problems caused by dependence on MNCs, whether Malaysia's political system is "extractive" or not, and how it has been reformed in recent years.

So far, we have examined the process of a country's transition from a low-income country to a high-income country, mainly from the production side (left side of the figure). On the other side is the demand side (right side of the figure), where the produced goods are consumed. Many developing Asian countries have achieved rapid economic development through export-oriented industrialization that relies on overseas markets. However, export-oriented industrialization may lead to competition to lower labor and environmental standards to attract companies, create international trade and financial imbalances, and cause trade friction with export destinations. However, it is not easy to transform an export-oriented economy into an economy led by domestic demand. Chapter 6 traces how Malaysia achieved export-oriented industrialization and shows that the Malaysian economy has successfully shifted to a domestic demand-led economy since the mid-2000s. It also discusses the policy and political factors behind this shift.

Looking at Malaysia's economic development over time, it can be said that the policies of the Malaysian government aimed at economic development were "generally successful." On the other hand, not all policies were successful, and policies necessary at one stage of development sometimes created obstacles at the next stage. In Chapter 7, we review the discussions in Chapters 2 through 6 and discuss the remaining issues that need to be addressed if Malaysia is to continue its economic growth after becoming a high-income country.

Notes

1. Felipe et al. (2012).
2. Another definition of the middle-income trap is when a country that had been growing at an annual rate of 3.5% or higher experiences a decline in its economic growth rate exceeding 2%. This definition is problematic because it would classify many Asian countries as "trapped" during major economic events such as Japan's 1974 oil shock and the Asian Financial Crisis. Ultimately, which countries are considered to be in the middle-income trap varies depending on the definition used.
3. This trap that low-income countries tend to fall into is called the "poverty trap."
4. Easterly and Levine (2001).

5. Following the Solow growth model, industrial upgrading includes both increasing per capita capital stock (capital deepening) and raising technological levels through innovation and imitation (technological upgrading).
6. Doner and Schneider (2016).
7. Doner and Schneider (2016).
8. Acemoglu and Robinson (2012).
9. Dollar (2016).
10. Gören (2013).
11. See the following literature: Alesina et al. (2003), Alesina and La Ferrara (2005), and Montalvo and Reynal-Querol (2005).

References

Acemoglu D, Robinson JA (2012) Why nations fail: the origins of power, prosperity, and poverty. Crown Business, New York

Alesina A, Devleeschauwer A, Easterly W et al (2003) Fractionalization. J Econ Growth 8:155–194

Alesina A, La Ferrara E (2005) Ethnic diversity and economic performance. J Econ Lit 43:762–800

Dollar D (2016) Institutional quality and growth traps. In: Hutchinson FE, Das SB (eds) Asia and the middle-income trap. Routledge, Abingdon, pp 161–178

Doner RF, Schneider BR (2016) The middle-income trap: more politics than economics. World Polit 68(4):608–644

Easterly W, Levine R (2001) It's not factor accumulation: stylized facts and growth models. World Bank Econ Rev 15(2):177–219

Felipe J, Abdon A, Kumar U (2012) Tracking the middle-income trap: what is it, who is in it, and why? Working Paper No. 715, Levy Economics Institute of Bard College, Annandale-on-Hudson

Gören E (2013) Economic effects of domestic and neighbouring countries' cultural diversity. ZenTra Working Paper in Transnational Studies No. 16/2013

Kumagai S (2015) The Middle-Income Trap from the Viewpoint of Trade Structures: Are the Geese Trapped or Still Flying? J Int Commer Econ Policy 06(03) 1550017-10.1142/S1793993315500179

Montalvo Marta, Reynal-Querol (2005) Ethnic diversity and economic development. J Dev Econ 76(2) 293–323

Todo Y (2015) Introduction to development economics [Kaihatsu Keizaigaku Nyūmon]. Shinseisha, Tokyo

Chapter 2
Challenges in the Low-Income Period and Their Solution

The Effects of the New Economic Policy (1960s–1980s)

Today, economic development is often synonymous with "industrialization" in developing countries. Most countries experience continuous income growth, or economic development, through industrialization, shifting from an economy centered on agriculture and primary commodities. Therefore, the critical aspect of economic development in the low-income period is the smoothness of transition from agriculture to industry.

This point has been analyzed in the classic model of development economics, the "dual sector model," or Lewis model.[1] The dual sector model assumes that a developing country's economy comprises agriculture (traditional sector) and industry (modern sector). In the early stages of economic development, the agricultural sector has a state of "disguised unemployment," where more people are working than actually needed for agricultural production. In essence, this disguised unemployment means two people share work that could be done by one person, rather than having one person employed and one unemployed. Industrialization is assumed to progress as this surplus labor from rural areas is employed at low wages in the modern sector, generating profits for capitalists, which are then reinvested.

Improved productivity in the agricultural sector is essential for industrialization to proceed smoothly. In developing countries, it is typical for the agricultural sector to account for more than 50% of GDP and employment during the low-income period. If the agricultural sector—the largest in the economy and the one that sustains people's lives through food production—lacks stability, subsequent economic development will be uncertain.

Increased agricultural productivity means fewer farmers are needed to produce the same amount of crops, allowing more labor freed from agricultural production to move to the industrial sector. Furthermore, if increased productivity generates a greater surplus of agricultural products, it can serve as a source of investment for industrial development, promoting industrialization. Conversely, if agricultural productivity does not improve, agricultural goods will become relatively scarce compared to industrial goods, leading to higher prices for agricultural goods

S. Kumagai and M. Nakamura, *Economic Development Strategies*, Emerging-Economy State and International Policy Studies, https://doi.org/10.1007/978-981-95-6899-4_2

and higher wage levels necessary for urban workers to live, which may hinder the expansion of the industrial sector.[2]

Moreover, when labor moves from rural to urban areas, it is not always smoothly employed in the urban modern sector. In many developing countries, large slums are formed in cities, and labor from rural areas often flows into these areas first.[3] Expanding this informal sector of the urban economy can negatively impact subsequent economic development.

Additionally, when utilizing the surplus from the agricultural sector as a resource for the development of the industrial sector, the commercialization of agriculture and the existence of a financial system covering rural areas become essential. Even when agricultural surplus exists, it cannot fuel industrial development if farmers cannot convert it to cash, or if the money remains in rural areas as "under-the-mattress savings."

When these various problems are overcome—agricultural productivity increases, investment in the industrial sector expands, and smooth transfers of labor and capital occur between the two sectors—a balanced growth process between agriculture and industry begins, and economic development is expected to proceed smoothly.

However, in some developing countries during the latter half of the twentieth century, resources for industrialization were extracted by exploiting rural areas rather than increasing agricultural productivity. In tropical African countries such as Ghana, Nigeria, Kenya, and Senegal, government agencies purchased cash crops at low prices and channeled export profits into development projects and manufacturing subsidies.[4] In Thailand, Malaysia's neighboring country, an export tax was imposed on rice to supply food cheaply to urban residents in addition to securing tax revenue. If such urban-biased policies hinder the improvement of agricultural productivity, it will also impede industrialization. Even if industrialization proceeds, urban-biased policies will lead to income disparities and structural conflicts of interest between urban and rural areas. If serious income disparities and conflicts between urban and rural areas emerge early in economic development, they will hinder further progress even when a country reaches middle-income status through industrialization.

So, what kind of growth strategy was adopted in Malaysia immediately after independence?

2.1 The Malaysian Economy from the 1960s to the 1970s

2.1.1 Favorable Initial Conditions

Before analyzing Malaysia's economic development, let us first confirm its starting point. If Malaysia had been a privileged country initially, then subsequent economic development would have been easier. Conversely, if it reaches today's income level despite deplorable conditions, we must carefully analyze what policies were used to achieve it.

In reality, it can be said that Malaysia was relatively well-off at the starting point of economic development. Malaysia had been steadily developing its economy since immediately after independence in 1957 by exporting abundant natural resources such as rubber and tin. Looking at the footage of the independence declaration ceremony, tens of thousands of well-dressed people gathered at the newly completed Merdeka Stadium in the capital, Kuala Lumpur, with many cars parked in the parking lot. From this evidence, it can be inferred that Malaysia was already a relatively prosperous country at the time of independence. From independence in 1957 to the 1960s, Malaysia was in the take-off period of economic development, with import-substitution industrialization centered on cities and rural development, such as land development and relocation projects progressing in parallel. The economic growth rate in the 1960s averaged 6.1% annually, which is by no means low.

Malaysia was also fortunate to have had an exceptionally high-quality administrative structure for a developing country. Figure 2.1 shows the relationship between government quality and income level (nominal GDP per capita) for 89 countries worldwide in 1984, based on the QOG dataset[5] from the University of Gothenburg, a comprehensive government quality dataset. The government quality data is a composite index of three indicators (corruption, law and order, and bureaucratic quality), normalized to a maximum value of 1 and a minimum value of 0, with higher values indicating better quality.[6] There is a relatively strong positive correlation between government quality and GDP per capita ($n = 89$, $r = 0.7574$).[7] Countries with higher income levels tend to have higher government quality. The upward-sloping line represents the average trend between the two variables.

In 1984, Malaysia's GDP per capita was $2234, while its government quality index value was 0.79. Malaysia's position well above the trend line shows that its government quality was very high relative to its income level. Among countries with a GDP per capita below $5000, only South Africa ($2429, 0.83) and Taiwan ($3203, 0.79) scored higher than Malaysia.

By 1984, it had been only 20 years since Malaysia was formed in 1963, and less than 30 years from the independence of the Federation of Malaya in 1957. The young nation of Malaysia had a high-quality administrative structure primarily due to historical circumstances. Malaysia's administrative and judicial organizations were established during the British colonial period and were handed over to Malaysians in their entirety. In Malaysia, independence meant that the colonial state would be run by locals instead of bureaucrats from the suzerain state. Unlike neighboring Indonesia and the three Indochinese countries that experienced wars of independence or revolutions, Malaysia achieved independence through negotiations and didn't need to rebuild its governance system.

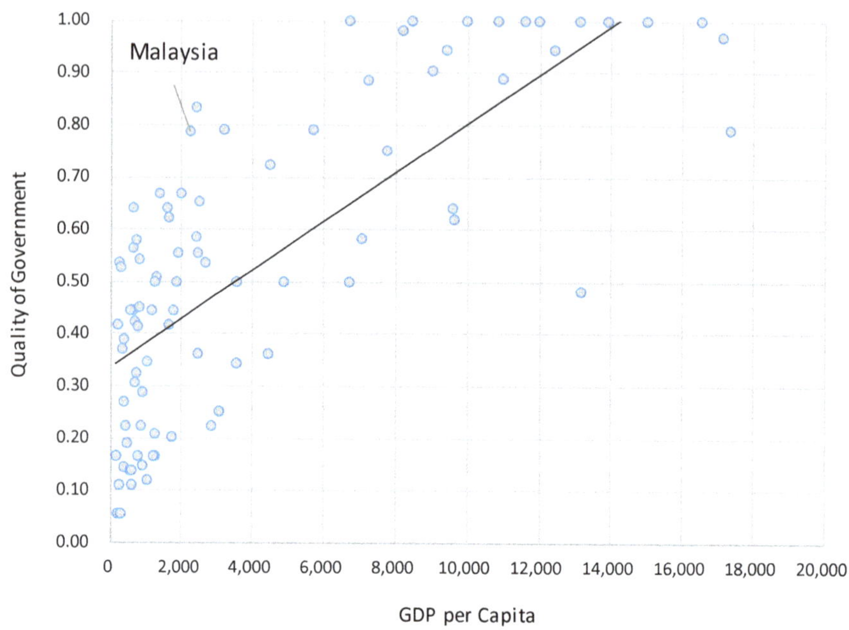

Fig. 2.1 Relationship between government quality and GDP per capita (1984). *Source:* Created by the author based on Dahlberg et al. (2021)

2.1.2 *Ethnic Issues, Dependence on Primary Commodities, and Youth Employment Problems*

However, Malaysia also had its own unique disadvantages. Originally, Malaysia, predominantly populated by the Malay people, saw a large influx of Chinese and Indian immigrants under British colonial rule from the late nineteenth century, becoming a multi-ethnic nation by the time of independence. Additionally, it faced a potential "time bomb" because rural Malays were being left behind in economic development. This would lead to the "ethnic riots" of May 13, 1969.

In 1971, Malaysia's nominal income per capita was \$390, about 7% of the US income per capita (\$5620). When compared to 2019 figures, it is close to Indonesia (6.2% of the US income per capita). At this point, Malaysia was considered a lower-middle-income country rather than a low-income country. At the same time, Malaysia's population was 11.16 million, only about one-third of the 32.58 million in 2019, making it a relatively small country in terms of population for a densely populated Asian nation. This would become a constraint in terms of small market size under import-substitution policies and a constraint in terms of labor shortages under the subsequent export-oriented industrialization policies.

In 1970, the manufacturing sector accounted for 13.7% of Malaysia's GDP. Since Indonesia's manufacturing sector also accounted for 13.7% of its GDP in 2019, it can be said that Malaysia had achieved a certain level of industrialization. However, rubber and tin, two commodities, accounted for 53.8% of Malaysia's exports, making it a typical primary commodity-exporting country. This indicates that the manufacturing sector had developed under import-substitution policies with high tariff protection, focusing mainly on domestic demand while lacking the international competitiveness needed for large-scale exports.

The history of oil production in Malaysia is long, having started in Sarawak by Shell in 1910. Despite this long history, crude oil became a major export item only in the late 1970s. Therefore, in the early 1970s, Malaysia was a primary commodity-exporting country but not an oil-producing country where crude oil or natural gas accounted for more than half of its exports.

From this perspective, it can be seen that Malaysia was no longer a low-income country in 1971 when it started the New Economic Policy (NEP), which will be discussed later. Although it relied on primary commodities for more than half of its exports, it was not an oil-producing country, and its domestic manufacturing industry had reached a certain scale through import-substitution policies. The economic growth rate of over 6% per year on average in the 1960s indicates that Malaysia's economic development was progressing relatively smoothly during this period.

Nevertheless, in 1970, Malaysia's poverty rate was 49.3%, meaning about half of the population living in poverty. In particular, the poverty rate among Malays was high at 64.8%, with two out of three living in poverty. At that time in Malaysia, ethnicity, residence, occupation, and income were strongly interlinked, with wealthy urban Chinese in commerce and industry contrasting sharply with poor rural Malays in agriculture.

In addition, the ratio of capital ownership by ethnicity in Malaysia at that time deviated significantly from the population composition ratio of each ethnic group. In 1969, despite being the population majority in Peninsular Malaysia, Malays owned only 1.5% of capital, while Chinese owned 22.8%, Indians 0.9%, and foreigners 62.9%. In response, the New Economic Policy set a goal: "within a period of 20 years, Malays and other indigenous people will manage and own at least 30% of the total commercial and industrial activities in all categories and scales of operation."

Malaysia's unemployment rate in 1970 was 7.8%, which may not seem very high. However, as mentioned earlier, disguised unemployment is common in developing countries, and Malaysia was in a similar situation. The unemployment rate by ethnicity was 8.1% for Malays, 7.0% for Chinese, and 11.0% for Indians. Half of the unemployed were under age 20, with a high 17% unemployment rate for those aged 15–19, compared to merely 2%–4% for those over 25.[8] For Malaysia at that time, the unemployment problem was not an issue for the entire workforce but rather a result of the inability to provide sufficient employment opportunities for the rapidly increasing young population. Education had evidently expanded ahead of the economy's ability to provide quality employment, as the unemployment rate for primary school graduates was 5%–9%, while that for secondary school graduates reached about 20%.

2.2 Urbanization and Industrialization Support Through the New Economic Policy

2.2.1 *Aiming to Correct the Ethnic Division of Labor Structure*

Many policies that have promoted Malaysia's economic development to date can be said to have started with the New Economic Policy in 1971. The New Economic Policy is a development policy that aims to correct the ethnic division of labor structure built under the colonial system, where the majority of Malays are farmers, and the commercial and industrial sectors are occupied by the Chinese, and to eradicate poverty regardless of ethnicity. Although government economic development policies existed before that, the first Prime Minister Rahman, who took power immediately after independence, adopted a "laissez-faire" stance. His policies remained limited to general economic approaches typical in a market economy system. It can be said that the government began to intervene strongly in the economy only after the second Prime Minister Razak implemented the New Economic Policy.

The Second Malaysia Plan (1971–1975), which outlined the specifics of the New Economic Policy, classifies and analyzes the Malaysian economy into five blocks[9]: the "traditional rural sector," "modern rural sector," "traditional urban sector," "modern urban sector," and "government sector." In terms of income, the "modern urban sector" is classified as high-income, the "government sector" and "modern rural sector" as middle-income, and the "traditional urban sector" and "traditional rural sector" as low-income. Figure 2.2 shows a rough estimate of the population size and percentage of Malays in the five sectors. Many Malays belonged to the "traditional rural sector," while the Chinese occupied most of the modern urban sector.

As mentioned earlier, before the New Economic Policy, Malaysia had been exporting primary commodities such as rubber and tin while promoting import-substitution industrialization, achieving certain results. At the same time, the government had also been focusing on rural development, providing infrastructure such as electricity, water supply, roads, and educational opportunities in rural areas. The government also established the Federal Land Development Authority (FELDA) and initiated resettlement schemes aimed at rural modernization. However, the benefits of import-substitution industrialization were mainly enjoyed by the Chinese in the modern urban sector. Although the government was carrying out rural development, the population in the traditional rural industry was increasing, and many people were living below the poverty line. There was a significant wage gap between rural and urban areas, but the movement of labor from rural to urban areas was hindered by ethnic barriers, with cities being Chinese-centered and rural areas being Malay-centered. Many Malays in the traditional rural sector were believed to be stuck in disguised unemployment.

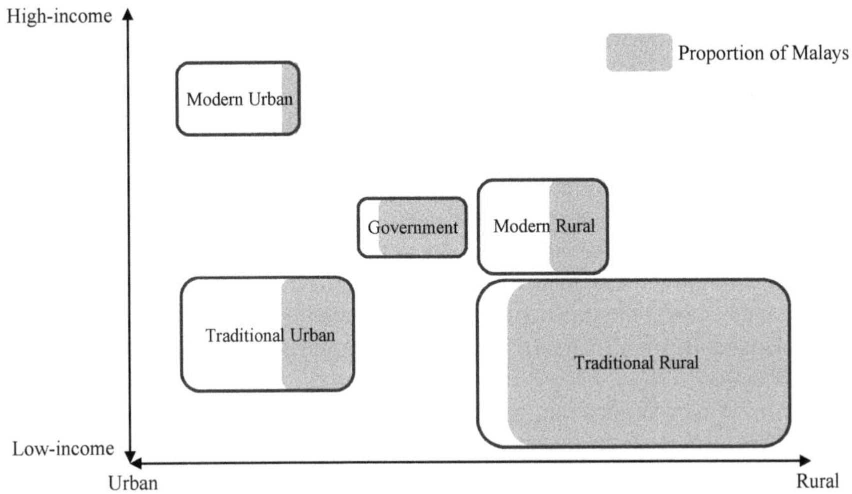

Fig. 2.2 Five economic blocs of Malaysia: population distribution and approximate Malay demographic composition. *Source* Compiled by the author from Malaysia (1971)

If there had been a natural large-scale population movement from rural to urban areas before the New Economic Policy, the Malaysian government would not have made the migration of Malays from rural to urban areas such an important policy issue. The Third Malaysia Plan (1976–1980) points out that "Socio-political stability could not be maintained for long in situations where, for example, a Malay farmer coming to town, even with an increased income, felt somewhat alienated, somewhat an outsider, simply because he saw so few Malays in the shops, restaurants and factories of the town.[10]"

The New Economic Policy provided employment opportunities for these rural Malays, especially youth, in the modern urban sector and the government sector while promoting their migration to cities. The New Economic Policy can be said to have been the driving force behind the economic growth of the 1970s, which promoted both industrialization and urbanization. The import-substitution industrialization of the 1960s, which preceded this, had progressed mainly in the modern urban sector but was reaching its limits of development due to the smallness of the market. For market expansion and labor supply, Malaysia needed to continue its economic growth by involving rural Malays in industrialization and urbanization. The New Economic Policy is a government-led "big push"[11] to promote industrialization and urbanization in Malaysia, which was difficult to naturally progress due to racial barriers, even if there was a wage gap.

2.2.2 *Start of Export-Oriented Industrialization*

Malaysia's economic growth rate reached an average of 7.5% per year in the 1970s, the first decade of the New Economic Policy. Throughout the 1970s, the number of people employed in the agricultural sector increased by a mere 1.9% annually. In contrast, the manufacturing sector saw a 7.6% increase, and the service sector experienced growth of around 6%. In the manufacturing sector, the number of people employed in labor-intensive industries such as the electronics and electrical industry and textile industry grew by more than 10% per year on average. In the service sector, civil servants created the most employment. In agriculture, there was a shift from rubber plantations, which had provided the most employment, to palm oil plantations and other crops.

In terms of industrialization, while import-substitution industries drove growth in the 1960s, export-oriented sectors such as the electronics and electrical industry and the textile industry became significant contributors in the 1970s. Export growth averaged 5.9% per year from 1971 to 1975, then accelerated to 9.4% from 1976 to 1980. As a result, the share of manufactured goods in exports reached 27.5% in 1980.

Agricultural exports accounted for 52.1% of total exports in 1970 but declined to 35.8% in 1980. Natural rubber's share in agricultural exports fell from 33.4% to 17.1%, while palm oil exports rose from 9.8% to 25.3%. The 1970s witnessed a shift in the agricultural sector's leading crop from rubber to palm oil.

The mining sector's share in exports increased from 22.8% in 1970 to 34.5% in 1980, with crude oil accounting for most of this increase. The share of crude oil in mining sector exports increased from 13.9% in 1970 to 73.3% in 1980, while the share of tin significantly decreased from 86.1% to 25.5%. The leading player in Malaysia's mining sector shifted significantly from tin to crude oil in the 1970s.

Thus, during the 1970s in Malaysia, export-oriented manufacturing industries, primarily labor-intensive ones, expanded significantly. In the primary commodity sector, there was also a shift from rubber to palm oil and from tin to crude oil. It can be said that the economic growth structure that led to the current Malaysia began to take shape in the 1970s, triggered by the implementation of the New Economic Policy.

Had the New Economic Policy not been implemented, the Malaysian economy would likely have followed a very different trajectory. Considering this point, it must be said that the New Economic Policy was the key to opening the door to Malaysia's stable economic development thereafter. The May 13 incident in 1969 demonstrated that the conventional economic policies preceding the New Economic Policy were inadequate to address Malaysia's urban-rural disparities, which were deeply intertwined with ethnic issues, or to effectively promote urbanization and industrialization. If left unaddressed, the situation would likely have resulted in the steady development of Chinese-centered urban commerce and industry, while rural Malays remained trapped in low-income conditions. This would have further deepened the political divide. Furthermore, from the late 1970s, crude oil exports began in earnest, and had a combination of Malay elites, Chinese businesses, and foreign capital monopolized the profits from oil-related industries, the country's stability would have been significantly undermined.

As mentioned earlier, the New Economic Policy's primary objectives were "eradication of poverty irrespective of race" and "restructuring of society," with the goal of achieving them by 1990. By 1990, Malaysia's poverty rate had decreased from 49.3% in 1970 to 17.1%, demonstrating that the goal of "eradication of poverty irrespective of race" was achieved to a considerable extent. The unemployment rate had also dropped to 4.5% by 1990, effectively reaching a state of full employment.

Regarding the other goal of "restructuring of society," the share of capital ownership by Bumiputeras (indigenous peoples), including Malays, reached 20.3% in 1990, falling short of the 30% target but increasing significantly from 1.5% in 1969. The proportion of Malays in the urban population reached 47.3% in 1991, and in terms of occupational categories, the ethnic distribution became close to the population ratio in many occupations (see Chapter 3). The share of manufacturing in GDP also reached 27% in 1990, and The New Economic Policy transformed the Malaysian economy significantly over the 20-year period from 1971 to 1990.

Considering that the majority of people experiencing poverty were Malays at the start of the New Economic Policy in 1971 and that the restructuring of society essentially meant the advancement of Malays into commerce, industry, and urban areas, it is reasonable to view the New Economic Policy as a pro-Malay policy. However, since most Malays lived in rural areas and worked in agriculture in 1971, the New Economic Policy effectively functioned as a pro-rural policy for the entire country. As we will see later, generous support measures such as rice price subsidies were implemented for rice farmers, whose poverty rate was particularly high (see Section 5 of this chapter). The government also provided education to farmers, developed infrastructure in rural areas, promoted rural development to raise the living standards of farmers, actively provided employment opportunities for farmers in the commerce and industry sectors, and promoted their migration to urban areas. In essence, the New Economic Policy can be viewed as a policy that strongly promoted the process of economic development assumed in the dual sector model, where surplus labor from rural areas moves to the urban commercial and industrial sectors through government intervention.

Before the New Economic Policy, the movement of labor from agriculture to commerce and industry and the migration from rural to urban areas in Malaysia were hindered by ethnic barriers. Despite a significant wage gap between rural and urban areas, which typically drives urbanization, the situation in Malaysia at that time was characterized by rigid links between ethnicity, place of residence, and occupation. If these ethnic barriers had remained unaddressed, Malaysia could not have entered the process of economic development assumed in the dual sector model. The New Economic Policy removed these ethnic barriers through decisive government intervention, thereby promoting industrialization and urbanization.

From this perspective, the New Economic Policy was not merely an affirmative action based on ethnicity, but also a radical industrialization and urbanization policy.

2.3 Incorporating Rural Surplus into the Financial System

2.3.1 *Achieving High Savings Rates*

Malaysia was among the first developing countries to recognize the importance of rural financial systems and implemented policies to improve rural access to financial services. For example, the Postal Office Savings Bank[12] was established as early as 1948. Additionally, leading Malaysian economist Ungku Aziz observed that rural Malays kept their savings at home rather than in bank deposits when saving for the Hajj pilgrimage to Mecca, as they sought to avoid the interest payments prohibited in Islam. To incorporate these savings into the formal financial system, he proposed establishing the Pilgrims Fund (Tabung Haji) in 1962,[13] which provided Muslims with an interest-free way to save for the Hajj pilgrimage.

In addition, Malaysia established the Employees Provident Fund (EPF) in 1951 to save a portion of wages for retirement. Furthermore, as part of the New Economic Policy, Malaysia began encouraging the ownership of company shares by Bumiputeras. However, when Bumiputeras individually owned company shares, they often quickly sold them to members of other ethnic groups, particularly the Chinese. To prevent the quick sale of shares to non-Bumiputeras, Malaysia established the national holding company Permodalan Nasional Berhad (PNB) in 1978 and created investment trusts available exclusively to Bumiputeras.[14]

With the development of access to the financial system in rural areas, Malaysia's savings rate was the highest among the advanced ASEAN4 countries from the 1970s to the early 2010s (Fig. 2.3).

2.4 Problems Generated by Economic Growth in the 1970s

2.4.1 *Four Structural Problems Emerged*

It is important to note that the New Economic Policy, both in ideology and in practice, did not aim for direct redistribution from the wealthy Chinese to the poor Malays, except for the rice distribution industry discussed later. The Second Malaysia Plan, which helped the New Economic Policy materialize, states, "The strategy is founded on the philosophy of active participation, not on disruptive redistribution. It works in an ever expanding economy in which the growing volume of goods and services is enjoyed by all groups in the Malaysian society in such a manner that there is no feeling of deprivation by any group, and also in a manner which contributes to national unity.[15]"

Malaysia's economic growth rate reached an average of 7.5% per year in the 1970s, the first decade of the New Economic Policy. This shows that the New Economic Policy was not a "destructive redistribution" as its ideology stated. However, the

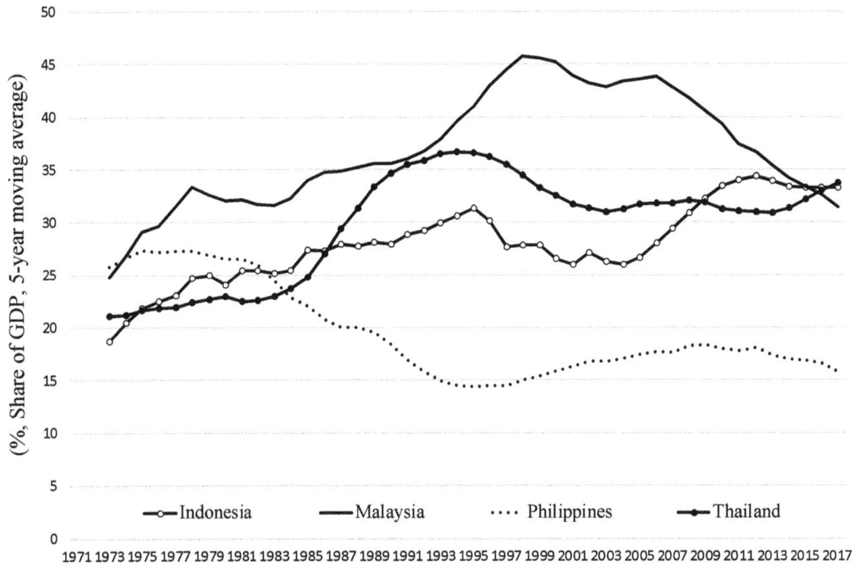

Fig. 2.3 Trends in savings rates of ASEAN-4 countries (1973–2017, 5-year moving average). *Source:* Author's compilation based on World Development Indicators (WDI)

economic growth led by the New Economic Policy in the 1970s created several structural issues that later became problematic legacies for the Malaysian economy. These include (1) the over-expansion of the public sector, (2) the over-emphasis on labor-intensive industries, (3) the dependence of the manufacturing sector on foreign capital, and (4) the (excessive) preferential treatment of Bumiputeras.

However, these four structural aspects were also necessary for Malaysia's economic development in the 1970s. The "over-expansion of the public sector" was inevitable during early economic development when private investment was weak, and the economy required public sector support. Moreover, in the early stages of the New Economic Policy, since Chinese and foreign-owned companies conducted a large part of commerce and industry, the public sector needed to actively engage in these sectors and create opportunities for Bumiputeras to promote their participation. The government also actively expanded employment in public sectors such as administration, education, healthcare, the military, and police to create opportunities for Bumiputeras.

The "over-emphasis on labor-intensive industries" was also unavoidable before achieving effective full employment in the 1990s. Job creation, particularly for the younger generation, remained a major challenge during this period. The Second Malaysia Plan also explicitly states that "labor-intensive technologies will be actively adopted." From the Seventh Malaysia Plan (1996–2000) onward, the need for economic development supported by enhanced economic value-added, transition to a knowledge economy, and productivity improvement was clearly stated. Before that, however, labor-intensive industry was considered desirable for creating more employment.

The "dependence of the manufacturing sector on foreign capital" was also an inevitable approach for Malaysia, which had a small manufacturing base, to leverage foreign capital for its development. The New Economic Policy aimed to increase the Bumiputera share of capital ownership, while simultaneously calling for increased foreign investment, especially in the manufacturing sector.[16] The first free trade zone (FTZ) opened in the Bayan Lepas area of Penang in 1972, eliminating import duties on parts used in export products. This approach to attracting labor-intensive foreign companies to FTZs proved highly successful and was subsequently expanded throughout Malaysia. Subsequently, the dependence of Malaysia's manufacturing sector on foreign capital was further strengthened by three factors: the wave of Japanese companies' overseas relocation following the strong yen after the Plaza Accord in the late 1980s; the 1986 Promotion of Investments Act that granted various incentives to foreign capital; and the guidelines announced in September of the same year that allowed 100% foreign capital investment if more than 50% of the products were exported or if more than 350 Malaysians were employed full-time.

Following the 1969 ethnic riots, the Malaysian government found the "preferential treatment of Bumiputeras" to be an unavoidable policy. In particular, from the adoption of the New Economic Policy in 1971 until the initial planned period of 1990, preferential policies for Bumiputeras were necessary in all aspects, including education, employment, participation in business management, and capital ownership. As mentioned earlier, the preferential treatment of Bumiputeras served dual purposes: correcting income disparities between ethnic groups and mobilizing rural farmers into the modern urban sector.

To date, the Malaysian government has continuously attempted to address the four structural problems mentioned above in its economic development process. However, because these problems are intertwined—where resolving one often exacerbates another—no fundamental solution has been achieved to this day. However, Malaysia's economic growth trends indicate that these four problems have been sufficiently controlled to prevent serious impacts on economic development. These issues will be addressed in the following chapters and examined in detail in the final chapter as ongoing challenges for the future.

2.5 The Political Background of the Rural Bias

2.5.1 The Political Process Leading to the Ethnic Riots

As we have seen, the Malaysian government promoted industrialization and urbanization by encouraging rural Malays to advance into commerce and industry while pursuing rural development through the New Economic Policy introduced in 1971. However, in developing countries in the latter half of the twentieth century, there were many cases where industrialization was attempted by exploiting farmers. This occurred because there were no other means to obtain resources for industrialization, and politically, urban residents posed a more significant threat to the rulers than rural farmers did. The practice of overly favoring urban residents, resulting in an unfair and inefficient allocation of resources for economic growth, is called "urban bias." Why, then, did Malaysia avoid urban bias during its low-income period and instead implement a New Economic Policy that significantly supported rural residents?

First, let us briefly review the political developments from independence to the introduction of the New Economic Policy.

The government that took power immediately after independence was the "Alliance Party," led by Prime Minister Tunku Abdul Rahman. The Alliance Party was a coalition of three parties[17]: the United Malays National Organisation (UMNO), the Malayan Chinese Association (MCA), and the Malayan Indian Congress (MIC). In the federal legislative election held 2 years before independence, the Alliance Party won 51 out of 52 seats in a landslide victory. In the multi-ethnic society of Malaya, political parties were established along ethnic lines, and these ethnic-based parties then formed a coalition. Around the same time, leaders of major ethnic groups gathered to establish the multi-ethnic Independence of Malaya Party (IMP), but it failed to gain significant voter support. The Alliance Party, having won the election, became the main negotiator for independence with the British and led the constitution-making process.

One of the main issues in drafting the constitution was establishing conditions for granting citizenship to Chinese and Indian residents. Before World War II, in Penang and Malacca, which were under direct British colonial rule, citizenship as British subjects was granted based on the principle of *jus soli*. However, areas under indirect rule through Malay rulers imposed strict conditions on non-Malays seeking citizenship. The constitution enacted at the time of independence recognized the "special position" of the Malays while granting broad citizenship to Chinese and Indians based on the principle of *jus soli* and guaranteeing their rights to use their mother tongues and practice their religions freely. The constitutional provisions stipulating these ethnic and religious rights are commonly referred to as the "Merdeka (independence) Compact."

After the Federation of Malaya gained independence in 1957, the validity of the Merdeka Compact established by the Alliance Party became the central political issue. The opposition parties that emerged after independence pursued ethnic interests more radically to counter the Alliance Party. On the Malay side, the Pan-Malaya Islamic Party (PMIP), later known as PAS, gained significant support in the first general election in 1959, taking control of state governments in Kelantan and Terengganu, both states with Malay-majority populations. On the non-Malay side, after Singapore, Sabah, and Sarawak joined Malaysia in 1963, the People's Action Party (PAP) led by Lee Kuan Yew of Singapore expanded to the peninsula and shook the existing political framework. Lee Kuan Yew advocated the slogan "Malaysian Malaysia" and argued that Malaysia was not a "Malay country," directly opposing UMNO, the core component of the Alliance Party. This political struggle worsened inter-ethnic relations, ultimately leading to Singapore's separation and independence in August 1965.

After Singapore's independence, the remaining members of the PAP in Malaysia changed their party name to the Democratic Action Party (DAP) and continued their political activities. The DAP continued to use the slogan "Malaysian Malaysia" and announced its opposition to "classifying citizens into 'Bumiputras' and 'non-Bumiputras' and discriminating against citizens in matters of appointments and promotions, particularly in the public sector ... on grounds of race.[18]" At that time, this stance was perceived as a direct challenge to the special position of the Malays guaranteed by the constitution.

On May 13, 1969, riots erupted following escalating inter-ethnic tensions during the third general election held three days earlier. In this election, caught between Malay and non-Malay extremists, the Rahman government saw its Alliance Party lose a significant number of parliamentary seats. The Malay community was particularly shocked by the fact that the DAP, which strongly opposed pro-Malay policies, made significant electoral gains while the MCA, the Chinese party within the ruling coalition, suffered a major defeat.

Meanwhile, supporters of the DAP and the Parti Gerakan Rakyat Malaysia (Gerakan, or Malaysian People's Movement Party), another predominantly non-Malay opposition party, held a "victory" parade in central Kuala Lumpur to celebrate their success. Malay residents perceived this celebratory act as provocative, generating strong resentment among them. When clashes broke out between UMNO supporters who had gathered to stage a counter-demonstration and Chinese passersby, the riots quickly spread throughout the city.[19] The following day, a state of emergency was declared nationwide, but it took three days for the unrest to subside. In these riots, which manifested as inter-ethnic conflict, Chinese shops became the primary targets of arson and looting. Government reports stated that 196 people died in the riots, with Chinese victims constituting over 70% of the fatalities.[20]

2.5.2 The Beginning of the New Economic Policy

The large-scale riots made promoting national integration the government's top priority. Deputy Prime Minister Abdul Razak Hussein, who took over the responsibility of restoring public order from Prime Minister Rahman, established the Department of National Unity (DNU) just 6 weeks after the riots and proposed a policy of promoting economic development under government leadership to achieve national integration. The New Economic Policy was formulated with the DNU playing a central role. In March 1970, the DNU issued guidelines to all ministries for formulating the Second Malaysia Plan (5-year plan). This document established three primary government goals in order of priority: (1) reduction of racial economic disparities, (2) creation of employment opportunities, and (3) promotion of overall economic growth.[21] After coordination within the government, the introduction of the Second Malaysia Plan announced in 1971 included the statement, "in the implementation of this policy, the Government will ensure that no particular group will experience any loss or feel any sense of deprivation.[22]"

The idea that the government should actively intervene in the economy to correct inter-ethnic disparities existed even before the riots. In June 1965, the first "Bumiputera Economic Congress" was held under the auspices of the Ministry of National and Rural Development to discuss measures to support capital accumulation and the advancement of Malays into commerce and industry. In response to the conference recommendations, several institutions were established or reformed: Bank Bumiputra was created as a credit institution for Malays; the underperforming Rural Industrial Development Authority (RIDA) was reorganized into the stronger Majlis Amanah Rakyat (MARA); and State Economic Development Corporations (SEDCs) were progressively established across all states. The Bumiputera Economic Congress is considered a turning point that changed the content and direction of the government's economic policies toward the Malays.[23]

The May 13 incident made this trend decisive and irreversible. After the violent clash between ethnic groups, a strong consensus emerged within the government to strengthen policies aimed at reducing inter-ethnic disparities. Government leaders recognized that preventing future riots required national unity, which in turn necessitated correcting inter-ethnic disparities. The riots effectively shifted governmental power from Rahman, who favored minimal economic intervention, to the more interventionist Razak. Razak had previously led the Bumiputra Economic Congress in his capacity as Minister of National and Rural Development. In September 1970, Razak became the second Prime Minister and vigorously implemented these development policies.

2.5.3 The Rural Sector as the Ruling Party's Vote Bank

It should be noted that the New Economic Policy, both in its stated principles and implementation, did not aim for direct redistribution from wealthy Chinese to poor Malays, except for the rice distribution industry discussed later. The Second Malaysia Plan, which implemented the New Economic Policy, states that the strategy promotes active participation in an expanding economy where all societal groups share in increasing prosperity, avoiding feelings of deprivation while fostering national unity.

The New Economic Policy promoted rural interests primarily because many Malays lived in rural areas while Chinese predominantly occupied urban centers.

This residential segregation by ethnicity was primarily a result of urban development patterns dating back to the nineteenth century. Many of Malaysia's cities developed from waterborne commerce hubs or around tin mines. Penang and Malacca exemplify the former category, while Kuala Lumpur represents the latter. Tin mine development, which began in earnest in the nineteenth century, was carried out almost entirely by immigrant workers from China. Consequently, the towns that formed around these mines inevitably had a predominantly Chinese population. Port towns like Penang prospered as Chinese merchants engaged in international trade established businesses there. As urbanization progressed in this manner during the colonial period, Malays largely remained in rural areas.

At the time of the May 13 incident, Razak and other government leaders considered measures to address unemployment and poverty in rural areas an urgent priority, and consequently, the initial stage of the New Economic Policy focused on rural development. For rice farmers in particular, who experienced a high poverty rate, drastic measures were implemented to raise their income levels.

Even before the implementation of the New Economic Policy, Malaysia did not suppress rice prices—the staple food—to benefit urban residents, unlike many other developing countries. On the contrary, government policy deliberately maintained the producer price of domestically produced rice above the import price of Thai rice.[24] Despite this price support, rice farmers remained poor. In 1970, while the overall poverty rate in Peninsular Malaysia was 49.3%, the poverty rate among rice farmers—95% of whom were Malays—reached an alarming 88.1%.[25]

A primary reason for the poverty of rice farmers was the exploitative distribution system. In 1949, during British rule, authorities introduced a minimum guaranteed price system for paddy to ensure a stable rice supply. However, rice millers and distributors largely ignored this system and continued to exploit producers. Rice farmers accumulated substantial debts to rice millers and distributors, effectively leaving them without bargaining power. The vast majority of these rice millers and distributors were Chinese.[26]

Upon launching the New Economic Policy in 1971, the government established Lembaga Padi dan Beras Negara (LPN, or the National Padi and Rice Board) and entered the rice milling business directly. This intervention aimed to dismantle the exploitative structure in which Chinese distributors took advantage of Malay farmers. In 1974, the government banned rice importation by the private sector and established a system to manage rice trade uniformly through LPN. This policy shifted substantial profits from rice imports and sales away from Chinese distributors and into government control. Additionally, in response to the soaring prices of chemical fertilizers caused by the first oil shock, the government resumed fertilizer subsidies, which had been temporarily suspended.

This series of policies constituted a direct redistribution of economic benefits from Chinese distributors to Malay farmers.[27] Despite these interventions, the income level of rice farmers did not improve significantly. The predominance of small-scale farming operations and insufficient increases in yield per unit area prevented substantial income improvements. Even by 1976, the poverty rate among rice farmers remained alarmingly high at 80.3%.[28]

In response to this persistent poverty, the government implemented direct income support measures for farmers. In 1980, a subsidy system was introduced to pay 10 ringgit per picul (60.48 kg) to producers who sold paddy to LPN or government-designated distributors. The producer price of rice (premium grade) in the previous year was 30 ringgit per picul, so the introduction of this rice price subsidy effectively raised the actual producer price by 33%. By 1984, a striking 69% of the average annual net profit from rice farming came from rice price subsidies. While this policy imposed a substantial fiscal burden on the government and reduced efficiency in rice production and distribution, its redistributive effect was significant. As a result, the poverty rate among rice farmers dropped to 57.7% by 1984.[29]

There was a political incentive behind the Malaysian government's implementation of such bold redistribution policies. Unlike tropical African countries and Thailand, where fear of urban protests led to urban-biased policies, Malaysia deliberately developed rural-favoring policies. This approach was driven by the large number of rural constituencies and fierce political competition for rural support.

The preponderance of rural constituencies originated in the constituency delimitation implemented by the colonial government. When conducting the first federal legislative election 2 years before independence, the colonial government prioritized balancing urban and rural areas over equalizing the weight of each vote. After independence, the first general election in 1959 used the same constituency delimitation as the pre-independence election, where each of the 52 districts was divided into two. Consequently, the overrepresentation of rural areas continued. In Peninsular Malaysia, this district delimitation remained in use until the third general election in 1969.

Following the riots and before the fourth general election in 1974, the government increased the number of seats and redrew constituency boundaries, deliberately strengthening rural overrepresentation. This change was influenced by the entry of UMNO's rival, PAS, into the ruling coalition. Following the riots, the Alliance Party formed the "Barisan Nasional" (BN, or National Front) on January 1, 1973, incorporating several opposition parties. PAS also joined the BN, resulting in all major Malay parties becoming part of the ruling coalition, with the DAP remaining as the only powerful opposition party in the peninsula. Under this party system, any increase in rural seats would almost certainly benefit the ruling coalition. In the 1974 election, the BN's share of seats reached an overwhelming 87.7%.

This constituency redistricting heavily favored the ruling coalition and significantly undermined electoral fairness. Such electoral distortions are among the primary reasons why many analysts do not consider the post-riot political system truly democratic. However, PAS left the BN in 1977 and reemerged as UMNO's principal rival in the fifth general election held the following year. The introduction of a rice price subsidy of 10 ringgit per picul in 1980 was driven by pressure from farmer movements supported by PAS.

For UMNO, the core party of the ruling coalition, rural areas with a large Malay population constituted its main support base, and there was fierce competition with PAS to secure rural votes. Consequently, post-riot Malaysian governments consistently implemented policies that directed substantial benefits to rural areas. From the late 1970s through the late 1980s, these policies significantly narrowed income gaps between urban and rural areas and between Malays and Chinese. The next chapter examines these trends and their long-term implications in detail.

Notes

1. The dual sector model is discussed in Lewis (1954) and in the model by Ranis and Fei (1961) who built upon Lewis's work.
2. The mechanisms by which agricultural production stagnation impedes economic development include the "Malthusian trap," where living standards stagnate at subsistence levels as population growth outpaces agricultural production growth, and "Ricardo's trap," where agricultural productivity declines due to the use of inferior land as the agricultural area expands, thereby hindering industrialization.
3. Harris and Todaro (1970) modeled this reality.
4. Bates (1981).
5. Dahlberg et al. (2021).
6. The original data come from the International Country Risk Guide (ICRG). The earliest ICRG data available are from 1984. While the World Bank's Worldwide Governance Indicators (WGI) are widely used as an international indicator of government quality, WGI data are only available from 1996 onwards.
7. This was calculated excluding the UAE (32,310 dollars, 0.48) as an extreme outlier.
8. Malaysia (1981, p. 53).
9. Malaysia (1971, p. 37).
10. Malaysia (1976, p. 6).
11. The "Big Push" theory suggests that developing countries in a poverty trap need a powerful push, such as large-scale government infrastructure investment, to get on the path of economic development.
12. Reorganized into Bank Simpanan Nasional in 1974.
13. Muhammad Syafiq Borhannuddin (2015, pp. 1–15).
14. Investment trusts that non-Bumiputeras could purchase were also established later.
15. Malaysia (1971, p. 43).
16. Malaysia (1971, p. 91).
17. After the formation of Malaysia in 1963, MCA's name was changed to Malaysian Chinese Association and MIC's to Malaysian Indian Congress, along with the country's name change. The same applies to PAS mentioned shortly afterward.
18. Democratic Action Party (1969, p. 19).
19. NOC (1969: 51); Straits Times, May 14, 1969.
20. NOC (1969, pp. 88–90, 96).
21. Faaland et al. (1990, pp. 305–318).
22. Heng (1997, pp. 265–266).
23. Horii (1989, p. 33).
24. Ishida (2001, pp. 60–61).
25. Malaysia (1981, p. 33).
26. Ishida (2001, p. 104).
27. Ishida (2001, pp. 107–110).
28. Malaysia (1986, p. 86).
29. Malaysia (1986, pp. 86, 90) and Ishida (2001, p. 112).

References

Bates RH (1981) Markets and states in tropical Africa: the political basis of agricultural policies. University of California Press, Berkeley

Dahlberg S, Sundström A, Holmberg S et al (2021) The quality of government basic dataset, version Jan 21. University of Gothenburg, The Quality of Government Institute

Democratic Action Party (1969) Who lives if Malaysia dies? Democratic Action Party, Petaling Jaya, Selangor
Faaland J, Parkinson JR, Saniman R (1990) Growth and ethnic inequality: Malaysia's new economic policy. Dewan Bahasa dan Pustaka, Kuala Lumpur
Harris JR, Todaro MP (1970) Migration, unemployment and development: a two-sector analysis. Am Econ Rev 60(1):126–142
Heng PK (1997) The new economic policy and the Chinese community in Peninsular Malaysia. Dev Econ 35(2):262–292
Horii K (1989) Historical characteristics of Bumiputera policy and the role of state capital (Bumiputera Seisaku no Rekishiteki Seikaku to Kokka Shihon no Yakuwari). In: Horii K (ed) Social restructuring and ethnic issues in Malaysia: the results of 20 years of bumiputera policy (Malaysia no Shakai Saihen to Shuzoku Mondai). Institute of Developing Economies, Tokyo
Ishida A (2001) Political dynamics of Malaysian agriculture (Malaysia Nōgyō no Seiji Rikigaku). Nihon Keizai Hyōronsha, Tokyo
Lewis WA (1954) Economic development with unlimited supplies of labour. Manch Sch 22(2):139–191
Malaysia (1971) Second Malaysia Plan 1971–1975. Government Press, Kuala Lumpur
Malaysia (1976) Third Malaysia Plan 1976–1980. Government Press, Kuala Lumpur
Malaysia (1981) Fourth Malaysia Plan 1981–1985. National Printing Department, Kuala Lumpur
Malaysia (1986) Fifth Malaysia Plan 1986–1990. National Printing Department, Kuala Lumpur
Muhammad Syafiq B (2015) Ungku Aziz's perspective on development. Turk J Islamic Econ 2(1):1–15
National Operations Council (NOC) (1969) The May 13 tragedy: a report. National Operations Council, Kuala Lumpur
Ranis G, Fei JCH (1961) A theory of economic development. Am Econ Rev 51(4):533–565

Chapter 3
Quantitative and Qualitative Expansion of the Labor Force

Urbanization, Disparities, and Education (1970s to 1990s)

In recent decades, countries that have achieved remarkable economic development, particularly those in East Asia, have attained economic growth during their lower-middle-income period by focusing on labor-intensive, export-oriented industries such as textile manufacturing and the assembly of electronic and electrical products. This growth was primarily supported by workers who migrated from rural to urban areas, as a large labor force is required to sustain labor-intensive industries, which are often located in or near urban areas.

In the early stages of economic development, when unemployment is a significant problem, expanding employment is a top priority for the government, and the fact that an industry is labor-intensive is considered a desirable characteristic. However, as economic development progresses and the economy approaches full employment and enters a phase of labor shortages, it becomes unsustainable to continue economic growth by relying on labor-intensive industries. At this point, a shift to higher value-added, capital- and technology-intensive sectors becomes necessary. To step up from labor-intensive to high-value-added industries, companies need to invest in mechanization and labor-saving technologies while improving workers' quality through education and training to increase productivity.

If a country neglects this transition and continues to depend on labor-intensive industries even after becoming an upper-middle-income country by suppressing wage increases through informal employment and hiring low-cost foreign workers, its economic growth rate will decline. Furthermore, if the labor share of income, the proportion of corporate profits paid to workers mainly as wages, remains low for an extended period, wealth will be concentrated among a small wealthy class, widening income disparities among the population and causing domestic demand to stagnate.

In countries with authoritarian political systems, policies that restrict labor movements or suppress wage increases are often implemented in the early stages of economic development as these regimes prioritize investment over consumption. Moreover, if labor-intensive industries have developed, relying on foreign direct

S. Kumagai and M. Nakamura, *Economic Development Strategies*, Emerging-Economy State and International Policy Studies, https://doi.org/10.1007/978-981-95-6899-4_3

investment by multinational corporations, then wage increases are viewed as a negative factor for management, and management is more likely to demand wage restraints or the introduction of foreign workers. In this situation, multinational corporations that employ a large number of workers in large factories and have the option to relocate to other countries have strong bargaining power against the host country government.

Generally, it is understood that wage increases occur after labor productivity rises, creating room for management to raise wages. However, historically, there have been many cases where wages increased first, followed by a corresponding increase in labor productivity. For example, in eighteenth century England, wages were relatively high, while capital and energy were cheap. This increased the return on investment for spinning machines in England, driving the Industrial Revolution.[1]

In Singapore, the National Wages Council recommended wage increases exceeding 20% in 1979,[2] which was in line with the national policy called the "Second Industrial Revolution" that aimed to promote high-value-added industries. Subsequently, government-led wage increases of over 50% were implemented over the next three years. Judging from the trend of economic growth rates, the negative impact of these wage increases on the economy was minimal, and they later became the foundation for Singapore's transition to a high-income country.

It is desirable for increases in labor productivity and wages to occur simultaneously. However, if workers' bargaining power is weak, they may not receive the benefits of increased labor productivity. On the other hand, wage increases lead to the exit of companies that cannot keep up, resulting in increased labor productivity for the surviving companies.

Opponents of minimum wage systems often argue that raising the minimum wage will lead to higher unemployment rates. However, recent research in the United States suggests that raising the minimum wage does not necessarily reduce employment.[3] Therefore, historical examples and recent academic studies suggest that it is reasonable for the government to take the lead in raising wages at a certain stage of economic development.

For a lower-middle-income country to continue growing and advance to an upper-middle-income country after achieving economic growth through the quantitative expansion of its labor force, it is essential to shift from emphasizing the quantity to the quality of the labor force. However, it is not easy for a country that has grown by relying on low-wage labor to achieve productivity improvements while allowing wage increases rather than depending on low-wage labor. It is important for the government to improve the quality of workers through education and training. One policy option is to raise wages proactively to provide incentives for the private sector to mechanize and improve efficiency. Conversely, policies that artificially suppress wages or compensate for labor shortages with foreign workers without limits risk delaying productivity improvements.

So, how has Malaysia tackled the challenge of shifting from the quantity to the quality of its labor force, and to what extent has it succeeded? Has it achieved a virtuous cycle where wage increases lead to expanded domestic demand and improved labor productivity? This chapter first shows that in the early stages of economic development, the New Economic Policy mobilized Malay workers from rural areas into the commercial and industrial sectors, resolving the problem of labor quantity and that the introduction of foreign workers supplemented remaining shortages. We also point out that the initial New Economic Policy led to a reduction in income disparities. Furthermore, it shows that after the problem of labor quantity was resolved, a shift in development policy was pursued to address labor quality issues. Higher education reforms were implemented to improve the quality of labor, and we will clarify the political background that enabled this policy shift.

3.1 Malay Workers Supported High Economic Growth

3.1.1 Malays Advancing into Cities

Among Asian countries, Malaysia is considered relatively small in terms of population, with just 32.66 million people in 2021. This is the smallest population among the advanced ASEAN5 countries (excluding Singapore), and is notably small when compared to Indonesia (approximately 270 million), the Philippines (110 million), and Thailand (approximately 70 million).

However, Malaysia's population is still growing slowly. According to the United Nations' medium variant projection, Malaysia's population is expected to exceed 35 million in 2027 and 40 million in 2047, peaking at around 42 million in 2070 before slightly declining thereafter.[4] Japan's population in 2070 is projected to be approximately 90 million, meaning Malaysia's population size, currently about one-fourth of Japan's, is expected to expand to about half of Japan's in 50 years.

According to Malaysian government statistics, the population of Peninsular Malaysia in 1911 was only 2.32 million. Despite the massive influx of Chinese and Indian laborers into tin mines and rubber plantations under British colonial rule, the population of Peninsular Malaysia remained extremely low. The population was 6.28 million at the time of independence in 1957, 8.92 million when Malaysia was formed in 1963 with the addition of Sabah, Sarawak, and present-day Singapore (Singapore seceded in 1965), and just over ten million in 1970.[5] Considering that the majority were Malays, many of whom were confined to rural areas, it can be said that without mobilizing rural Malay workers into the commercial and industrial sectors in urban areas, it would have been impossible to secure the labor force necessary for industrialization, and Malaysia's economic growth since the 1970s would not have been realized.

As mentioned in Chapter 2, at that time in Malaysia, commerce and industry, primarily conducted by the Chinese, were centered in urban areas. In contrast, the majority of Malays were involved in agriculture in rural areas. Due to the "ethnic barrier" between urban and rural areas, Malays in rural areas did not naturally migrate to urban areas in search of higher wages and engage in commerce and industry, even when wages in urban commercial and industrial sectors increased. The New

Economic Policy is also known as the "Malay (Bumiputera) preferential policy," and indeed, this is one of its essential aspects. However, the New Economic Policy also provided primary and secondary education to rural Malays, which strongly supported their migration to cities and employment in the commercial and industrial sectors. Without the New Economic Policy, Malaysia would have encountered a severe labor shortage during the early stages of economic development.

In line with the New Economic Policy, the Malaysian government strongly supported the advancement of Malays into the commercial and industrial sectors,[6] which accelerated the influx of Malays into urban areas. During this period, it was reported that at least 24% of Kuala Lumpur's total population was living in squatter settlements built on illegally occupied land.[7] As a countermeasure, the Malaysian government focused on providing low-cost housing,[8] resulting in a relatively small urban informal sector in Malaysia. According to World Bank statistics, in 2010 the percentage of the urban population living in slums was 27% in Thailand, 23% in Indonesia, and 41% in the Philippines. In contrast, the slum population in Kuala Lumpur in 2013 was only 12,868, less than 1% of the total population.[9]

In the 1980s, Malaysia's urbanization and industrialization further accelerated, and by 1991, 51.1% of the total population lived in urban areas. The percentage of Malays living in urban areas nearly doubled, increasing from 21.3% in 1980 to 39.4% in 1991. Subsequently, in 2000, the percentage of Malays living in urban areas surpassed 50.1%, exceeding the percentage living in rural areas, and Malays accounted for 53.1% of the urban population. In 1970, the Chinese accounted for 59% of the urban population. Thus, over 30 years, Malaysia's cities underwent a significant transformation from a situation where the Chinese constituted the majority of residents to one where Malays constituted the majority (Fig. 3.1).

One characteristic of Malaysia's urbanization is that, in addition to the migration of people from rural areas into existing cities, the expansion of existing urban areas and the construction of new cities also played a significant role. The number of townships increased from 72 in 1980 to 170 in 2000. Townships with a population of 150,000 or more tripled from 9 to 27, while relatively small townships with a population of 15,000 to 25,000 doubled from 39 to 80.[10] Furthermore, from the mid-1990s, the new administrative city of Putrajaya and the IT-specialized city of Cyberjaya were constructed south of Kuala Lumpur, expanding the metropolitan area. This expansion can be considered one of the reasons why large-scale slums did not form in Malaysia's existing major cities.

3.1.2 Towards the Eradication of Ethnically Stratified Labor Systems

During this period, the rigid ethnic segregation of occupations—where Chinese dominated commerce and industry while Malays worked primarily in agriculture—also decreased significantly. In 1970, Malays accounted for 67.6% of those involved in the

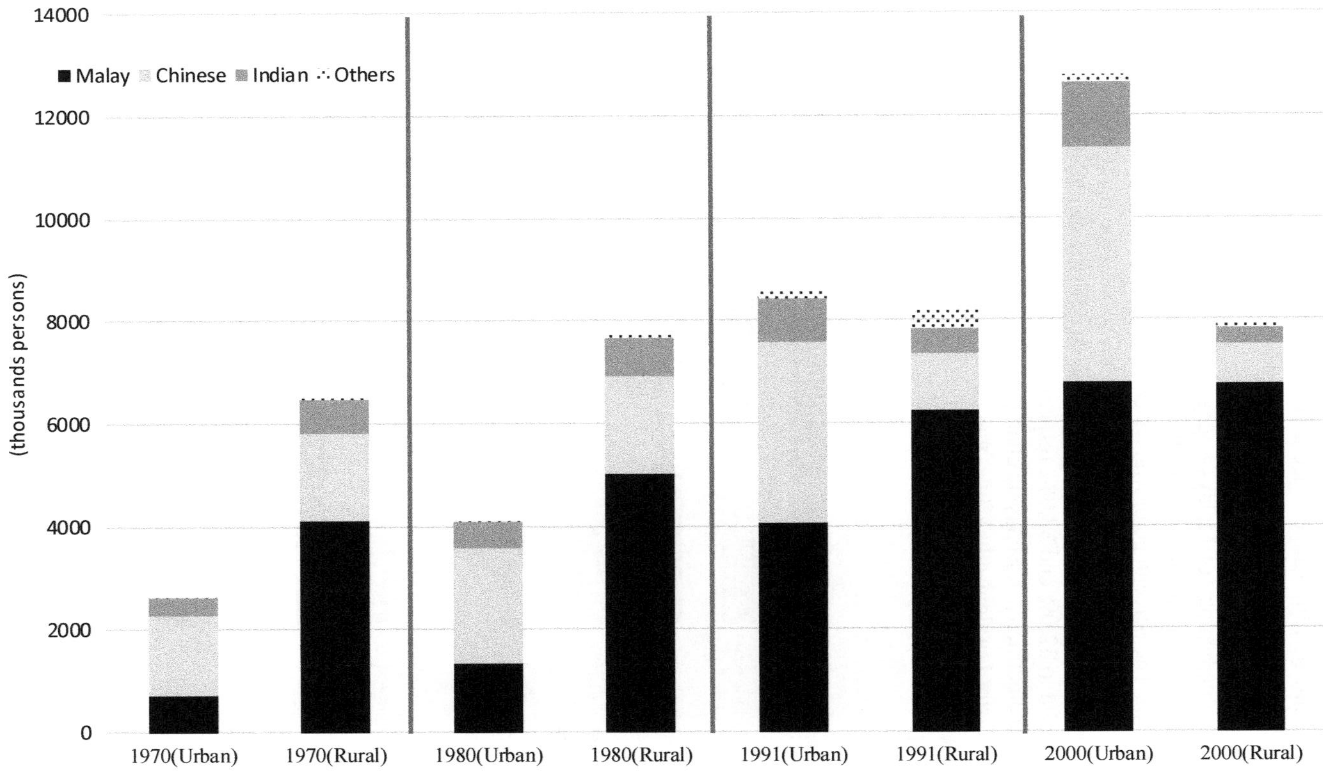

Fig. 3.1 Urban and Rural Population by Ethnicity, 1970–2000. *Source* Created from the Five-Year Plans (Malaysia [various years]) and Population Census data. *Note* 1970 and 1980 data cover Peninsular Malaysia only. For 1991 and 2000, "Malay" includes other Bumiputera ethnic groups

primary sector, exceeding their population share, while their share in the secondary industry was 32.1% and in the tertiary industry 42.6%, falling below their population share. Meanwhile, the Chinese accounted for 58.7% of those engaged in the secondary industry and 45.5% in the tertiary industry, both figures far exceeding their population share.

By 2000, the percentage of Malays engaged in the primary industry had fallen to 61.5%, below their population share (with 21% classified as "Others," namely foreign workers). The percentage of Malays engaged in the secondary industry was 46.6%, and in the tertiary industry 52.0%, both surpassing the percentages for the Chinese. Conversely, the percentage of Chinese engaged in the secondary and tertiary sectors decreased to 32.0% and 33.9%, respectively. The rigid relationship between employment and ethnicity in Malaysia changed significantly over 30 years, and the occupational distortion along ethnic lines was considerably reduced. This represented a remarkable rate of change (Fig. 3.2).

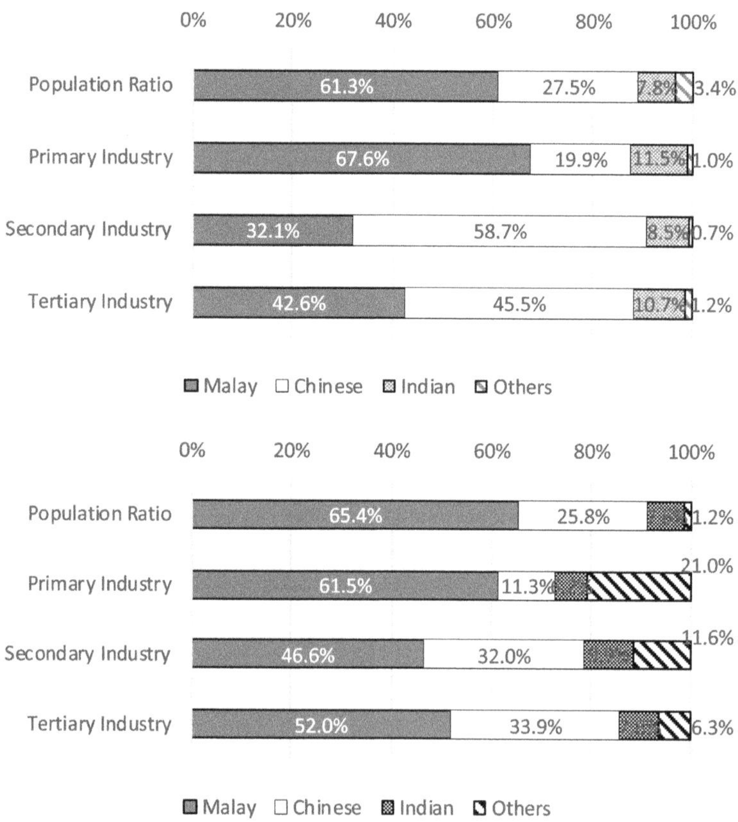

Fig. 3.2 Ethnic Composition of Employment by Industry: (a)1970 (b)2000. *Source* Created by the author based on data from Five-Year Plans (Malaysia [various years]). *Note* 1970 data covers Peninsular Malaysia only. For 2000, "Malay" includes other Bumiputera ethnic groups

3.2 The Issues Surrounding Foreign Workers

3.2.1 Foreign Workers in the Informal Sector

In many developing countries, the informal sector has a significant presence in the economy. In contrast, the informal sector involving Malaysian nationals is relatively small in Malaysia. As mentioned earlier, this is because the New Economic Policy actively promoted population migration from rural to urban areas and provided low-cost housing.

However, since the 1990s, foreign workers have dominated Malaysia's informal sector. According to the Department of Statistics Malaysia, in 2017, there were 1.36 million workers in the informal sector[11] in Malaysia, accounting for 9.4% of total employment. Although the definition differs, this figure is significantly smaller compared to the International Labour Organization (ILO) estimates for Indonesia (84.2%) and Thailand (67.5%).[12] Furthermore, Malaysia's definition of the informal sector closely resembles that of non-regular employment. The ILO's definition of "workers not protected by law" more accurately reflects the situation of foreign workers in Malaysia, particularly undocumented workers. At one point, estimates suggested that there were 2 to 3 million undocumented workers in Malaysia, more than double the number of informal sector workers reported by the Department of Statistics Malaysia.

Historically, Malaysia has had a small population relative to its land area and economic activities, which contributed to the influx of Chinese and Indian workers into Malaysia as laborers from the nineteenth to the early twentieth century. When full-scale industrialization progressed in the late 1980s, labor shortages became severe despite the rapid mobilization of Malay workers from rural areas into the commercial and industrial sectors. In response, in 1992, the Malaysian government expanded the employment of foreign workers to the manufacturing and service industries—having previously limited it to plantations, construction sites, and domestic work—and began the full-scale introduction of foreign workers.

Malaysia's foreign worker employment system is designed on the premise of fixed-term repatriation and is clearly distinguished from immigration. The acceptance of unskilled foreign workers is limited to those aged 18 to 45, and they are not allowed to bring their families. Work permits for unskilled foreign workers are renewed annually and, in principle, can currently be renewed for up to 3 years, with a maximum total stay of 10 years.[13] In addition, foreign workers can be accepted from only 15 countries, and the industries in which they can work are designated for each source country.

However, this system, designed to address short-term labor shortages, does not match the reality of persistent labor shortages. Consequently, Malaysia's foreign worker system is characterized by the constant and large-scale presence of over-stayers (who remain after their visas have expired) and undocumented workers (who enter the country without obtaining work permits).

As of December 2019, the largest proportion of foreign workers in Malaysia came from Indonesia (34.7%), followed by Bangladesh (28.6%), Nepal (14.9%), Myanmar (8.0%), and India (5.5%).[14]

3.2.2 *One in Four Workers is a Foreigner*

A key characteristic of Malaysia's foreign worker issue is the large proportion of the labor force they represent. According to statistics for the fourth quarter of 2020, foreign workers numbered 2.202 million out of a total labor force of 15.922 million, accounting for 13.8%. Estimates suggest that Malaysia has as many undocumented workers (who don't appear in official statistics) as—or even more than—documented foreign workers. Assuming there are approximately the same number of undocumented workers, foreign workers would constitute about one-quarter of Malaysia's workforce.

Figure 3.3 shows the number of foreign workers and their percentage of the total workforce. Since the 2010s, foreign workers have consistently constituted more than 15% of the total workforce. If this percentage were applied to Japan, it would be equivalent to more than 10 million foreign workers.[15]

While the influx of foreign workers continues to increase due to both supply factors (wage disparities with neighboring countries) and demand factors (labor shortages in some industrial sectors), the Malaysian government aims to limit the total number of foreign workers. In a speech in August 2005, then-Prime Minister Abdullah stated that Malaysia was "addicted to foreign workers" and called for reducing this dependence, arguing that it hindered industrial upgrading.[16]

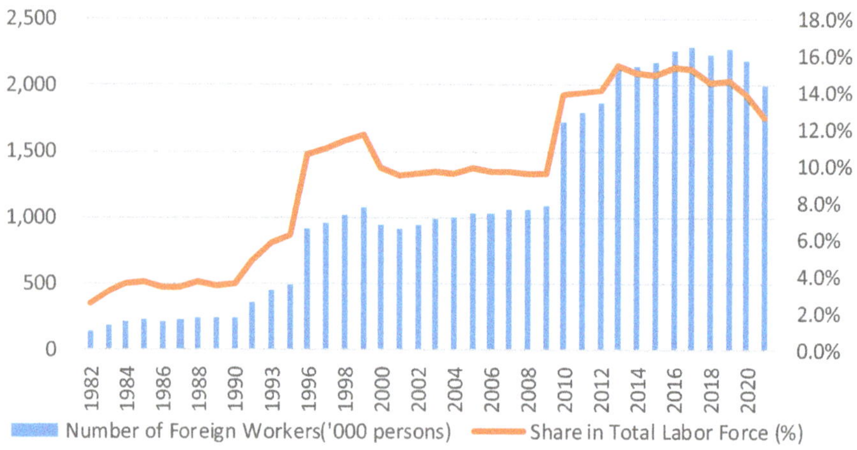

Fig. 3.3 Number of Foreign Workers and Their Share in Total Labor Force (1982–2021). *Source* Created by the author based on data from Department of Statistics Malaysia website (Labor force by ethnic group, Malaysia/states, 1982–2021)

The Malaysian government has repeatedly raised taxes on the employment of foreign workers, suspended and resumed new hires, granted amnesty to undocumented workers, and both legalized and repatriated them. For example, from October 2011 to January 2014, an amnesty and legalization program for undocumented workers (commonly known as the 6P Program) was implemented. Under this program, 1.3 million people applied, of whom 500,000 were legalized and 330,000 were deported. In Malaysia, such crackdowns, deportations, and legalization of undocumented workers are carried out regularly, and the number of foreign workers in official statistics fluctuates with the timing of these actions. In Fig. 3.3, there are two significant jumps (in 1996 and 2010) in the number of foreign workers.

3.2.3 The Pros and Cons of Dependence on Foreign Workers

There is an ongoing debate about whether foreign workers have a positive or negative impact on the Malaysian economy. The World Bank argues that foreign workers are essential for Malaysia's economic development, estimating that a 10% increase in unskilled foreign workers boosts Malaysia's real GDP by 1.1% and that for every ten foreign workers accepted, 5.2 jobs are created for Malaysians. It also estimates that while a 10% increase in foreign workers reduces the wages of unskilled workers by 3.94%, it simultaneously increases the overall wages of Malaysians by 0.14%. The World Bank concludes that while the fiscal burden of foreign workers is minor, there are problems with Malaysia's foreign worker management system and reforms are necessary.[17]

Undeniably, foreign workers are filling employment mismatches. Foreign workers are typically employed in what are known as 3D (Dirty, Dangerous, and Demanding) jobs that Malaysians are reluctant to take. While 39.8% of foreign workers are employed in occupations classified as elementary occupations, only 8.1% of Malaysians are employed in these categories.

According to JETRO's Investment Cost Comparison (2020–2021),[18] the monthly salary of manufacturing workers in Dhaka, Bangladesh, is $115, while in Kuala Lumpur, it is $431—about four times higher. If workers' rights are sufficiently guaranteed, the presence of foreign workers who fill occupations unpopular among Malaysian citizens due to wage differences with their home countries can be beneficial for both sides.

On the other hand, Bank Negara emphasized the disadvantages of foreign workers in a box article titled "Low-Skilled Foreign Workers' Distortions to the Economy" in its 2017 annual report. Bank Negara argues that dependence on low-skilled foreign workers reinforces Malaysia's image as a low-cost investment destination, and multinational corporations increasingly exploit the ease of hiring foreign workers. As a result, the low-value-added segments of multinational corporations' value chains are located in Malaysia, while the high-value-added segments are shifted to Singapore and China.[19]

The social and economic problems associated with the increase in foreign workers include: (1) the negative impact on the income of domestic workers who compete with them in the labor market; (2) the increased burden on public expenditures such as education, healthcare, and social security; and (3) the potential for increased crime rates and social and cultural frictions. In the case of Malaysia, by limiting foreign workers to fixed-term unskilled labor and not allowing them to bring their families, the problems described in points (1) and (2) are minimized. Furthermore, due to Malaysia's historical background as a trade hub frequented by foreigners, the issues in point (3) have also remained relatively minor.

However, continuing to supplement the labor shortage (originally filled by rural Malays) in the commercial and industrial sectors with a large number of foreign workers is likely to have a negative impact on Malaysia's economic development in the long run. Foreign workers are necessary at construction sites and on plantations where mechanization is difficult, as well as in jobs that Malaysians are reluctant to take. However, accepting a large number of foreign workers on manufacturing shop floors risks reducing incentives for companies to invest in mechanization and product upgrading. It may also suppress the demand for skilled workers that would normally be required through such modernization efforts.

As Bank Negara also points out, a mutually reinforcing relationship exists between dependence on foreign workers and dependence on foreign companies in the manufacturing sector. For example, in the electronics and electrical industry, some multinational corporations employ a large number of foreign workers. In contrast, locally owned companies and multinational corporations with localized management tend to have a relatively lower dependence on foreign workers.[20]

Of course, there are exceptions: locally owned companies such as Top Glove, which exports rubber gloves in a highly price-competitive market where differentiation is difficult, also employ many foreign workers. However, even in the electronics and electrical industry, where there is potential for increasing value-added, multinational corporations whose management has not been localized tend to rely heavily on foreign workers. This is likely because sufficient authority has not been transferred to local subsidiaries, preventing management from operating according to local conditions and resulting in a bias toward wage restraint for management efficiency. This situation suggests that dependence on foreign capital in the manufacturing sector is a factor that reinforces dependence on foreign workers.

Furthermore, it is necessary to address the human rights issues concerning foreign workers in Malaysia. In Malaysia, human rights issues include the exploitation of foreign workers by brokers and the abuse of domestic workers. In the Trafficking in Persons Report released in June 2014, the United States downgraded Malaysia to the lowest rating. A particular concern is that a large number of undocumented workers are placed in a vulnerable position in relation to employers and brokers, often forced to work without pay or having their passports confiscated.

In July 2020, the United States banned the import of rubber gloves from Top Glove, citing forced labor. In January 2021, COVID-19 clusters emerged at four of the company's factories, forcing them to suspend operations. The underlying issue was that more than 5000 foreign workers were forced to live in substandard conditions in employee dormitories.[21] As a result of these incidents, such companies have begun to improve the treatment of foreign workers.

3.3 Trends in Economic Disparities

3.3.1 *The Effects of the New Economic Policy*

As we have seen, the New Economic Policy promoted the advancement of Malays into urban areas and employment in commerce and industry, rapidly overturning the rigid employment structure of "commerce and industry for the Chinese, agriculture for the Malays." So, did this change result in a reduction in income disparities? Let us examine the trends and changes in income disparities here.

Figure 3.4 shows the trends in the Gini coefficient (which is 0 when there is no disparity and approaches 1 as disparity increases), representing the degree of disparity, along with the share of income of the bottom 40%, middle 40%, and top 20% of households in total income from 1957/58 to 2019.[22] From this figure, we can see that income disparities: (1) rapidly widened from independence in 1957 to the mid-1970s; (2) narrowed continuously from a peak in 1976 until the late 1980s[23]; (3) remained at almost the same level until the mid-2000s; and (4) have been gradually narrowing since then, particularly since the 2010s.

What stands out first is the rapid expansion of disparities after independence. Immediately after independence, in 1957/58, the Gini coefficient was 0.412, which was not exceptionally high among developing countries in East Asia. During this period, the Gini coefficient was 0.558 in Taiwan (1955) and 0.48 in the Philippines (1956).[24] However, while disparities narrowed in Taiwan and remained flat in the Philippines, the income gap widened in Malaysia, with the Gini coefficient reaching 0.513 in 1970. Income disparities in Malaysia continued to widen after that, with the

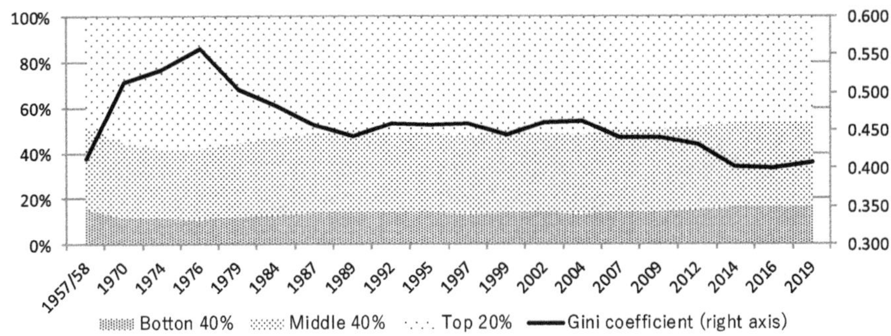

Fig. 3.4 Trends in Income Inequality in Malaysia (1957–2019). *Source* Created by the author based on Snodgrass (1980) and DOSM (various years)

Gini coefficient reaching 0.557 in 1976. However, this marked a turning point, after which disparities began to narrow rapidly.

It is challenging to analyze the factors behind the widening income disparities in Malaysia from independence to the mid-1970s due to the lack of detailed data. However, it is generally accepted that income disparities in a country tend to widen in the early stages of economic development and narrow as economic development progresses (known as the Kuznets hypothesis).[25] Kuznets explains that income disparities widen due to urbanization and industrialization in the early stages of economic development because urban incomes are higher than rural incomes, and income disparities also tend to be more pronounced in urban areas. In Malaysia, before the effects of the New Economic Policy became apparent, urbanization did not progress significantly. However, income disparities may have widened both between urban and rural areas and within urban areas as the incomes of the wealthy urban residents—who benefited from import-substitution industrialization and primary commodity exports—increased.

So, were the two main objectives of the New Economic Policy—poverty reduction and the reduction of inter-ethnic disparities—achieved? First, the poverty rate (Fig. 3.5) was very high at 49.3% in 1970, the year after the May 13 incident, and was exceptionally high among Bumiputeras at 64.8%. After that, the poverty rate declined steadily, reaching 17.5% for Bumiputeras and 12.4% overall in 1992, when Malaysia attained upper-middle-income status. The poverty rate continued to decline, reaching 0.6% in 2014. However, the poverty line was revised in 2020 and applied retroactively to the previous two surveys, resulting in a poverty rate of 7.6% in 2016 and 5.6% in 2019. The new poverty line is set at a monthly household income of 2208 ringgit.

The World Bank defines the poverty line for upper-middle-income countries as $6.85 per person per day (in 2017 purchasing power parity) (as of 2022). When Malaysia's poverty line is converted to the same format, it equals $11.45 per person

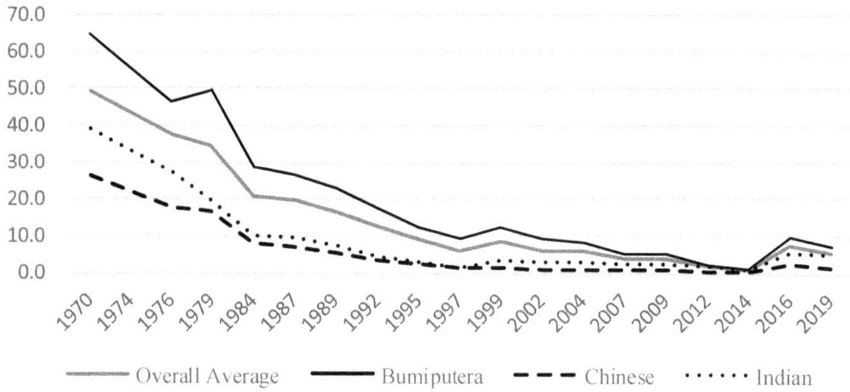

Fig. 3.5 Trends in Poverty Rates in Malaysia (1970–2019). *Source* Created by the author based on DOSM (various years)

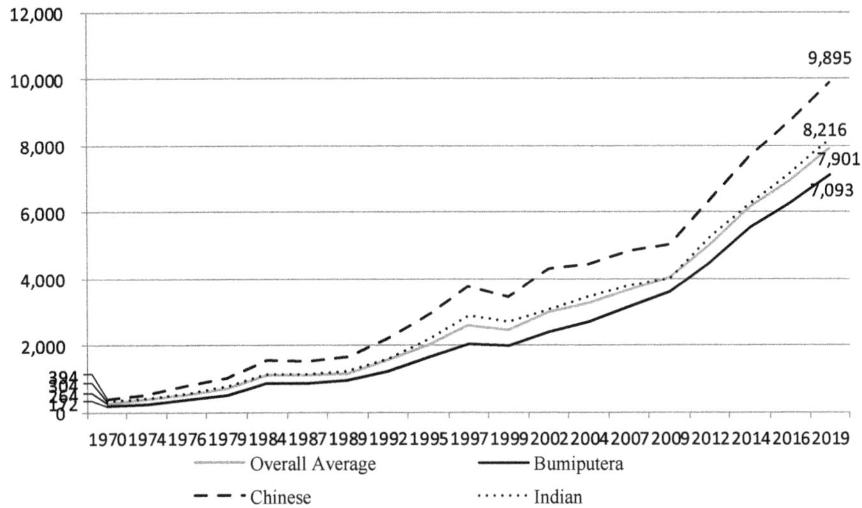

Fig. 3.6 Trends in Average Monthly Household Income by Ethnic Group (1970–2019). *Source* Created by the author based on DOSM (various years)

per day, considerably higher than the World Bank's $6.85. The Malaysian government has reset the poverty line to match the current price level and has renewed its focus on poverty reduction.

Income disparities between ethnic groups also began to narrow after the introduction of the New Economic Policy (Fig. 3.6). In 1970, the average monthly household income for all households was 264 ringgit, while that for Bumiputera households was only 172 ringgit (65% of the overall average). From the 1970s to the 1980s, inter-ethnic income disparities narrowed rapidly, with Bumiputera household income reaching 80% of the overall average in 1987.

However, inter-ethnic disparities did not improve further for a while after that, and the level remained stagnant throughout the 1990s. Then, in the mid-2000s, inter-ethnic disparities began to narrow again, with Bumiputera household income reaching 90% of the overall average by 2009.

Looking again at the long-term trend of income disparities, Malaysia's Gini coefficient remained high at around 0.45 from the late 1980s (when high economic growth began), through the 1990s (when it became an upper-middle-income country), and even into the mid-2000s, spanning the 1997–98 Asian Financial Crisis. This was also a period when urbanization progressed alongside industrialization, and disparities between urban and rural areas became more pronounced.

Therefore, when examining the trends in the Gini coefficient alongside the trends in urban-rural disparities and the disparities between the Chinese and Bumiputeras (Fig. 3.7), we see that both urban-rural disparities and Chinese-Bumiputera disparities, like the Gini coefficient, began narrowing from 1976 onward. From the late 1970s through the 1980s, regional and ethnic disparities narrowed simultaneously, contributing to the reduction of overall disparities.

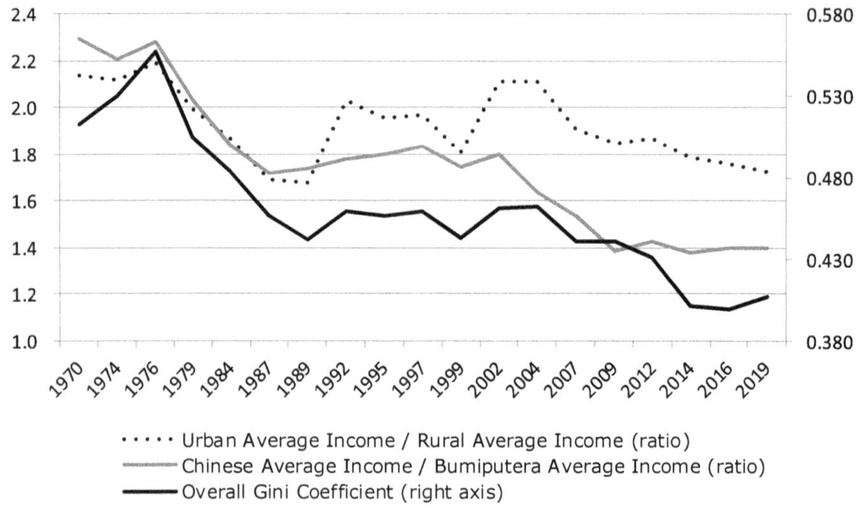

Fig. 3.7 Trends in Gini Coefficient, Urban-Rural Disparity, and Chinese-Bumiputera Income Gap (1970–2019). *Source* Created by the author based on DOSM (various years)

However, a significant change emerged in the 1990s. While ethnic disparities remained essentially flat, urban-rural disparities expanded rapidly in the early 1990s, reverting to the level of a decade earlier. Subsequently, urban-rural disparities widened further in the early 2000s, a period that included the Asian Financial Crisis.

Underlying these changes in trends is a shift in the emphasis of disparity reduction measures. As discussed in the previous chapter, when the New Economic Policy began, the government recognized that resolving the unemployment problem in rural areas, where many Malays resided, was an urgent issue. Therefore, the initial phase of the New Economic Policy focused on rural development. Poverty eradication and the reduction of inter-ethnic disparities could not be achieved without resolving the employment problem in rural areas.

However, as the government pushed ahead with industrialization policies in earnest in the 1980s, the emphasis of the New Economic Policy shifted toward supporting the advancement of Bumiputras into commerce and industry. From the late 1980s, as high economic growth was achieved through export-oriented industrialization—specifically the development of the electronics and electrical industry led by foreign companies—urban-rural disparities began to widen.

Urban-rural disparities widened while ethnic disparities remained unchanged and overall disparities stayed high. This pattern indicates that income disparities within each ethnic group also remained substantial during this period.

3.3.2 *Narrowing Inter-Ethnic Disparities and Persistent Intra-Ethnic Disparities*

Let us examine the trends in inter-ethnic and intra-ethnic income disparities in Malaysia. Figure 3.8 shows the Theil index, one of the inequality indices, calculated by combining average household income and population data by ethnicity (Bumiputra/Chinese/Indian) and income class (top 20%, middle 40%, bottom 40%). The Theil index has the advantage of being able to decompose inequality into contributions by category. First, the Theil index for Malaysia as a whole shows a trend similar to that of the Gini coefficient: peaking in 1976, then declining, leveling off in the 1990s, and declining again in the 2010s.

What is particularly interesting is the trend in the contribution of each of the nine categories (formed by ethnicity (Bumiputera/Chinese/Indian) × income level (high/middle/low)) to overall inequality. Looking at the contribution of "Chinese-high income" to overall inequality, it was remarkably high in the early 1970s. It is fair to say that the problem of income disparity in Malaysia at that time was almost entirely attributable to the high relative income of the Chinese high-income group. However, the contribution of the Chinese high-income group decreased significantly from the late 1970s onward, declining to about half of its initial level by 1989. On the other hand, the contribution of the Bumiputera high-income group increased, rising gradually with the implementation of the New Economic Policy, catching up with the contribution of the Chinese high-income group in 2004, and becoming the highest contributor since 2007.

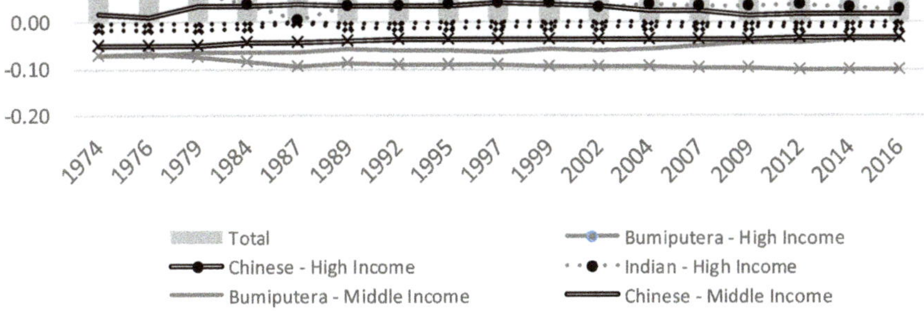

Fig. 3.8 Trends in Theil Index (By Ethnicity and Income Class, 1974–2016). *Source* Created by the author based on Ministry of Economy, Median of monthly household gross income of household group by ethnic group and strata, Malaysia

Since the 2000s, it has been widely recognized that the focus of Malaysia's income disparity problem has shifted from inter-ethnic disparity to intra-ethnic disparity. However, it is clear that even in 1970, intra-ethnic income disparities were already extremely large. Malaysia's income disparity problem can be better understood as having shifted from the concentration of high income among the Chinese high-income group in the 1970s to the concentration of high income among the Bumiputera high-income group in the 2000s. This makes sense if we consider that the majority of Bumiputeras once perceived a disparity with the Chinese high-income group (termed "inter-ethnic" income disparity), whereas now many Bumiputeras perceive a disparity with the Bumiputera high-income group (termed "intra-ethnic" income disparity). In other words, from the perspective of Bumiputeras, the income disparity problem has shifted from inter-ethnic disparity to intra-ethnic disparity. On the other hand, from the perspective of the Chinese middle- and low-income groups, they previously experienced significant "intra-ethnic" income disparity with the Chinese high-income group, whereas now they perceive significant "inter-ethnic" income disparity with the Bumiputera high-income group.

How have government policies influenced these trends in income disparities between ethnic groups, between urban and rural areas, and in society as a whole? If we focus on the fact that the extreme disparities of the mid-1970s significantly improved by the late 1980s, we can conclude that the New Economic Policy was effective. Ragayah, who examined the factors behind the disparity changes since 1970, summarized the findings of previous studies and argued that four key factors implemented during the New Economic Policy period contributed to disparity reduction and poverty alleviation: rural development, education and employment policies, export-oriented industrialization policies, and capital formation support for Bumiputeras.[26] According to Ragayah, rural development—specifically, support measures such as agricultural infrastructure development and subsidies—improved incomes in rural areas where many of the poor resided. Bumiputera support measures in education and employment promoted their advancement into the secondary and tertiary industries. This movement was further accelerated by the growth of export-oriented, labor-intensive manufacturing industries. Those who left rural areas to work in factories in urban areas sent money back to their hometowns, which also improved income levels in rural areas. In addition, government-established low-risk, high-return investment trust schemes for Bumiputeras contributed to promoting savings among the Bumiputra population.

On the other hand, if we focus on the persistence of intra-ethnic disparities, we can conclude that the New Economic Policy did not contribute significantly to narrowing the gap between the rich and the poor. Some critics argue that economic policies should not continue to focus on the "illusion" of inter-ethnic disparities,[27] given that intra-Malay disparities rapidly expanded from independence to 1970 and that the pace of disparity reduction within Bumiputeras has been slow since the 1980s.

Ragayah also acknowledges that government economic policies failed to reduce disparities from 1990 to the mid-2000s. She attributes this to two factors: industrial upgrading that led to wage disparities, and the increase in foreign workers that coincided with sluggish growth in the agricultural sector, widening the urban-rural gap.

Summarizing the above discussion, we can conclude that: (1) the initial phase of the New Economic Policy, which emphasized rural development, likely contributed to reducing income disparities that had continually widened since independence; however, (2) the government's disparity reduction measures had little notable effect from the 1990s to the mid-2000s.

3.4 Development of the Education System

3.4.1 Improved Secondary Education Enrollment During the New Economic Policy Period

For developing countries to initiate industrialization and subsequently transition from labor-intensive industries to high value-added industries, it is necessary to continuously expand the education system. In Malaysia, primary education expanded from an early stage, but the development of subsequent levels, particularly higher education, was delayed.

Under British rule in Malaya, only English schools provided a complete education pathway from primary through secondary to higher education. There were also vernacular schools—Malay, Chinese, and Tamil—but these offered only primary education before World War II. After the war, Chinese secondary schools were actively established, but there were no secondary schools with Malay as the language of instruction.[28] Consequently, students from Malay primary schools seeking secondary education had no choice but to first enter special English language courses at English schools before transferring to secondary education.[29]

After independence, education policies in the 1960s focused on strengthening primary education and expanding secondary education. Free primary education was implemented in 1961.[30] According to the World Bank's World Development Indicators (WDI), the net enrollment rate for primary education in 1971, when the New Economic Policy began, reached 86.7%. The average for OECD member countries was 88.2%, indicating that Malaysia had achieved a primary education enrollment rate nearly on par with developed countries at this point.

However, regarding secondary education, the gross enrollment rate[31] in 1971 was 41.2%, significantly below the 70.7% for OECD member countries. It also lagged behind the Philippines (47.5%), a country where formal education was established early in Southeast Asia. Twenty years later, in 1990, the secondary education enrollment rate had increased to 63.4%, narrowing the gap with OECD member countries (84.7%). Considering that Malay secondary schools did not exist at the time of independence, the government's efforts to strengthen Malay language education under the New Economic Policy clearly contributed to the increase in secondary education enrollment rates. At this point, Malaysia's rate still fell short of the Philippines (72%) but far surpassed Indonesia (46.6%) and Thailand (28.5%).

3.4.2 *Expansion of Higher Education Opportunities with the Revision of the New Economic Policy*

However, the situation regarding higher education was completely different. For Malaysia, the earliest comparable data available in the WDI is from 1979. At that time, the gross enrollment rate for higher education was only 3.8%. This was far below OECD member countries (29.5%) and the Philippines (23.5%) and less than half of Thailand (8.5%). Even in 1990, the situation had changed little, with Malaysia's rate (7.2%) being merely one-fifth of OECD member countries (37.5%) and less than half of Thailand's rate (15.9%).

The delay in the expansion of higher education in Malaysia can be attributed to two factors: first, the historical absence of universities during the colonial period; and second, the government's prioritization under the New Economic Policy of improving the relative position of Malays over expanding higher education opportunities.

There were no universities in what is now Malaysia until independence. In 1949, two colleges in Singapore were merged to form the University of Malaya, and in 1959, after independence, the Kuala Lumpur campus of the University of Malaya was established. This became Malaysia's first university. It took another ten years for the second university to be established, and even by 1990, there were only seven national universities.

The number of universities remained limited because the government restricted the establishment of private universities. While the government permitted the establishment of private educational institutions that granted certificates or diplomas (such as colleges and polytechnics), it prohibited the establishment of degree-awarding private universities for a long time. In the 1970s, Chinese education officials applied for approval to establish a Chinese-medium private university, but the government rejected this proposal. The applicants filed a lawsuit seeking approval, but the court ruled against them in 1982, finalizing their defeat.[32]

After the May 13 incident, education policy became an area strongly influenced by Malay nationalism. From 1970, the conversion of English schools to Malay schools began. By 1982, the conversion of all English schools to Malay schools—from elementary and secondary schools to pre-university courses—was completed. Furthermore, in 1983, Malay became the language of instruction even in universities that had predominantly used English until then. In addition, an ethnic quota system was introduced for university admissions. Through a ruling party agreement in 1979, the ratio was set at 55% for Bumiputeras and 45% for non-Bumiputeras (35% for Chinese and 10% for others).[33]

For a quarter of a century, policy prioritized correcting inter-ethnic disparities over expanding higher education. This approach continued until the mid-1990s, when

Malaysia attained upper-middle-income status and the policy was revised. In 1996, the Private Higher Educational Institutions Act was enacted, and the Universities and University Colleges Act and other laws were amended, allowing the establishment of private universities. Lectures could also be conducted in English with the permission of the Minister of Education. As a result, most private universities adopted English as the language of instruction.[34]

With this policy change as a turning point, the higher education enrollment rate increased significantly, reaching 43.1% in 2019 (Fig. 3.9). Within Southeast Asia, excluding the city-state of Singapore (91.1%), Malaysia has surpassed the Philippines (35.5% in 2017), which has struggled since the 1980s and is second only to Thailand (49.3% in 2016).

If the strict regulations on higher education had continued even after Malaysia became an upper-middle-income country in the mid-1990s, human resource development would have stagnated and become an obstacle to industrial upgrading. What, then, made possible the policy change that led to the expansion of higher education opportunities?

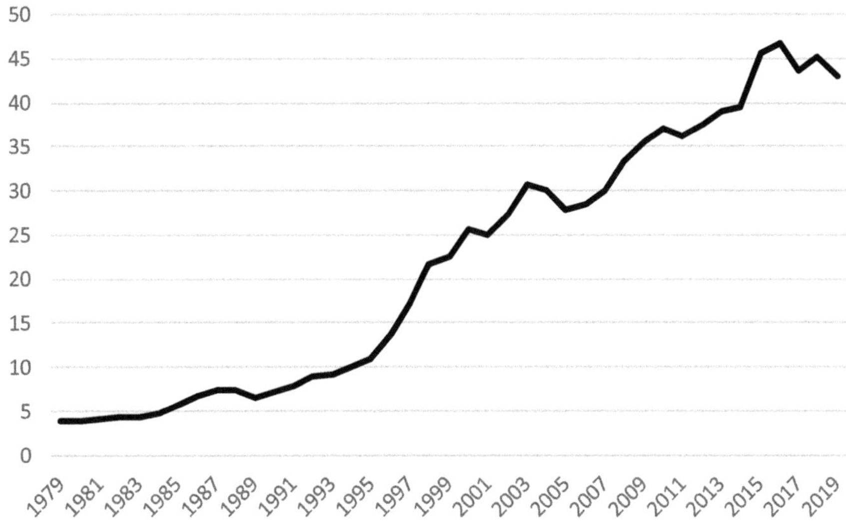

Fig. 3.9 Trends in Gross Enrollment Rate in Higher Education (1979–2019). *Source* Created by the author based on WDI. *Note* Data for 1981, 1996, and 1997 are unavailable. Estimated values based on average rate of change are used

3.5 The Political Process Leading to the Establishment of the Economic Growth-Oriented Policy

3.5.1 The Struggle over "Development Policy after 1990"

Policy shifts, such as the approval of private university establishment, were realized as the development policy review progressed—a shift from prioritizing Malay support measures to emphasizing economic growth that began in the mid-1980s.

The New Economic Policy was defined in the Outline Perspective Plan (OPP), formulated by the government in 1973, as a 20-year plan from 1971 to 1990.[35] In other words, the various goals, such as increasing the share of Bumiputera corporate stock ownership to 30%, were positioned as targets to be achieved by 1990. Therefore, discussions on the successor policy began in earnest in the late 1980s.

The trigger for this was the seventh general election in August 1986. The Malaysian Chinese Association (MCA), a key member of the ruling coalition Barisan Nasional (BN), demanded to "decommunalise" economic policy and stated its position before the election that it would not agree to a unilateral extension of the New Economic Policy. The Malaysian People's Movement Party (Gerakan), another Chinese-majority ruling party, also called for abolishing the ethnic quota system. The opposition Democratic Action Party (DAP), in its election manifesto, called for an end to the New Economic Policy and argued that the division of citizens into Bumiputeras and non-Bumiputeras should be abolished. These demands from the Chinese side were unacceptable to the United Malays National Organisation (UMNO), a major Malay political party. The BN coalition promised in its manifesto to strive for broad consensus on development policy after 1990 but avoided mentioning the specifics of the policy.[36]

The following year, 1987, UMNO, MCA, and Gerakan all held leadership elections, and development policy after 1990 became the main point of contention there as well. The UMNO leadership election in April saw Prime Minister Mahathir and Deputy Prime Minister Ghafar Baba team up against Razaleigh Hamzah, Minister of Trade and Industry, and Musa Hitam, former Deputy Prime Minister, in the fiercest battle in the party's history. Although the Mahathir camp won, the margin of victory was narrow, and the power struggle within the party continued after the election. In the run-up to this leadership election, Deputy Prime Minister Ghafar had set a goal of "increasing the share of Bumiputera corporate stock ownership to 35% by 2020." On the other hand, MCA decided at its youth convention the day before its leadership election to oppose the extension of the New Economic Policy, and the incumbent president of Gerakan also pledged in the party's leadership election to implement a renewed development policy after 1990.

As the rift between BN component parties deepened over development policy after 1990, Chinese parties and organizations clashed with UMNO in October of the same year over personnel issues at Chinese primary schools. The trigger was an incident where a teacher without qualifications in Chinese language education was appointed to a managerial position at a Chinese primary school in Malacca. Chinese education organizations opposed this appointment and demanded that the Ministry of Education withdraw it. Chinese political parties, both ruling and opposition, supported this movement and held a protest rally of about 5000 people in Kuala Lumpur. On that occasion, Lee Kim Sai, MCA Deputy President, stated that cooperation with DAP would be possible if the issue was not resolved. At the rally, a hard-line tactic of having Chinese primary school students boycott classes was decided, and boycotts were carried out at 45 Chinese primary schools.[37]

The moves by Chinese organizations and parties stimulated Malay society, particularly UMNO, which considers itself the representative of Malay interests. The party's youth wing held a rally mobilizing 15,000 people to counter the Chinese side, demanding the dismissal of Lee Kim Sai, the Minister of Labour, and the expulsion of MCA from the ruling coalition. As anti-Chinese sentiment rose among Malays, Sanusi Junid, UMNO Secretary-General, and others hastily planned a mass rally to commemorate the 40th anniversary of UMNO's founding, raising concerns among Chinese society that the rally might trigger a recurrence of riots.[38]

The government resorted to authoritarian tactics to defuse worsening ethnic tensions. The police began preventive detention under the Internal Security Act and arrested 104 people within a little over two weeks. Those detained in this crackdown named Operation Lalang included politicians from the ruling and opposition parties, Chinese education organizations, intellectuals' organizations, consumer groups, environmental groups, and other NGO activists.

3.5.2 The Advocacy of "Vision 2020"

After suppressing and calming the overheated debate on ethnic interests, the government resumed its moves to formulate development policy after 1990 at the end of the following year. In December 1988, the establishment of the National Economic Consultative Council (NECC) was announced to formulate recommendations on post-1990 development policy. In January 1989, the NECC was launched, consisting of 150 members, including leaders of ruling and opposition parties, representatives of economic organizations, trade unions, Chinese education organizations, religious organizations and other NGOs, intellectuals, and lawyers. Ghazali Shafie, a former Foreign Minister who had led the formulation of the New Economic Policy as Director-General of the Department of National Unity (DNU), was appointed as the chairperson, and 75 Bumiputeras and 75 non-Bumiputeras were selected as members. Lim Kit Siang, Secretary-General of DAP, and other individuals who had been temporarily imprisoned in Operation Lalang were also appointed as members.

The NECC meetings were held behind closed doors, both in subcommittees and plenary sessions, and the details of the discussions were not made known to the public. However, from the comments of the members to the media and other sources, it was clear that there was a large gap between the opinions of Malays and non-Malays; representatives of Chinese education organizations and DAP, dissatisfied with the way consensus building was being carried out, withdrew from the council.

In addition, although the report was initially scheduled to be prepared by the end of 1989, the work was significantly delayed. Although a draft was discussed at a plenary session for a week in August 1990, no agreement was reached.

In response, Mahathir declared that the government would not be bound by the NECC's recommendations, and he called a snap general election in October 1990 without revealing the specifics of the new development policy. In the eighth general election, the ruling coalition BN struggled in both Malay and Chinese constituencies. Still, it maintained its two-thirds majority in the lower house by leveraging its centrist strength in ethnically mixed constituencies.

In the Parliament session convened after the election, Mahathir reiterated that the government was not obligated to accept all of the NECC's recommendations because some members had withdrawn from the council. However, the NECC was not entirely useless in building consensus on the new development policy. A certain level of agreement had been reached among the members through discussions inside and outside the NECC.

One of these was the promotion of economic growth through the utilization of market mechanisms. Kamal Salih, an economist who served as the chairperson of the NECC report drafting committee, announced his policy concept, the "Income Doubling and Distribution Plan,"[39] in July 1989, when NECC activities were active. This plan, which aimed to double per capita national income by 2000 through 9% annual growth, proposed deregulation, which Chinese economic organizations had long been calling for, to achieve the goal. Regarding redistribution and employment restructuring policies to eliminate inter-ethnic disparities, the plan stated that "growth rate improvement is essential before redistribution" and advocated the necessity of policies that do not hinder growth.

Another point of agreement was the strengthening of national consciousness that transcends the boundaries of ethnicities such as Malay, Chinese, and Indian. In August 1988, Mahathir spoke at a seminar hosted by the Department of National Unity under the Prime Minister's Department about the need to create a "Malaysian Nation" (Bangsa Malaysia). On the other hand, Chinese political parties and Chinese organizations also recognized the need to strengthen "Malaysian Nationalism," as they acknowledged that various policies based on Malay nationalism had actually hindered national integration. In its policy document, MCA argued that "to enhance Malaysian nationalism, the government should also choose to emphasize national symbols that all ethnic groups can identify with, especially the Malay language, the King, and the flag, and downplay those symbols that exclude some citizens, especially religion."[40] This can be said to be an expression of the Chinese community's willingness to accept the Malay language as the national language and the King as the constitutional monarch as their own symbols.

In this way, 20 years after the start of the New Economic Policy, the recognition that accelerating economic growth should be the next priority and that national consciousness should be nurtured without being too caught up in the framework of ethnicity began to be shared by Malays and non-Malays. Building on this consensus, Mahathir articulated a national vision called 'The Way Forward,' which he announced in February 1991. This proposal, which called for Malaysia to become a developed country by 2020 and for the realization of a "Malaysian Nation (Bangsa Malaysia)" coexisting in harmony and equality, was later named "Vision 2020."

Vision 2020 was welcomed by MCA and Gerakan, as well as the leaders of the opposition parties DAP and Parti Islam Se-Malaysia (PAS). From the late 1980s, Malaysia had entered a period of high economic growth, and no forces directly opposed the government's policy of taking the necessary measures to accelerate economic growth further. The people also supported the government, and in the ninth general election in 1995, the ruling party received a record high vote share (65.2%) and won 84% of the seats in the lower house. The shift in higher education policy in 1996 was realized in the context of the people endorsing the government's deregulation policy to become a developed country.

During its lower-middle-income period, Malaysia achieved the quantitative expansion of the labor force necessary for export-oriented industrialization and the reduction of income disparities through the New Economic Policy. However, in the 1990s, when Malaysia became an upper-middle-income country, a shift from quantity to quality of the labor force became necessary for further development. Still, it cannot be denied that the industrial sector's dependence on foreign workers has become an obstacle. On the other hand, the establishment of private higher education institutions, which had been strictly regulated until the 1980s to prioritize correcting inter-ethnic disparities, was liberalized, and the higher education enrollment rate rapidly increased. This policy shift was made possible by voters' support for the government, which set a course for prioritizing economic growth by presenting "Vision 2020."

Notes

1. Allen (2009).
2. Asano and Takeshita (1980).
3. Ito (2019).
4. UN Population Division, World Population Prospects (https://population.un.org/wpp/Download/Standard/Population/). Accessed on 30 Sep 2022.
5. Department of Statistics, Malaysia, Population Statistics.
6. During 1971–80, MARA built 1147 business premises for Malays, trained about 50,000 entrepreneurs, and provided consulting services to over 15,000 Malays. Additionally, UDA, SEDCs, and FELDA provided 7138 office spaces for Malays (Malaysia 1981: 194).
7. Malaysia, Fourth Malaysia Plan 1981–1985, p. 242.
8. Of the 744,000 housing units built between 1971–80, the public sector constructed 207,590 units.
9. Keuk, Yusfida, and Hazlina (2016).
10. Abdul Rahman and Nair (2014).
11. The Department of Statistics Malaysia defines the informal sector as: 1) unregistered enterprises, 2) producing goods/services for sale or exchange, 3) employing 10 or fewer people, and not covered by any social security, and 4) engaged in non-agricultural sectors (Department of Statistics Malaysia 2020).
12. The ILO defines informal sector workers as "all remunerative work (self-employment and wage employment) that is not registered, regulated or protected by existing legal or regulatory frameworks, as well as non-remunerative work undertaken in an income-producing enterprise. Informal workers lack secure employment contracts, employment benefits, social protection

and workers' representation." International Labour Organization, Statistics on the informal economy (https://ilostat.ilo.org/topics/informality/). Accessed on 30 Sep 2022.
13. Immigration Department of Malaysia, Official Portal.
14. Ministry of Home Affairs, Malaysia (2019).
15. In reality, Japan's foreign worker population was approximately 1.73 million as of October 2021, accounting for only 2.6% of Japan's employed population.
16. Nakamura and Umezaki (2006).
17. World Bank (2015).
18. JETRO Investment Cost Comparison (https://www.jetro.go.jp/world/search/cost.html). Accessed on 30 Sep 2022.
19. Bank Negara Malaysia (2018).
20. This is according to the author's (Kumagai) field research in Penang State in November 2018.
21. "Malaysia's Top Glove reports COVID-19 outbreak at four factories," Reuters, January 16, 2021.
22. The Malaysian government has conducted household surveys twice every five years since 1974, with the latest published data being from the 2019 survey. Prior to this, only three surveys were conducted in 1957/58, 1967/68, and 1970. The 1967/68 survey was excluded from Fig. 2.4 as it only covered cash income. For 1957/58, modified values by Snodgrass (1980) were used.
23. It should be noted that Malaysian household surveys covered different geographical areas before and after 1976. Until 1976, only Peninsular Malaysia was surveyed; from 1979, Sabah and Sarawak states were included. However, examining Gini coefficients by state between 1976 and 1979 shows decreases in all states except Pahang. Therefore, the reduction in inequality during this period was not merely due to the expansion of survey coverage.
24. Mizoguchi (1985).
25. Kuznets (1955).
26. Ragayah (2008).
27. Chakravarty and Abdul-Hakim (2005).
28. Sugimura (2000).
29. Chai (1977: 17–18).
30. Malaysia (1965: 163–166).
31. The gross enrollment ratio is calculated by dividing the number of students enrolled by the population of the corresponding school age, while the net enrollment ratio is calculated by dividing the number of only those students within the appropriate age group by the population of that age group. The gross enrollment ratio may exceed 100% because the numerator includes students studying beyond the corresponding age due to reasons such as grade repetition or returning to education.
32. Sugimura (2000: 117–123).
33. Soda (2006: 266–268).
34. Soda (2006: 275–276).
35. The Outline Perspective Plan (1970–1990) was published as part of Chapter 4 of the Mid-Term Review of the Second Malaysia Plan (Malaysia 1973).
36. For a detailed discussion on the successor policy to the New Economic Policy, see Nakamura (2006).
37. Sugimoto (2005: 134); Sugimura (2000: 127–130); *New Straits Times*, October 12, 1987.
38. Kimura (1988: 356–357); *New Straits Times*, October 16–24, 1987.
39. Kamal and Zainal Aznam (1989).
40. Kok et al. (1990: 168).

References

Abdul Rahman H, Nair PL (2014) Urbanisation and growth of metropolitan centres in Malaysia. Malays J Econ Stud 51(1):87–101

Allen RC (2009) The British industrial revolution in global perspective. Cambridge University Press, Cambridge

Asano Y, Takeshita H (1980) Battle formation toward the 1980s: Singapore in 1979 (1979 nen no Singapore). In: Institute of Developing Economies (ed) Ajia Dōkō Nenpō 1980 (Yearbook of Asian affairs 1980). Institute of Developing Economies, Tokyo, pp 423–454

Bank Negara Malaysia (2018) Box article: low-skilled foreign workers' distortions to the economy. Bank Negara Malaysia Annual Report 2017. Bank Negara Malaysia, Kuala Lumpur, pp. 35–43

Chai HC (1977) Education and nation building in plural societies: the West Malaysian experience. Australian National University, Canberra

Chakravarty SP, Abdul-Hakim R (2005) Ethnic nationalism and income distribution in Malaysia. Eur J Dev Res 17(2):270–288

Department of Statistics Malaysia (2020) Informal sector in Malaysia. DOSM Newsletter, DOSM/BPTMS/3.2020/Series 51

International Labour Organization. Statistics on the informal economy. https://ilostat.ilo.org/topics/informality/

Ito S (2019) Impact of minimum wage increases (part 1): employment does not seem to decrease in the United States (Saitei Chingin Hikiage no Eikyō). IDE Square. http://hdl.handle.net/2344/00051459

Kamal S, and Zainal AY (1989) Overview of the new economic policy and framework for the post-1990 economic policy. Paper presented at the national conference on post-1990 economic policy, Putra World Trade Centre, Kuala Lumpur, 31 July–1 Aug 1989

Keuk JN, Yusfida AA, Hazlina H (2016) Eradicating squatters through resettlement programme: a conceptual paper. MATEC Web of Conf 66(2):00023

Kimura M (1988) Malaysia in 1987: forced breakthrough induces ethnic confrontation (1987 nen no Malaysia). In: Institute of Developing Economies (ed) Yearbook of Asian Affairs 1988 (Ajia Dōkō Nenpō 1988). Institute of Developing Economies, Tokyo, pp 356–357

Kok WK, Ling LS, Fong CO, Chua JM, Yeoh M (1990) The Malaysian challenges in the 1990's. Pelanduk Publications, Kuala Lumpur

Kuznets S (1955) Economic growth and income inequality. Am Econ Rev 45(1):1–28

Malaysia (1965) First Malaysia Plan 1966–1970. Government Printing Office, Kuala Lump

Malaysia (1981) Fourth Malaysia Plan 1981–1985. National Printing Department, Kuala Lumpur

Ministry of Home Affairs, Malaysia (2019) Penerbitan statistik kementerian dalam negeri. Bahagian Perancangan Strategik, KDN

Mizoguchi T (1985) Economic development policy and income distribution: the experience in East and Southeast Asia. Dev Econ 23(4):307–324

Nakamura M (2006) Political process surrounding the post-1990 issue: background of Vision 2020 (Post 1990 Nen Mondai o Meguru Seiji Katei). In: Torii T (ed) Malaysia under the Mahathir administration (Mahathir Seiken-ka no Malaysia). Institute of Developing Economies, Tokyo, pp 69–113

Nakamura M, Umezaki S (2006) Malaysia in 2005: long road to structural reform (2005 nen no Malaysia). In: Institute of Developing Economies (ed) Yearbook of Asian Affairs 2006 (Ajia Dōkō Nenpō 2006). Institute of Developing Economies, Tokyo, pp 341–372

Ragayah Haji Mat Zin (2008) Income inequality in Malaysia. Asian Econ Policy Rev 3(1):114–132

Snodgrass DR (1980) Inequality and economic development in Malaysia. Oxford University Press, New York

Soda N (2006) Higher education reform during the Mahathir administration: national vision, policy shift, and political debate (Mahathir Seiken Ki no Kōtō Kyōiku Kaikaku). In: Torii T (ed) Malaysia under the Mahathir administration (Mahathir Seiken-ka no Malaysia). Institute of Developing Economies, Tokyo, pp 266–268

Sugimoto H (2005) International educational relations in Malaysia: global impact on education (Malaysia ni okeru Kokusai Kyōiku Kankei). Toshindo, Tokyo

Sugimura M (2000) Malaysia's education policy and minorities: national integration and Chinese schools (Malaysia no Kyōiku Seisaku to Mainoriti). University of Tokyo Press, Tokyo

World Bank (2015) Malaysia economic monitor: immigrant labor. World Bank

Newspapers and Online Media

New Straits Times
Reuters

Chapter 4
Key Players in Economic Development

Domestic Private Companies, Foreign Companies, and Government-Linked Companies (1980s to 2000s)

For developing countries with less advanced corporate sectors than those in developed nations, the roles played by domestic private companies, foreign companies, and government-linked companies (GLCs) in driving economic development are crucial. Countries like Japan, South Korea, and Taiwan, which had dynamic domestic private sectors from the early stages of economic development, faced fewer issues. However, in many developing countries, the growth of domestic private companies is insufficient, and they inevitably rely on foreign companies and GLCs to promote industrialization and economic development.

Contemporary middle-income countries, particularly those in East Asia, have achieved economic growth during their lower-middle-income stage by focusing on labor-intensive, export-oriented industries. Foreign capital, especially in the form of direct investment, has financially supported this growth. Export-oriented economic development relying on foreign capital differs significantly from the economic growth achieved by today's developed countries, which primarily utilized domestic capital.

For developing countries, accepting direct investment can be a double-edged sword for their future economic development. On the one hand, direct investment offers a shortcut to industrial development and technology acquisition. Many companies in developing countries lack the ability to participate in global value chains (GVCs) that involve cross-border transactions of components and products without the support of overseas multinational corporations. Developing countries can also benefit from technology spillovers when multinational corporations guide local subcontractors to produce specific components at lower costs and transfer know-how.

On the other hand, multinational corporations deliberately control the flow of knowledge and technology to developing countries to protect their own interests, hindering the accumulation of industrial knowledge and technology in these countries.[1] Compared to domestic companies that primarily conduct research and development (R&D) in their home countries, the transfer of knowledge and technology from overseas multinational corporations to developing countries is naturally

S. Kumagai and M. Nakamura, *Economic Development Strategies*, Emerging-Economy State and International Policy Studies, https://doi.org/10.1007/978-981-95-6899-4_4

slower. Although multinational corporations are expected to promote technological upgrading in developing countries, this effect diminishes as developing countries' income levels rise and the technological gap with developed countries narrows.

Another key factor in the economic development of contemporary middle-income countries is the presence of GLCs. In developing countries where private companies are underdeveloped, GLCs are often established and expected to play a key role in driving economic development. Why do many countries establish GLCs even within market economy systems? The concept of "market failure" is at the root of arguments justifying the existence of GLCs. Government intervention is deemed necessary to address situations where optimal equilibrium cannot be achieved through market mechanisms alone, such as in cases of economies of scale, information asymmetry, provision of public goods, and uncertain large-scale investments.

However, government intervention to correct market failure can lead to other problems. From a management perspective, GLCs tend to lack external monitoring to oversee managers compared to private companies (notably, due to the absence of diverse private shareholders), which reduces managers' incentives to pursue efficiency. From a political perspective, it is pointed out that managers of GLCs pursue employment maximization or political fame rather than management efficiency.[2] Additionally, state-owned enterprises often face a situation called "soft budget constraints,"[3] which makes it difficult to discipline management. Soft budget constraints refer to situations where state-owned enterprises receive additional government funds through subsidies or loss compensation, unlike private companies that operate within their revenue constraints, leading to a lack of discipline in spending.

The balance between the three types of companies—foreign companies, large domestic private companies, and state-owned enterprises—is sometimes called the "tripod structure"[4] of the dominant capital supporting a country's economy. This tripod structure varies by country and era, and the balance among the three types as well as policies toward each significantly influence the path of economic development in developing countries.

With regard to corporate activities, the occurrence of bubbles and the "resource curse" can hinder the economic development of developing countries as they continue industrialization. These phenomena can occur separately, and in resource-rich countries, the resource curse and bubbles can co-occur due to the surge in resource prices. If the profitability of investing in primary commodities or real estate continues to be higher than investing in manufacturing, it is natural for companies to direct their investments towards non-manufacturing sectors. However, it is difficult to continuously improve productivity in primary commodities and real estate sectors compared to manufacturing. The outflow of management resources from manufacturing, which can serve as the axis of continuous economic development, may have a long-term negative impact on the economic growth of developing countries.

What, then, was the relationship between domestic private companies, foreign companies, and GLCs in Malaysia? Were the disadvantages of foreign dependency and the negative aspects of GLCs adequately managed? Furthermore, how did the government's policies to promote Bumiputera participation in the commercial and industrial sectors affect the activities of these three types of companies? First, let us examine how the balance among these three types of companies has changed over time.

4.1 Changes in the Key Players of Malaysia's Economic Development

4.1.1 Setting Bumiputera Capital Ownership Targets in the New Economic Policy

Before the implementation of the New Economic Policy, economic activities in Malaysia were primarily carried out by foreign companies, mainly from the former colonial power Britain and Chinese companies. In 1969, foreign companies held 62.1% of corporate stock ownership, Chinese 22.8%, and Malays only 1.5%. Considering that Malays constituted 52.7% of Malaysia's population in 1970, their 1.5% share of capital ownership was remarkably low.[5] Moreover, Bumiputera participation in corporate management was even lower than their capital ownership share. Considering that "Ali-Baba" businesses became problematic later on (arrangements where Bumiputeras were nominally the owners or contracting parties of companies while Chinese businesspeople carried out the actual management and business operations), it is reasonable to infer that there were very few genuine Bumiputera corporate managers before the New Economic Policy.

Regarding Bumiputera capital ownership and management participation, the Second Malaysia Plan stated the goal: "Within a period of 20 years, Malays and other indigenous people will manage and own at least 30% of the total commercial and industrial activities in all categories and scales of operation."[6] However, significantly increasing the capital ownership share of a specific ethnic group within just 20 years is not easy in a country with a market economy system. It is also challenging to force Bumiputeras, who had little involvement in business, to participate in corporate management.

After the implementation of the New Economic Policy, various methods were attempted to realize Bumiputera capital ownership and management participation, as will be discussed below.

4.1.2 Joint Ventures with Chinese and Foreign Capital

As part of the New Economic Policy, the Razak administration enacted the Industrial Coordination Act (ICA) in 1975 to promote Bumiputera capital ownership and management participation. The ICA included guidelines for companies to obtain manufacturing licenses, requiring Bumiputera participation in all aspects of capital, employment, and management at the individual company level. For example, the ICA guidelines stipulated that: (1) capital should be 100% Malaysian-owned in principle, with 30% owned by Bumiputeras; (2) the board of directors should be composed according to the ethnic ratio of capital ownership; and (3) employment should be based on the ethnic ratio of the population at each occupational level.[7]

Had the ICA been strictly enforced at the individual company level, the goal of 30% Bumiputera capital ownership would eventually have been achieved. However, implementing a policy that mandates allocating 30% of shares in existing and new companies to Bumiputeras is not easy. Chinese and foreign companies strongly opposed the ICA, and in response, the scope of application and requirements of the ICA guidelines were relaxed.[8] Additionally, under this scheme, Bumiputeras would hold less than a majority of shares in each company, making it difficult for them to gain management control. In practice, Chinese businesses responded to the ICA by developing "Ali-Baba" arrangements, in which Bumiputeras formally owned capital but had little involvement in management, or where Chinese entrepreneurs bought out licenses that had been preferentially issued to Bumiputeras.

4.1.3 Government Acquisition of Existing Companies

Alongside promoting joint ventures between Bumiputeras and non-Bumiputeras through the ICA, the Malaysian government used public funds to acquire existing companies. The national corporation Perbadanan Nasional Berhad (PERNAS) was established in 1969 to acquire high-performing British and Chinese companies and to involve Bumiputeras in their management. Notable companies acquired by PERNAS include the Malaysian Mining Corporation (MMC) and Sime Darby. Later, companies acquired by PERNAS were transferred to the government-linked investment company Permodalan Nasional Berhad (PNB), and through Bumiputera-focused national unit trust schemes like Amanah Saham Nasional (ASN), broader Bumiputera individual capital ownership was realized. When PNB made acquisitions, it could obtain funds from the government under favorable conditions such as interest-free loans without collateral requirements.[9]

There are several issues with this Bumiputera policy approach to corporate acquisition. First, acquiring numerous high-performing companies was not easy. The number of such companies is limited, and their shares come at a high price. If the intention to purchase becomes apparent, the stock price may surge, and cooperation from existing shareholders may not be forthcoming. On September 7, 1981, PERNAS successfully carried out a surprise hostile takeover of the British plantation company Guthrie Corporation in the London market. This action, known as the "Dawn Raid," led to a deterioration in relations between Malaysia and Britain. This incident demonstrates that acquiring high-performing companies through conventional methods was not easy.

The approach of using national capital to acquire high-performing companies, transform their management to be Malaysian-led, and sell them to Bumiputeras through unit trusts achieved some success. However, to rely solely on this method to achieve the New Economic Policy's goal of 30% meant Bumiputera capital ownership would require enormous funds and that was unrealistic.

4.1.4 Establishment of Government-Linked Companies

A more direct approach to increasing Bumiputera capital ownership is establishing GLCs. While this direct government involvement in business yielded some results in raising Bumiputera capital ownership, properly managing these GLCs proved challenging. From the late 1970s to the early 1980s, many GLCs experienced poor performance and bankruptcy.[10]

The heavy industrialization policy implemented under the Mahathir administration in the early 1980s extended this public enterprise-based Bumiputera policy. The Malaysian government established the Heavy Industries Corporation of Malaysia (HICOM) in 1983. Under HICOM's umbrella, the government established heavy industry companies such as the national car manufacturer Proton and the steel company Perwaja Steel, with Japanese companies serving as the primary technical partners. Except for Proton, which enjoyed a market share of over 70% in the passenger car market for a time due to generous protection and preferential policies, these heavy industry projects performed poorly in the following years. Throughout the 1980s, 45–50% of GLCs operated at a loss, and half of these loss-making companies were excessively indebted.[11]

In the mid-1980s, while GLCs continued to perform poorly, the Malaysian economy entered a recession due to factors such as declining primary commodity prices. In response, the Mahathir administration shifted its policy toward privatizing GLCs and attracting export-oriented foreign investment. The approach of establishing public enterprises to support Bumiputera advancement into commerce and industry effectively came to a halt.

4.1.5 Privatization and Sale of Government-Linked Companies

In the 1980s, GLC privatization was carried out worldwide, with the United Kingdom serving as a model. In Malaysia, privatization began in 1983 under the Mahathir administration, which was relatively early by global standards. Initially, Malaysia's privatization policy aimed to improve the management efficiency of GLCs and reduce fiscal deficits. However, from the late 1980s, the main objective of the privatization policy shifted to nurturing Bumiputera corporate groups, which became particularly clear after the announcement of the "Privatization Master Plan" in 1991.[12] The recipients of privatized companies and projects were selected from entrepreneurs considered close to the then-Prime Minister Mahathir Mohamad (1981–2003), Deputy Prime Minister and Finance Minister Anwar Ibrahim (1993–98, 1991–98), and Finance Minister Daim Zainuddin (1984–91). Riding the wave of the economic boom from the late 1980s, the policy of nurturing Bumiputera corporate groups through privatization appeared to have achieved some success. For example, the DRB-HICOM Group, which controlled the national car manufacturer Proton, surprised the world in 1996 by acquiring the prestigious British sports car maker Lotus.

On the other hand, the close relationship between the nurturing of Bumiputera entrepreneurs through privatization and influential politicians and political parties has often been criticized as crony capitalism.[13] However, this approach has a certain rationality given the assumption of implementing the Bumiputera policy. At the UMNO party conference held in 1988, then-Prime Minister Mahathir pointed out that "despite the promotion of the Bumiputera policy, very few Bumiputera entrepreneurs with management capabilities have been nurtured" and stated that "...from now on, the focus will be on the selective nurturing of Bumiputera entrepreneurs based on their management capabilities."[14] In other words, due to the limited number of excellent Bumiputera managers, the government would sell privatized companies to a small number of elite Bumiputera entrepreneurs.

Furthermore, during the same period, the Malaysian government was concerned about the potential long-term decline in Bumiputera ownership percentage in privatized companies. If the sale of GLCs were to be carried out to a large number of individual Bumiputeras through the securities market, it would be difficult for the government to monitor and regulate the subsequent resale of shares by individual Bumiputeras to other ethnic groups or foreigners. Conversely, if only a small number of Bumiputera entrepreneurs hold the shares of companies that receive privatization projects, monitoring and regulating the resale of shares becomes easier. Moreover, if those entrepreneurs are close to the government and the ruling party, monitoring share ownership and management becomes even more effective.

4.1.6 Re-Nationalization Progresses During the Asian Financial Crisis

The Asian Financial Crisis, which began with the Thai baht's depreciation in July 1997, had a significant impact on the Malaysian economy and led to the economic crisis of 1998, during which Malaysia recorded its worst economic growth rate since independence at minus 7.4%. During this period, major Bumiputera corporate groups that had acquired privatized GLCs had expanded through aggressive acquisitions, using bank loans with shares as collateral. When stock prices fell due to the Asian

Financial Crisis and the subsequent economic downturn, while interest rates simultaneously rose due to monetary tightening policies, these corporate groups faced imminent business failure.

At this point, the problems inherent in the privatization-based Bumiputera policy became apparent. Because the managers of the failed corporate groups were also major shareholders, replacing the management was not easy. If the managers remained major shareholders after resigning, they could still maintain substantial influence over management. Therefore, replacing the managers effectively required simultaneously compelling them to sell their company shares.

For example, the Renong Group, which had received numerous privatization projects, was dismantled, and its core company, UEM, was re-nationalized by the government-linked investment company Khazanah Nasional. Later, however, Halim Saad, the owner-manager, filed a lawsuit against the government, claiming that this process was unfair.[15] Also, Malaysia Airlines (MAS), which had been privatized and sold off to the Naluri Group, was re-nationalized by the Minister of Finance Incorporated (MoF Inc.). This action drew strong public criticism for buying back the shares at their original privatization price, despite their significant depreciation following the currency crisis.[16]

4.1.7 The "Tripod Structure" of Malaysia after the Currency Crisis

In 1969, corporate activities in Malaysia were primarily dominated by two groups: British foreign companies and Chinese domestic capital. Subsequently, as part of the New Economic Policy, British companies were acquired and Malaysianized, while Bumiputera capital participation and acquisitions of Chinese companies were actively pursued. As a result, the percentage of Bumiputera companies, especially GLCs, in economic activities expanded. Furthermore, as many GLCs were privatized in the 1980s, and the introduction of 100% foreign-owned companies in the manufacturing sector was actively promoted from the late 1980s onwards, the presence of domestic private companies and foreign companies increased. Later, after the 1997–98 Asian Financial Crisis, major privatized companies that had suffered deterioration in assets were re-nationalized, and the presence of GLCs expanded again. In this way, the "tripod structure" of foreign companies, GLCs, and domestic private companies in the Malaysian economy has undergone significant changes over time.

As the aftermath of the Asian Financial Crisis subsided by the mid-2000s, a certain balance was established in the tripod structure of the Malaysian economy, which has continued to the present. Since 1990, the Malaysian government has excluded government-owned shares from the published capital ownership ratios by ethnicity, making it difficult to grasp the "tripod structure" in Malaysia. Therefore, by combining several statistics to estimate the presence of foreign companies, GLCs, and domestic private companies in the Malaysian economy, it is estimated that in the mid-2000s, the percentage of domestic private companies in the stock ownership ratio of the Kuala Lumpur Stock Exchange was about 50%, of which about 60% was accounted for by Chinese companies.[17] It is also estimated that foreign and GLCs each accounted for 25% of the remaining 50%. However, not all GLCs are listed, and considering the presence of the national oil company Petronas,[18] whose estimated market capitalization is enormous, the presence of GLCs is likely to be even more significant in reality than these figures suggest.

In Thailand, Indonesia, and South Korea, which were significantly affected by the Asian Financial Crisis, the presence of foreign capital expanded after the currency crisis.[19] In contrast, in Malaysia, the acquisition of domestic companies by foreign capital after the Asian Financial Crisis was minimal, and many of the Bumiputera large companies among domestic private companies were re-nationalized. Therefore, a significant characteristic is that the presence of GLCs in the tripod structure increased.

4.2 New Economic Policy, GLCs, and GLC Reform

4.2.1 Commencement of the GLC Transformation Program

In the 1960s, private companies centered on Chinese capital existed in Malaysia. However, due to the special circumstances of the goal of increasing Bumiputera share ownership in the New Economic Policy, it was not possible to actively support Chinese private companies and entrust them with economic development. Therefore, GLCs played a significant role initially, followed by privatized companies from the late 1980s and again by GLCs from the 2000s onwards. GLCs are difficult to manage appropriately, and there are examples where they hinder economic development. In Malaysia, the government has also been seeking a better management style for GLCs through trial and error.

Around 2003, the Malaysian government began to refer to government-linked companies as GLCs. GLCs are companies operated for commercial purposes, for which the Malaysian government has direct control.[20] In neighboring Singapore, GLCs are also called GLCs. Although the Malaysian government has not explicitly stated it, it is believed that there was an intention to model GLCs after those in Singapore, such as Singapore Airlines, which boasts good performance despite being a government-linked company.

The Malaysian government decided not to re-privatize GLCs but to improve their management while keeping them state-owned, and in 2004, it launched the "GLC Transformation Program." The most significant point of this program was that it limited the role of GLCs as "public institutions" and established a system for them to pursue profits as private companies. The GLC Transformation Program put forward the following three principles: (1) GLCs must focus on performance above all else, (2) GLCs can only become "part of the solution" to support the nation's development if they have performance and results, and (3) in implementing these two principles, GLCs are expected to operate within a clear governance structure and contribute to the interests of stakeholders.[21]

One of the main reasons why the management of state-owned enterprises and privatized enterprises did not go well before this program was that they were explicitly or implicitly required by the government and politicians to "contribute to national development," and they struggled with the conflict between this and the pursuit of corporate profits. The GLC Transformation Program established the primary goal of GLC management as the pursuit of profits as a for-profit company, with the contribution to the nation positioned as a secondary goal.

Furthermore, the GLC Transformation Program emphasizes corporate governance. Under the first Mahathir administration, privatized companies had too much influence from owner-managers. In public enterprises, until the 1970s, bureaucrats and politicians with no business experience often occupied positions on the board of directors. The GLC Transformation Program is considered to have significantly contributed to the improvement of management by stipulating the roles, selection policies, and evaluation indicators of the board of directors.

The Malaysian government considers the GLC Transformation Program, implemented over ten years from 2004, a great success. The market capitalization of the top 20 GLCs (G20) increased approximately threefold between 2004 and 2015.[22] Looking at the performance of individual companies in the G20, there is a tendency for larger companies to have improved management.[23] Among the GLCs that have enhanced their competitiveness through the transformation program, an increasing number of companies are expanding overseas, mainly in the ASEAN region.

On the other hand, there are differing views on the assertion that large GLCs are putting competitive pressure on the management of private companies competing with them in Malaysia.[24] While there is a quantitative analysis showing that private investment is negatively affected in industries where GLCs are dominant in Malaysia, the government has stated that "under the transformation program, government-linked investment companies (GLICs) and GLCs are shifting their role from investors to investment promoters, aiming to engage in 'crowding-in' investment by taking risks such as undertaking initial investments."[25] For example, in the regional economic corridor development plans formulated in the mid-2000s, the government selected one of the GLCs for each corridor and expected it to attract investments from other companies by taking the lead in investing.

As mentioned earlier, the issue of "soft budget constraints," which affects the performance of state-owned enterprises in general, has not been fundamentally resolved even in the GLC Transformation Program. The GLC Transformation Program does not state that if a GLC goes bankrupt, the government will not bail it out and will treat it the same as a private company. Instead, the GLC Transformation Program provides more direct incentives for GLC managers to conduct disciplined management. Specifically, it is indicated as a policy to introduce performance-based remuneration for GLC managers. There is a certain correlation between the performance of GLCs and the remuneration of their managers.[26]

The GLC Transformation Program can be understood as an attempt by the government to own companies as shareholders while employing professional managers to separate ownership and management and to discipline management through contracts with GLC managers, such as performance-based remuneration. To avoid ambiguity, key performance indicators (KPIs) are set for the content of "performance," and managers are evaluated based on their achievement of KPI-based targets.

As long as the goal of Bumiputera share ownership in the New Economic Policy continues, even if the government declares that it will not bail out GLCs when they go bankrupt, it inevitably becomes a "non-credible threat" in game theory. Once a GLC goes bankrupt, not bailing it out would decrease the Bumiputera share ownership ratio, so the government has no choice but to bail out the GLC after the fact. On the other hand, by establishing contracts with GLC managers, the government can predetermine that managers will suffer disadvantages in the event of poor performance. The government can also dismiss managers if their performance continues to be inadequate. The current approach of the government owning capital, employing Bumiputera professional managers, and disciplining them with performance-based remuneration seems to be the best way to discipline the management of GLCs, assuming that the goal of the Bumiputera share ownership ratio in the New Economic Policy persists.

4.2.2 A New Generation of Bumiputera Managers

During the GLC Transformation Program, many young and talented Bumiputera professional managers were appointed. One reason why managers close to the government were not appointed to GLCs as before was then-Prime Minister Abdullah's initiative to break away from "rent-seeking addiction" (discussed later). Also, Nor Mohamed Yakcop, who was entrusted with the GLC reform as Second Finance Minister by Prime Minister Abdullah, was a former executive of Bank Negara (Malaysia's central bank) and had led the debt restructuring after the Asian Financial Crisis as an advisor to Prime Minister Mahathir. The fact that Nor Mohamed was an economic bureaucrat rather than a politician was a factor in the appointment of professional managers connected to his network in the subsequent GLC reform.

As a typical example of a "young and talented Bumiputera professional manager," let us introduce Abdul Wahid Omar. Wahid was born in 1964 in Johor Bahru as the ninth of eleven siblings. He entered primary school around the same time as the start of the New Economic Policy. He later studied at the MARA Junior Science College (MRSM), established for Bumiputera secondary education. After graduating from MRSM, he received a MARA scholarship to study at a university in the United Kingdom and became a Fellow of the Association of Chartered Certified Accountants (FCCA). Returning to Malaysia, he started his career as an accountant at the consulting firm KPMG in 1987. From 1994 to 2001, he became the President of Amanah Capital Group's money market company, where he met Nor Mohamed, who was supervising the discount of bills at Bank Negara around that time. In 2001, at the age of 37, he was invited by Nor Mohamed to become the CEO of the re-nationalized UEM Group and led its restructuring. He served as CEO of Telekom Malaysia from 2004 to 2008, as CEO of Maybank from 2009 to 2013, and then as Minister in the Prime Minister's Department in charge of the Economic Planning Unit (EPU) under the Najib administration until 2016.

Many Bumiputeras have been involved as managers in corporate restructuring after the Asian Financial Crisis and the GLC Transformation Program. These individuals share common career paths: (1) they obtained degrees in accounting or management from overseas universities or graduate schools, (2) they have work experience at multinational corporations, and (3) they were under 50 years old when they were appointed as managers. These characteristics are similar to the career paths of managers of Malaysian multinational corporations and Chinese companies. Thirty years after the start of the New Economic Policy, in the 2000s, Bumiputera managers with qualifications comparable to other ethnicities had emerged as a result, and they were able to manage many GLCs. This starkly contrasts to the 1970s and 1980s, when "Ali-Baba" businesses were prevalent due to the lack of Bumiputera managers, and the 1980s and 1990s when GLCs were sold off to a small number of "cronies" close to politicians.

4.3 The Presence of Foreign Companies

4.3.1 Export-Oriented Industrialization and Foreign Companies

As mentioned earlier, foreign companies' presence in Malaysia decreased from over 60% in the late 1960s to about a quarter in the 2000s. However, foreign companies have not been declining unilaterally. Under the New Economic Policy, while British companies, the former colonial power, were acquired by PERNAS in the 1970s, new foreign companies appeared in Malaysia. This shift was triggered by the implementation of the export-oriented industrialization policy. Like many developing countries, Malaysia promoted industrialization using domestic demand through import-substitution policies in the 1960s, replacing imported goods with domestic production. However, at that time, the small size of the domestic market, in terms of both population and income levels, became a constraint. In the 1970s, Malaysia had to shift to export-oriented industrialization.

A representative example of Malaysia's export-oriented industrialization policy in the 1970s is the Free Trade Zone (FTZ) established in Penang. Malaysia's electronics industry was small in scale in 1970, with only 577 employees and a production value of 24.5 million ringgit. By 1980, the number of employees had increased 119-fold to 68,653, and the production value had increased 145-fold to 3.5593 billion ringgit.

In the 1980s, large-scale export-oriented direct investment flowed into Malaysia due to two factors: the rapid appreciation of the yen following the Plaza Accord in 1985 and the Malaysian government's 1986 relaxation of regulations on foreign capital ownership ratios. The Promotion of Investments Act, introduced in 1986, provided various incentives to foreign investors. The investment guidelines announced in September of the same year were groundbreaking, allowing 100% foreign capital ownership for companies that export more than 50% of their products or employ more than 350 Malaysians full-time. In response, many companies producing home appliances and audiovisual equipment entered Malaysia (Fig. 4.1). Malaysia became one of the world's leading production bases for audiovisual equipment such as televisions and VCRs.

The scale of direct investment in Malaysia can be seen by looking at the ratio of foreign investment to domestic investment. In 1985, the ratio of foreign investment to domestic investment (manufacturing sector) was 16.9%, but in 1989, 70% of domestic investment was foreign. The ratio of foreign investment to domestic investment subsequently declined slightly, but it remained at a high level of 40–50% before the Asian Financial Crisis.

As a result of this rapid inflow of direct investment, the presence of foreign companies in the manufacturing sector became very significant. As of 1995, foreign companies accounted for 32% of the number of companies, 53% of sales, and 73% of exports in the manufacturing sector. These figures are for the manufacturing sector as a whole, so the presence of foreign companies in export-oriented industries such as the electronics and electrical industry is thought to have been even higher.

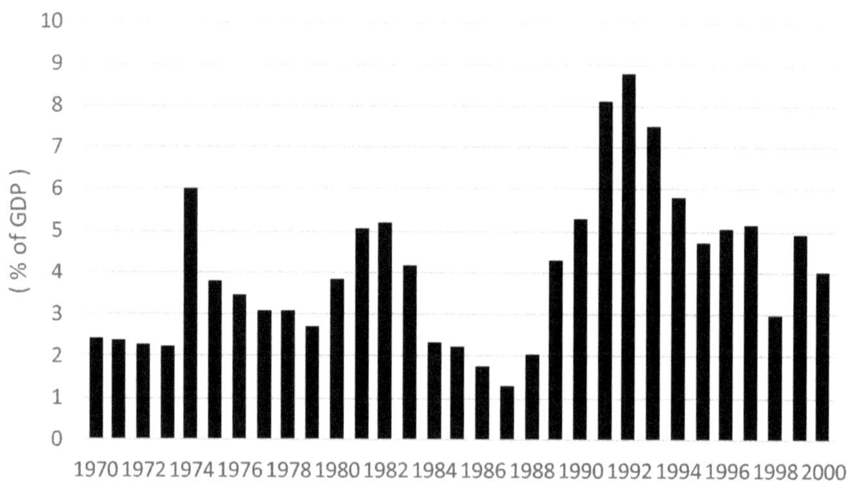

Fig. 4.1 Trends in Foreign Direct Investment Inflows in Malaysia (% of GDP). *Source* Created by the author based on World Development Indicators (WDI)

4.3.2 Government Investment Policies Differing by Sector

In this way, despite some twists and turns, Malaysia's foreign investment policy has become more open in response to changes in the global economic environment. For today's middle-income countries, where economic globalization is progressing and GVCs are developing, the option of "not attracting foreign investment" is hardly conceivable.

Although Malaysia has set a goal of increasing the share of Bumiputera stock ownership in the New Economic Policy, it has proceeded with reforms to accept foreign investment that contradict this goal. In doing so, there is room for choice regarding which industries actively accept foreign investment, and the Malaysian government's response is interesting.

Table 4.1 compares the foreign ownership ratio in Malaysia's stock ownership by industry sector in 1970 and 2004. During this period, the foreign ownership ratio declined in all industries except manufacturing, transportation and communication, and banking and insurance. Regarding the manufacturing sector, the Malaysian government has consistently and actively promoted the introduction of foreign capital from the import-substitution industrialization period to the export-oriented industrialization period. The Malaysian government has particularly expected foreign capital to play a leading role in export-oriented industries such as the electronics and electrical industry, which are labor-intensive and have high employment creation potential.

Contrary to the epithet "footloose," meaning that they can quickly relocate to other countries, foreign companies have invested in Malaysia, particularly in Penang, for half a century. Although gradual, their corporate activities have continued to become more sophisticated. For example, Intel Malaysia entered Penang in 1972 and has continued to invest in Penang Island and Kulim, Kedah, on the opposite shore, building a factory that handles the backend process of semiconductor manufacturing. By the early 2000s, it had begun undertaking some R&D, such as motherboard design.[27] In 2021, it announced that it would invest a massive 30 billion ringgit (US$7.1 billion) to expand its factory in Penang to handle the backend process of

Table 4.1 Foreign Ownership Ratio in Malaysian Stock Holdings. *Source* Compiled by the author based on Malaysia (1973, 2006)

Sector	1970	2004
Agriculture, Forestry & Fisheries	75.3	23.0
Mining	72.4	22.5
Manufacturing	59.6	64.7
Construction	24.1	14.9
Transport & Communications	12.0	31.3
Commerce	63.5	25.6
Banking & Insurance	52.2	59.5
Others	31.4	23.2
Total	60.7	32.5

semiconductor production, with operations to begin by 2024 employing an additional 4000 people on top of its current 13,000 employees.[28]

On the other hand, while the share of foreign ownership in the transportation, communication, banking, and insurance industries appears to have increased, it should be noted that the 2004 data does not include GLCs. Considering the significant presence of GLCs in these sectors (Pos Malaysia in the transportation sector, Telekom Malaysia and Axiata in the telecommunications industry, and large government-linked banks such as Maybank and CIMB in the banking sector), it is doubtful whether the presence of foreign companies has expanded when GLCs are included.

Looking at it this way, the Malaysian government seems to have accepted foreign capital dependence in the manufacturing sector, except for the heavy industrialization projects of the 1980s, represented by the national car manufacturer Proton. On the other hand, the government has not necessarily actively accepted foreign investment in primary and service industries. On the contrary, foreign capital was acquired in these sectors, and Malaysianization was promoted until the 1970s. The British company MMC, acquired by PERNAS, was a tin mining company, and the British company Sime Darby was a trading company handling primary commodities and heavy machinery.

Since the 2000s, prominent Malaysian companies have expanded overseas in the primary and service industries. The national oil company Petronas operates worldwide, and major plantation companies, both government-linked and private, have expanded into Indonesia and Africa. In the banking and telecommunications sectors, major government-linked and private companies are actively developing their businesses in ASEAN countries and India. For Malaysia, the fact that government-linked and Chinese companies have competitiveness, at least domestically, in high-value-added primary and service industries, particularly the financial sector, is thought to have a positive impact on economic development by reducing the leakage of value-added overseas.

4.4 The Occurrence of Bubbles and the "Resource Curse"

4.4.1 Bubble Occurrence as a Remote Cause of the Currency Crisis

When corporate investment is directed toward real estate due to the occurrence of bubbles or when it is intensively invested in the primary commodity sector due to the inducement of soaring natural resource prices, even if it brings about a temporary boom, it can hinder economic development in the long run. Unlike the manufacturing sector, it isn't easy to continuously improve productivity in these sectors.

In Malaysia, the period from the early 1990s to the Asian Financial Crisis can be identified as a time when bubbles occurred. During this period, Malaysia and developing countries in East Asia were on track for export-led economic growth and continued to experience high growth. Furthermore, as U.S. long-term interest rates significantly declined in the early 1990s, a large amount of investment and speculative funds flowed into developing countries in East Asia from overseas.

For Thailand, Indonesia, and South Korea, the three countries most affected by the Asian Financial Crisis, during this period, the basic balance, which adds the long-term capital account to the current account, was in significant deficit. Nevertheless, the overall balance, which includes the short-term capital account, was in substantial surplus.[29] This means that the inflow of short-term funds greatly exceeded the amount required to fill the current account deficit. In other words, short-term funds from overseas were flowing in, exceeding what was needed, to areas that required long-term funds.

In Malaysia's case, although the current account deficit was sufficiently covered by long-term funds such as direct investment, a large amount of short-term funds flowed in from overseas between 1992 and early 1994. In particular, the inflow of short-term funds in 1993 was large-scale, exceeding 8% of GDP, and became a major disruptive factor for Malaysia's monetary policy. To cope with this situation, Bank Negara lowered the high domestic interest rates that had been attracting short-term funds from overseas and implemented policies to curb short-term capital inflows.

However, as interest rates were lowered to curb the inflow of short-term funds, Malaysia's economy remained overheated for several years before the Asian Financial Crisis in 1997. Malaysia's real lending rate dropped sharply in 1994 and remained low until 1997, when monetary tightening was implemented in response to the Asian Financial Crisis. From 1995 to 1997, bank lending in Malaysia rapidly increased, particularly in the real estate and construction sectors. The interest rate cut by Bank Negara in 1994 prevented a currency crisis caused by excessive inflows of short-term capital from overseas, as in Thailand and South Korea. Still, it caused a bubble driven by domestic capital.

In this way, because today's developing countries, especially middle-income countries, are closely linked to international financial markets, it is essential for economic development that the central bank in charge of monetary policy can implement rational policies without arbitrary intervention from the government. Bank Negara proved its excellence through the successful introduction and management of both the fixed exchange rate system and short-term capital controls in response to the Asian Financial Crisis. However, at the same time, it is clear that its independence from the government was not secured, as evidenced by the resignation of then-Governor Ahmad Mohamed Don just before the introduction of the fixed exchange rate system due to a conflict with Prime Minister Mahathir over the response to the currency crisis. Although Prime Minister Mahathir's "political intervention" at this time worked in a positive direction, political intervention rarely leads to sound monetary policy.

Regarding this point, in 2009, under the leadership of then-Governor Zeti Akhtar Aziz, the Central Bank of Malaysia Act (CBA2009) was enacted, securing a considerable degree of independence for Bank Negara in terms of monetary policy decisions and the appointment of the governor (see Chapter 5). In 2016, when there was a tense relationship between the Najib administration and Bank Negara, the supervisory authority, over corruption related to the state investment company 1Malaysia Development Berhad (1MDB), the then-Deputy Governor of Bank Negara was promoted as the successor to Governor Zeti, whose term was expiring, rather than the candidate recommended by the Najib administration. In this case, the CBA2009, which stipulated the qualifications a governor should possess, is thought to have acted as a "brake." If a person close to the Najib administration had been appointed at this time, it would not have been surprising if the depreciation of the Malaysian ringgit, which had already fallen significantly due to the 1MDB issue, had continued unabated, taking on the appearance of a currency crisis.

4.4.2 *Malaysia's "Resource Curse" is Mild*

As one factor that has stagnated Malaysia's economic upgrading, let us touch on the "resource curse" here. From the perspective of Japan, which currently produces almost no natural resources, Malaysia, blessed with enough natural resources to export, may seem desirable. However, contrary to intuition, the economic development of countries that produce natural resources that should bring wealth to the nation is often unsatisfactory, a phenomenon called the "resource curse." Factors contributing to the resource curse include the instability of primary commodity prices, the crowding out of the manufacturing sector, the occurrence of "Dutch disease," where the exchange rate appreciates due to resource exports, and the difficulty of governance regarding natural resources and their benefits.[30]

Just as the relationship between the central bank and the government is crucial for a country's economy, the economic development of resource-rich countries is influenced by the relationship between the government and national resource companies. Even in countries with long prime ministerial tenures like Malaysia (an average of about nine years before the change of government in 2018), the development of mineral resources requires long-term investment decisions that exceed that tenure. If national resource companies are entirely under the control of politicians, there is a risk that short-term profits will be prioritized, leading to excessive extraction and underinvestment. Furthermore, suppose democracy is not functioning well in the first place. In that case, there is a danger that the profits from abundant natural resources will perpetuate the rule of a dictatorial regime, and civil war may break out over the enormous vested interests.

On this point, the World Bank has evaluated Malaysia as one of the few countries to have successfully overcome problems stemming from abundant natural resources. In addition to investing the profits from natural resources in productive capital and diversifying Malaysia's economic activities, the World Bank highly praises Petronas, stating that it "efficiently plays the role of a de facto national resource fund and has established a reputation for good governance."[31]

Nevertheless, as will be discussed in detail in Chapter 5, one of the reasons for the slowdown in Malaysia's industrial upgrading in the 2000s is thought to be the primary commodity boom. The price of crude oil (Brent), US$13 per barrel in 1998, rose to US$50 per barrel in 2005 and US$100 per barrel in 2008. This primary commodity boom promoted a shift in economic activity from manufacturing to the primary commodity sector in Malaysia.

In Malaysia, the five primary commodities (crude oil, natural gas, palm oil, rubber, and logs/timber) that once accounted for more than 80% of exports had decreased to less than 10% by 1998. However, by 2013, they had recovered to account for almost a quarter of total exports. Although Malaysia's trade structure differs significantly from the trade patterns of Latin America and other middle-income countries that are trapped in the middle-income trap, where the export competitiveness of primary commodities sometimes surpasses that of manufactured goods, it cannot be denied that the upgrading of the trade structure slowed down due to the impact of the surge in primary commodity prices in the 2000s. Malaysia seems to suffer from a mild "resource curse" due to its abundance of primary commodities.

4.5 Corporate Reform Brought About by a Change of Prime Minister

4.5.1 The Third Shift in the Tripod Structure

The balance between foreign companies, large domestic private companies, and GLCs, or the "tripod structure," in the Malaysian economy has undergone three significant changes.

The first change occurred from the 1970s to the early 1980s. As mentioned earlier, the government actively established public enterprises and acquired British companies and local Chinese companies through the national corporation PERNAS. As a result, the composition of the corporate landscape, which had traditionally been based on the "two pillars" of British companies and Chinese companies, evolved into a "tripod structure" that included these two groups plus GLCs. This change occurred as the government's economic policy shifted from a laissez-faire approach to a state-led New Economic Policy aimed at correcting inter-ethnic disparities. As seen in Chapter 2, this policy shift progressed after the ethnic riots of 1969.

The second major change occurred due to the relaxation of regulations on foreign companies and Chinese companies in the manufacturing sector (which began in the mid-1980s) and the privatization of GLCs. The relaxation of regulations primarily increased the presence of foreign manufacturing companies, while privatization created large domestic companies managed by Malays.

The relaxation of regulations on foreign companies and Chinese companies in the manufacturing sector began as a countermeasure to the recession, as seen earlier. For foreign companies, measures were announced in September 1986 to allow 100% capital ownership for companies that export more than 50% of their products or employ more than 350 Malaysians full-time. In addition, the operation of the Industrial Coordination Act (ICA), which obligated manufacturing companies to have 30%

of their capital owned by Bumiputeras, was relaxed, and the scope of exemptions was expanded twice in December 1985 and October 1986. As a result, it is estimated that the number of companies subject to ICA regulations decreased to about one-third of the previous level.[32]

These investment deregulation measures brought about an influx of foreign direct investment, predominantly from Japanese companies, and facilitated both the recovery from the recession and the subsequent high economic growth. However, the implementation of investment deregulation coincided with a heated debate over post-1990 development policy, as discussed in Chapter 3, and government leaders faced difficult political challenges. Investment deregulation potentially undermined policies supporting Bumiputera share acquisition, generating significant dissent within the ruling United Malays National Organisation (UMNO). Before the foreign investment deregulation in September 1986 and the relaxation of the ICA application in October, Prime Minister Mahathir indicated at the UMNO party conference in September of the same year that policies to achieve the 30% Bumiputera share ownership would continue beyond 1990. This declaration is widely interpreted as a preemptive measure taken to mitigate anticipated opposition within the party to investment deregulation. Still, it was an apparent deviation from the election pledge of the ruling coalition Barisan Nasional (BN) to formulate a successor policy to the New Economic Policy based on broad consensus. As seen in the previous chapter, it significantly contributed to deepening the conflict with the Malaysian Chinese Association (MCA) and other coalition partners.

As demonstrated in Chapter 3, the policy shift from "prioritizing Malay support" to "emphasizing economic growth" was not easily accomplished. Nevertheless, a substantial consensus had emerged through extensive discussions both within and outside the National Economic Consultative Council (NECC). When Mahathir proposed "Vision 2020" based on this consensus, various sectors of society, including opposition groups, rallied behind the goal of "becoming a developed country by 2020," which facilitated the implementation of multiple deregulation measures and private capital utilization initiatives to accelerate growth.

The privatization of public enterprises progressed within this evolving political and policy context. Although Malaysia was one of the first countries in the world to initiate privatization policies, the process began in earnest only in the late 1980s. To achieve the policy goal of Bumiputera advancement into the commercial and industrial sectors without significantly hindering the activities of foreign and Chinese companies, the government adopted the strategy of nurturing Bumiputera entrepreneurs through the strategic sale of public enterprises.

The third major transformation in the tripod structure occurred in the aftermath of the 1997–98 Asian Financial Crisis. Many of the large Bumiputera-owned companies that had emerged through the privatization of public enterprises were re-nationalized, and consequently, the presence of GLCs in the tripod structure increased once again.

As mentioned earlier, the Bumiputera companies created through privatization had owner-managers. When these companies faced financial difficulties after the Asian Financial Crisis, replacing management required compelling these owner-managers to sell their shares. If these owner-managers remained as major shareholders even after their resignation from management positions, they could still exert significant influence over corporate decisions. Therefore, government-linked investment companies like Khazanah Nasional and the Minister of Finance Incorporated (MoF Inc.) bought back the shares of these troubled companies and effectively re-nationalized them. Unlike neighboring countries such as Thailand, where the currency crisis similarly damaged corporate balance sheets but led to numerous foreign acquisitions, Malaysia experienced very few takeovers by foreign companies. This was partly because many Malaysian domestic companies were predominantly domestically oriented and operated in protected sectors such as infrastructure and services, making them less accessible for foreign acquisition.

Moreover, unlike the previous privatization wave, the government chose not to re-privatize these re-nationalized companies to Bumiputera entrepreneurs. Instead, in 2004, the GLC Transformation Program was launched, aiming to improve the performance of each company while maintaining government ownership. This comprehensive program clearly defined the roles, selection policies, and evaluation indicators of the board of directors, which is widely considered to have significantly contributed to improving corporate governance and performance.

4.5.2 Political Reform-Minded New Prime Minister Led the Reforms

Why did the government choose to continue managing the re-nationalized companies as GLCs instead of pursuing a second wave of privatization? Re-nationalization was primarily a crisis response measure, and it would have been logical to expect moves to return to the pre-crisis privatization model once corporate restructuring and management rebuilding were completed.

The primary catalyst for the government's decision to implement the GLC Transformation Program rather than pursue re-privatization was a significant change in leadership. Mahathir, who had served as Prime Minister for 22 years and initiated the policy of nurturing Bumiputera entrepreneurs through privatization, retired in October 2003. The new Prime Minister was Abdullah Badawi, who was widely nicknamed "Mr. Clean" for his reputation for integrity.

This change of Prime Minister was the outcome of the political turmoil precipitated by the Asian Financial Crisis. During the currency crisis, Deputy Prime Minister Anwar Ibrahim, who also served as Finance Minister, championed the "IMF policy without the IMF" that embraced tight monetary controls and fiscal austerity. At the same time, Prime Minister Mahathir vocally opposed these measures, attracting considerable international attention and speculation. The friction between the two leaders eventually escalated into a full-blown power struggle, with the Anwar faction publicly criticizing the Bumiputera entrepreneur rescue measures spearheaded by the Mahathir faction as blatant cronyism. The rescued entrepreneurs were widely known to be close associates of former Finance Minister Daim Zainuddin, a longtime confidant of the Prime Minister, and close allies of the Prime Minister himself. This perceived betrayal incurred the wrath of the Prime Minister, leading to the dramatic dismissal of Deputy Prime Minister Anwar in September 1998, followed shortly thereafter by his arrest.

The dismissal and subsequent arrest of Anwar, who was immensely popular among the Malay masses, fundamentally transformed the landscape of Malaysian politics. Parti Keadilan Nasional (later renamed Parti Keadilan Rakyat), formed by Anwar's supporters, successfully mediated the first direct alliance between the Parti Islam Se-Malaysia (PAS) and the Democratic Action Party (DAP), which had been traditional adversaries until then, leading to the historic formation of the opposition coalition Barisan Alternatif (Alternative Front). In the run-up to the pivotal tenth general election in 1999, the three opposition parties presented a unified manifesto calling for the eradication of corruption and the promotion of comprehensive democratization, strategically fielding unified candidates in every constituency in Peninsular Malaysia. As a result of this unprecedented cooperation, although DAP and Keadilan did not significantly increase their parliamentary representation, PAS made a historic breakthrough by winning control of state governments in two states. In this landmark election, analysts widely believe that for the first time, a majority of Malay voters cast their ballots for opposition candidates rather than the ruling coalition.

In 2002, as the cleanup from the currency crisis turned the corner, Mahathir unexpectedly announced his intention to retire during a dramatic UMNO party conference, shocking both party members and the general public. This announcement ultimately led to Abdullah, who had been appointed deputy prime minister following Anwar's downfall, being confirmed as Mahathir's designated successor. Acutely aware of the groundswell of public opinion calling for substantial political reform that had emerged during the watershed 1999 election, Abdullah strategically positioned the eradication of corruption and the restoration of public trust in government as his administration's top priorities upon assuming the prime ministership. Four months after taking office, Abdullah strategically dissolved parliament and called a general election. Riding a wave of public optimism and high expectations for the new Prime Minister's reform agenda, the ruling coalition secured a landslide victory, capturing an overwhelming 90% of the seats in the lower house.

It was Abdullah who initiated the comprehensive GLC Transformation Program in 2004, just one year after becoming prime minister. Keenly mindful of strong public sentiment calling for political cleanup and greater transparency, Abdullah recognized the urgent need to fundamentally review and restructure the relationship between the ruling party and the business community. His landmark speech delivered at the Harvard Club in May 2005 illustrates this fundamental shift in approach particularly well. During this high-profile occasion, Abdullah candidly told the assembled business leaders that Malaysian companies must overcome three critical "addictions" that were hindering the country's economic development. Along with over-dependence on foreign workers and excessive reliance on government subsidies, he specifically problematized what he termed "rent-seeking addiction" as the most detrimental to Malaysia's economic future. "Rent-seeking addiction," as Abdullah explained it, refers to the widespread tendency of Malaysian companies to neglect crucial efforts to develop management expertise and technical know-how, instead focusing primarily on forming political connections (what he termed "know-who") with influential government figures. With this pointed critique, he was directly warning entrepreneurs who had built their business models around seeking preferential treatment and special favors from well-connected politicians rather than developing genuine competitive advantages.

In such a collusive system where politicians and businesses form mutually beneficial arrangements, politicians inevitably receive some form of direct or indirect compensation from these businesses in return for their political patronage. In parallel with the rampant rent-seeking behavior that characterized the high-growth period of the 1990s, vote-buying practices became increasingly prevalent and systematic in UMNO leadership elections, fundamentally corrupting the party's internal democratic processes. This troubling pattern strongly suggests that the substantial financial resources flowing back from favored businesses were being systematically channeled into funding factional power struggles within UMNO, creating a self-perpetuating cycle of political patronage and corruption. Mahathir himself had publicly acknowledged that money politics had become rampant within the party and, in a dramatic moment that underscored the severity of the issue, once shed tears at a party conference while explaining its destructive effects on UMNO and the nation. In line with his reform agenda, Abdullah also decisively cracked down on high-ranking party leaders involved in vote-buying practices. In a move that sent shockwaves through the political establishment, he subjected Mohd Isa Abdul Samad, the prominent Federal Territories Minister who had obtained the post of Vice President in the September 2004 leadership election, to an investigation by the party disciplinary committee, ultimately resulting in Isa's suspension from office for three years.

In this way, the fact that a person who was aware of the changes in public opinion after the currency crisis and sought to gain support by advancing political reforms became prime Minister led to the formulation and implementation of the GLC Transformation Program rather than the revival of the privatization policy, which had been regarded as a hotbed of cronyism. However, the Abdullah administration's "reforms" did not meet the expectations of the public. Half-hearted reforms only bred disappointment, and opposition parties calling for bolder reforms gained support. This will be discussed in the following chapters.

In Malaysia's case, the government's policies promoting Bumiputera participation in the commercial and industrial sectors have strongly influenced the balance between domestic private companies, foreign companies, and GLCs. After the introduction of the New Economic Policy, GLCs initially expanded, but in the mid-1980s, the government shifted towards privatization in response to the recession. When the Asian Financial Crisis hit privatized companies, the government re-nationalized them and implemented the GLC Transformation Program, taking adjustment measures according to environmental change. The Malaysian government has also been actively accepting foreign manufacturing companies while paying attention to not becoming overly dependent on foreign capital in sectors such as finance. Although the goal of successive administrations, especially the Mahathir administration, to nurture Bumiputera private companies independent from the government has not been fully achieved, since the mid-2000s, Bumiputera professional managers have been appointed as managers of GLCs, realizing substantial Bumiputera involvement in corporate management.

Notes

1. Only 10–30% of multinational corporations' R&D activities are conducted in overseas subsidiaries (Hirst, Thompson, and Bromley 2009). Moreover, 80% of total global R&D is concentrated in OECD countries (Chen and Vang 2008).
2. Sheshinski and Lopez-Calva (2003).
3. Kornai (1986).
4. Suehiro (2014).
5. Malaysia (1971: 40).
6. Malaysia (1971: 41).
7. Institute of Developing Economies (1977: 414–416).
8. Institute of Developing Economies (1978: 396–397).
9. Horii (1990: 139–140).
10. Hara (1980).
11. Jomo and Tan (2011: 335).
12. Kumagai (2006a).
13. Gomez and Jomo (1999).
14. Kimura (1989: 360).
15. The Sun Daily, August 27, 2014.
16. Kumagai (2001: 335–336).
17. As of 2004, excluding government holdings, the ethnic ownership ratio of capital was: Bumiputera 18.9%, Chinese 39%, Indian 1.2%, and foreign 32.5%. This ethnic share ownership ratio is based on book value and includes all registered companies. Also, as of 2005, government-linked companies accounted for 36% of the market capitalization of Bursa Malaysia (Kuala Lumpur Stock Exchange). For the purpose of estimation, we assume that the remaining 64% of Bursa Malaysia's market capitalization (excluding government-linked companies) follows the same ethnic ownership distribution as the ratio excluding foreign ownership. Based on these calculations, domestic private companies account for 48.9%, government-linked companies for 27.5%, and foreign companies for 23.6% of total capital.
18. According to the author's estimates, if Petronas were to be listed on the stock exchange, it would account for 30–40% of Bursa Malaysia's market capitalization.
19. Suehiro (2014: 97–123).
20. The definition of GLCs in Malaysia is as follows: 1) GLCs are companies that have a primary commercial objective and in which the Malaysian Government has a direct controlling stake; 2) Controlling stake refers to the Government's ability to appoint BOD members, senior management, and make major decisions for GLCs either directly or through GLICs; 3) These include companies the Government controls through Khazanah, MOF Inc., KWAP, and Bank Negara Malaysia. They also include companies where GLICs and federal government agencies have joint control; 4) Subsidiaries and affiliates of GLCs are also considered GLCs.
21. PCG (2015: 7).
22. Additionally, GLC shareholders' returns increased by an average of 11.1% annually from 2004–2014, and G20's net profit reached RM26.2 billion in 2014, growing at an average annual rate of 10.2% from 2004–2014. G20 companies operate in 42 countries, with overseas operations accounting for 34% of total revenue (up from 28% in 2004) and overseas assets making up 26% of total assets (up from 11% in 2004).

23. Kumagai (2018).
24. Menon and Ng (2013).
25. PCG (2015: 214).
26. Kumagai (2018: 288–290).
27. Kumagai (2006b).
28. "Intel to invest $7 billion in new plant in Malaysia, creating 9000 jobs," Reuters, December 16, 2021.
29. The current account balance consists of the trade balance (the difference between exports and imports of goods), the services balance (including travel and transportation), and the income balance (including dividends and interest). The long-term capital account primarily reflects the balance of long-term funds such as direct investment, while the short-term capital account shows the balance of borrowing and lending with maturities of one year or less through stock markets and bank loans. Note that this classification of balance of payments has since been revised.
30. Frankel (2010).
31. World Bank (2013).
32. Yasuda (1988: 171).

References

Chen YC, Vang J (2008) MNCs, global innovation networks and developing countries: insights from Motorola in China. Int J Bus Manage Sci 1(1):11–30

Frankel JA (2010) The natural resource curse: a survey. NBER Working Paper No. 15836, National Bureau of Economic Research

Gomez ET, Jomo KS (1999) Malaysia's political economy: politics, patronage and profits, 2nd edn. Cambridge University Press, Cambridge

Hara F (1980) Public enterprises at a critical stage: Malaysia in 1979 (1979 nen no Malaysia). In: Institute of Developing Economies (ed) Yearbook of Asian affairs (Ajia Dōkō Nenpō). Institute of Developing Economies, Tokyo, pp 377–422

Hirst P, Thompson G, Bromley S (2009) Globalization in question, 3rd edn. Wiley, Hoboken

Horii K (1990) Public enterprises and Bumiputera (Kōkigyō to Bumiputera). In: Horii K (ed) Industrialization in Malaysia: development of industrialization in a multi-ethnic nation (Malaysia no Kōgyōka). Institute of Developing Economies, Tokyo, pp 128–158

Institute of Developing Economies (1977) Malaysia in 1976: the Hussein administration struggling to determine its course (1976 nen no Malaysia). In: Yearbook of Asian Affairs 1977 (Ajia Dōkō Nenpō 1977). Institute of Developing Economies, Tokyo, pp 414–416

Institute of Developing Economies (1978) Malaysia in 1977: the fluctuating state administrations (1977 nen no Malaysia). In: Yearbook of Asian Affairs 1978 (Ajia Dōkō Nenpō 1978). Institute of Developing Economies, Tokyo, pp 396–397

Jomo KS, Tan J (2011) Lessons from privatization. In: Institute of Strategic and International Studies (ed) Malaysia: policies and issues in economic development. Institute of Strategic and International Studies, Kuala Lumpur, pp 329–364

Kimura M (1989) Malaysia in 1988: toward building a post-90 system (1988 nen no Malaysia). In: Institute of Developing Economies (ed) Yearbook of Asian Affairs 1989 (Ajia Dōkō Nenpō 1989). Institute of Developing Economies, Tokyo, pp 355–386

Kornai J (1986) The soft budget constraint. Kyklos 39(1):3–30

Kumagai S (2001) Malaysia in 2000: struggling for soft landing (2000 nen no Malaysia). In: Yearbook of Asian Affairs 2000 (Ajia Dōkō Nenpō 2000). Institute of Developing Economies, Tokyo, pp 319–350

Kumagai S (2006a) Privatization policy and its impact on major corporate groups (Mineika Seisaku to Shuyō Kigyō Gurūpu eno Inpakuto). In: Torii T (ed) Malaysia under the Mahathir administration (Mahathir Seiken-ka no Malaysia). Institute of Developing Economies, Tokyo, pp 139–178
Kumagai S (2006b) Rise and fall of PC-related industries in Singapore and Malaysia: the outcome of multinational corporation-centered development (Singapore, Malaysia no PC Kanren Sangyō no Seisui). In: Imai K, Kawakami M (eds) IT hardware industry in East Asia (Higashi Ajia no IT Kiki Sangyō). Institute of Developing Economies, Tokyo, pp 171–216
Kumagai S (2018) Government-linked companies (GLCs) and Bumiputera policy: from corporate governance perspective (Seifu kei Kigyō to Bumiputera Seisaku). In: Nakamura M, Kumagai S (eds) Malaysia in the post-Mahathir era (Post-Mahathir Jidai no Malaysia). Institute of Developing Economies, Tokyo, pp 261–299
Malaysia (1971) Second Malaysia Plan 1971–1975. Government Press, Kuala Lumpur
Menon J, Ng TH (2013) Are government-linked corporations crowding out private investment in Malaysia? ADB Economic Working Paper Series No. 345, Asian Development Bank
Putrajaya Committee of GLC High Performance (PCG) (2015) GLC transformation programme graduation report, vol 1. PCG, Kuala Lumpur
Sheshinski E, López-Calva LF (2003) Privatization and its benefits: theory and evidence. CESifo Econ Stud 49(3):429–459
Suehiro A (2014) New emerging Asian economies: beyond catch-up (Shinkou Asia Keizai-ron). Iwanami Shoten, Tokyo
World Bank (2013) Malaysia economic monitor: harnessing natural resources. World Bank
Yasuda N (1988) Bumiputera policy and the Industrial Coordination Act (Bumiputera Seisaku to Kōgyō Chōsei Hō). In: Horii K, Hagiwara N (eds) Socio-economic change in contemporary Malaysia (Gendai Malaysia no Shakai Keizai Henyō). Institute of Developing Economies, Tokyo, pp 139–176

Chapter 5
The Reality and Challenges of Industrial Upgrading

The Struggle for Productivity-Led Economic Growth (1990s to 2010s)

In 1994, while the Asian economies were continuing their high growth, Paul Krugman, who later won the Nobel Prize in Economics, published "The Myth of Asia's Miracle."1 Krugman argued that many Asian countries had achieved high growth by quantitatively expanding labor and capital inputs and would soon face growth limitations. Even countries that achieved economic development centered on labor-intensive industries—such as garment manufacturing and electronics assembly—during their lower-middle-income period will eventually experience a decline in economic growth rates. This decline occurs due to the law of diminishing returns, where increasing labor or capital no longer results in proportional increases in production. While there is debate about whether Krugman's assertion was correct for each East Asian country, lower-middle-income countries generally must shift from quantitative expansion of capital and labor inputs to qualitative expansion—that is, productivity improvement—to escape the upper-middle-income stage and enter the high-income category.

This book has analyzed the improvement in labor quality (Chapter 3) and the improvement in the quality of corporate management that efficiently utilizes capital (Chapter 4), but whether these two are appropriately achieved is questionable for continued economic growth in the upper-middle-income period. Regarding the improvement of labor quality, policies that keep wages low out of concern for negative impacts on labor-intensive industries and rely on cheap foreign workers delay the improvement of worker quality, which in turn delays the rise in labor productivity. It is also essential to upgrade the level of training for workers and education for young people newly entering the labor market.

Improving the quality of corporate management is a challenge for local companies. Moreover, state-owned enterprises and foreign-affiliated companies face particular difficulties in conducting management that improves productivity. Even with proper management, it is not easy for state-owned enterprises to continue operations without incurring losses.

S. Kumagai and M. Nakamura, *Economic Development Strategies*, Emerging-Economy State and International Policy Studies, https://doi.org/10.1007/978-981-95-6899-4_5

Relying on foreign-affiliated companies for economic development and industrialization makes it easier for local subsidiaries and subcontractors in developing countries to participate in global value chains (GVCs). However, when entering GVCs through foreign-affiliated companies, it becomes difficult for local subsidiaries and subcontractors in developing countries to take on higher value-added portions.

Furthermore, authoritarian political systems may be favorable for economic growth at the lower-middle-income stage because they can quantitatively increase inputs such as labor and capital through forceful policies. However, their negative aspects become more pronounced when economic development enters a stage requiring productivity improvement, mainly research and development. Institutions that provide broad incentives for people and companies to engage in investment, innovation, and productivity improvement activities are called "inclusive economic institutions" and are considered essential for a country's economy to achieve long-term growth.2

Moreover, inclusive political institutions are necessary to make inclusive economic institutions stable over the long term. Under extractive political institutions where vested interests control power and oppress the majority of citizens, it is difficult to realize innovations that bring about creative destruction that threatens vested interests, and productivity-led economic growth cannot be expected to continue in the long term.

After entering the upper-middle-income category in the early 1990s, was Malaysia able to shift from growth driven by quantitative expansion of production factors to growth driven by productivity improvement? This chapter first analyzes the reality of productivity changes and industrial upgrading in Malaysia and points out challenges for improvement. Next, it shows that while Malaysia's political system has oppressive aspects, the government formulates and implements policies with elections in mind and has adjusted its development policies in response to social demands.

5.1 The Advancement of the Malaysian Economy

5.1.1 Slow Rise in Total Factor Productivity

A method often used to analyze what factors are driving a country's economic growth is called "growth accounting." Growth accounting decomposes the economic growth rate into three components: the increase in capital stock, the increase in labor input, and the rise in total factor productivity (TFP). Among these three elements of economic growth, while statistics on capital stock and labor input are available, it is difficult to grasp TFP directly, so in many cases, TFP is estimated as the "residual" of economic growth that cannot be explained by the quantitative increase of the other two factors. Generally, TFP is regarded as the contribution of technological progress and improvements in management efficiency beyond the quantitative increase in capital and labor. If its growth rate is high, the country's economic growth is considered to be led by productivity improvement. It is known that 30% to about half of the economic growth rate in developed countries is due to the rise in TFP.[3]

When per capita income growth rates for countries worldwide are decomposed into capital increase per worker and TFP, it is shown that the ratio of TFP growth rate to per capita income growth rate increases as income levels rise.[4] Moreover, when analyzing the economic growth rates of developing countries using growth accounting methods, it is known that the main factor behind the stagnation of income in Latin American countries in the 1980s was negative TFP growth. In contrast, in high-growth East Asian countries, TFP growth significantly contributed to economic growth rates.[5]

The World Bank pointed out that Malaysia's TFP growth rate averaged 1.8% annually from 1990 to 2014, lower than the average annual rates of 2.2% observed in both South Korea and Singapore.[6] Decomposing Malaysia's economic growth rate by era shows that while the contribution of labor input increase has gradually decreased, the contribution of capital stock increase has steadily increased after a significant drop following the 1997–98 Asian Financial Crisis. Regarding the contribution of TFP, it was highest before the Asian Financial Crisis, became negative during the crisis, and then recovered, but its growth has remained sluggish since then (Fig. 5.1).

Thus, it is difficult to say that the ratio of TFP growth rate in Malaysia's economic growth has increased with income level, and on average, it falls short of Asian countries that have achieved high-income status, such as Singapore and South Korea. In the 11th Malaysia Plan (2016–2020), the Malaysian government set a target TFP growth rate of 2.3%,[7] but it remained low at 1.0%.[8] The Malaysian economy seems to be still unable to transition from economic growth relying on quantitative expansion of labor and capital to productivity-led economic growth.[9]

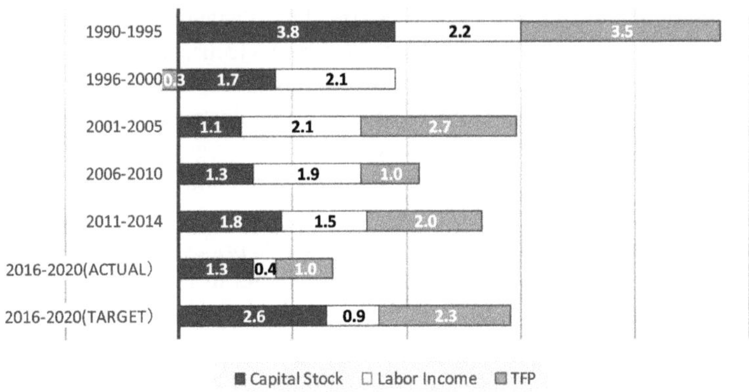

Fig. 5.1 Factor decomposition of Malaysia's economic growth rate. *Source* Compiled by the author based on World Bank (2016) Fig. 27 and Malaysia (2015, 2021)

5.1.2 *Stagnation in Industrial Upgrading as Seen in Export Structure*

In East Asia, long before the middle-income trap became a topic of discussion, industrial upgrading was discussed as necessary for middle-income countries to continue further economic growth. Industrial upgrading refers to the transition of a country's industries from labor-intensive and natural resource-intensive to capital-intensive and technology-intensive.10 The middle-income trap is sometimes defined as a state where "middle-income countries cannot compete with low-income, low-wage economies and cannot compete with advanced countries in high-skill innovation, "11 which, in simple terms, is nothing other than the "failure of industrial upgrading."

The Malaysian economy, driven by foreign investment, transformed from a primary commodity exporting country to an industrial product exporting country in a very short period from the 1980s to the 1990s. Figure 5.2 shows the change over time in Malaysia's exports classified into (1) five major primary commodities (crude oil, natural gas, palm oil, rubber, timber), (2) other primary commodities, (3) primary commodity-related products,12 (4) electronic and electrical products, and (5) other manufactured goods.

In 1980, primary commodities and related products accounted for over 70% of Malaysia's exports. In 1989, this fell below 50% for the first time, and by 1997, it had decreased to about 20%. In a very short period, the ratio of primary commodities and related products to exports and that of other manufactured goods completely reversed.

During the Asian Financial Crisis, the share of manufactured goods in Malaysia's exports exceeded 80%. This was due to the significantly improved price competitiveness of manufactured goods caused by the substantial depreciation of the ringgit during the currency crisis. Electronic and electrical products have been driving Malaysia's exports of manufactured goods, accounting for more than half of Malaysia's exports in 2000. However, the share of electronic and electrical products in exports began to decline, affected by the bursting of the IT bubble in the United States in 2001, and along with it, the share of manufactured goods as a whole also started to decrease.

Entering the mid-2000s, the global rise in resource prices became notable. While crude oil prices (Brent) averaged around $13 per barrel in 1998, they exceeded $50 in 2005 and surged to nearly $100 in 2008. The share of the five major primary commodities in exports, which had fallen below 10% in 1998, recovered to almost a quarter of exports by 2013 and exceeded one-third of exports together with primary commodity-related products. This slightly surpassed the export share of electronic and electrical products. However, this trend changed again with the fall in oil prices in late 2014. Crude oil prices, above $100 per barrel until early 2014, briefly fell below $30 in January 2016. The share of the five major primary commodities in exports decreased to 12.0% in 2020, and the share of manufactured goods is increasing again.

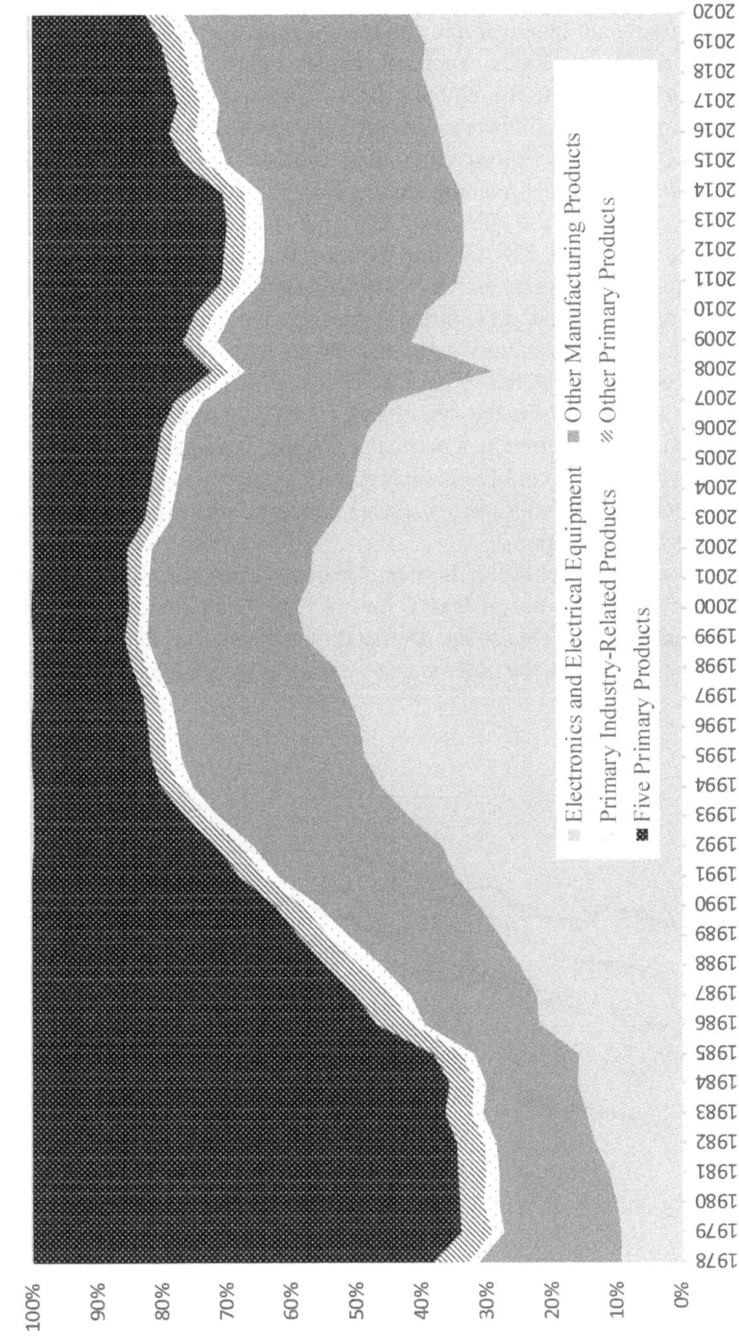

Fig. 5.2 Share of different product categories in Malaysia's exports (1978–2020). *Source* Compiled by the author based on UN COMTRADE (https://comtradeplus.un.org/) Accessed on 30 Sep 2023

Thus, Malaysia's exports were dependent on primary commodities before 1980, gradually shifted to manufactured goods throughout the 1980s and early 1990s, and became strongly reliant on electronic and electrical products during the Asian Financial Crisis. From the late 2000s, exports of primary commodities and processed goods grew significantly due to the global primary commodity boom, and in the 2010s, after the primary commodity boom subsided, the export structure transformed into a balanced one between primary commodities and related products, electronic and electrical products, and other manufactured goods.

There are indicators called PRODY and EXPY that show how sophisticated the goods exported by a country are. PRODY is an indicator based on the idea that "goods exported by high-income countries are more sophisticated." PRODY is a weighted average of the per capita income of countries exporting a particular good, weighted by the share of that good in the country's exports, and the higher the value, the more sophisticated the good is considered to be. PRODY is, in some sense, close to the concept of "export unit price." On the other hand, EXPY is a weighted average of the PRODY of each good exported by a particular country, weighted by its share in exports. EXPY can be an indicator of how sophisticated a country's export goods are as a whole and is conceptually close to a weighted average of the export unit prices of each good by its share in exports.

Figure 5.3 shows the trend of EXPY for East Asian countries from 1990 to 2015. From highest to lowest, the order of EXPY for six East Asian countries in 2015 is Japan, South Korea, China, Malaysia, Thailand, and Indonesia. Except for the reversal of China and Malaysia, the order matches the order of per capita income for each country.

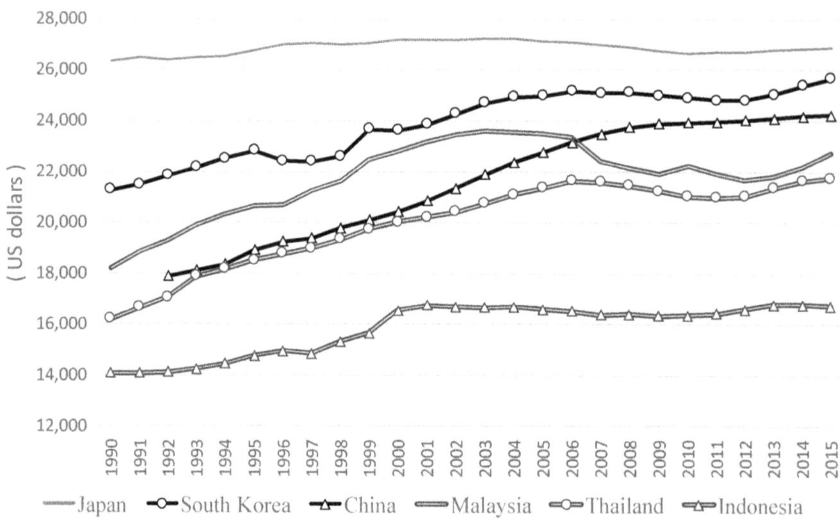

Fig. 5.3 Trends in EXPY for Asian countries (1990–2015). *Source* Kumagai and Kuroiwa (2020), Fig. 3

The significant rise in EXPY for the five countries excluding Japan in the 1990s corresponds to the development of manufacturing production networks in East Asia during this period, with each country beginning to export more sophisticated goods. Also, the fact that Japan and the three ASEAN countries' EXPY leveled off after entering the 2000s, while South Korea and China's EXPY continued to grow steadily, is intuitively understandable, as it coincides with the increased presence of Chinese and Korean brands like Samsung and Haier in the global market during this period. Thus, EXPY can be quite consistent with East Asia's reality as an indicator of export sophistication.

Furthermore, by calculating EXPY separately for five production stages—"capital goods," "parts," "consumer goods," "primary commodities," and "processed goods"—it becomes possible to conduct a more detailed analysis of industrial upgrading in each country.13 "Capital goods" include goods used in production, such as industrial machinery and construction machinery. "Parts" include components of industrial products such as semiconductors and automotive parts. "Consumer goods" include goods consumers purchase, such as food, home appliances, clothing, and passenger cars. "Primary commodities" include natural resources and agricultural products such as crude oil, natural gas, rubber, and grains. "Processed goods" include materials processed from natural resources, such as palm oil, chemical products, steel, and cement.

By aggregating EXPY first by the five stages and then totaling them in two steps, it becomes possible to decompose the changes in EXPY for each country into "within stages" and "between stages."

The rise in EXPY "within stages" occurs when, for example, the focus of exports shifts from simple consumer goods like clothing to more sophisticated goods like home appliances and passenger cars, even within the same "consumer goods" classification. The rise in EXPY within stages can be seen as gradual export sophistication.

The rise in EXPY "between stages" occurs when, for example, a country that primarily exports primary commodities industrializes and begins to export mainly consumer goods. The rise in EXPY between stages can be understood as structural export sophistication.

Table 5.1 shows the changes in Malaysia's EXPY, divided into changes in export shares for each stage, showing changes between stages, and changes in EXPY within each stage. The upper section shows changes from 1990 to 2000, and the lower section shows changes from 2000 to 2015.14 The export share on the left refers to the share of each stage in Malaysia's total exports. Changes in overall EXPY due to changes in this share are changes in EXPY "between stages."

The EXPY by stage on the right is the EXPY aggregated by stage, and it can be seen that the EXPY for primary commodities and processed goods is low, while the EXPY for capital goods and parts is high. Changes in EXPY for each stage become changes in EXPY "within stages." From 1990 to 2000, Malaysia's EXPY increased by $3858 between stages and $1741 within stages. The contribution of sophistication between stages is substantial due to the rapid shift of export items

Table 5.1 Changes in EXPY within and between production stages in Malaysia

	Export Share				EXPY			
	1990	2000	Change	Between-Stage	1990	2000	Change	Within-Stage
Capital Goods	9.0%	26.5%	+17.5%	+1124	24,991	27,997	+3006	+271
Consumer Goods	16.0%	11.3%	−4.7%	−1	19,147	20,231	+1084	+173
Processed Goods	28.7%	22.4%	−6.4%	+407	14,590	17,637	+3047	+876
Primary Products	24.2%	6.1%	−18.1%	+1064	14,684	16,229	+1544	+374
Parts & Components	22.1%	33.8%	+11.7%	+1264	27,520	27,737	+217	+48
Total				+3858				+1741
	Export Share				EXPY			
	2000	2015	Change	Between-Stage	2000	2015	Change	Within-Stage
Capital Goods	19.0%	12.9%	−6.1%	−470	26,815	28,801	+1986	+362
Consumer Goods	12.5%	13.1%	+0.6%	−10	18,664	19,840	+1176	+167
Processed Goods	22.1%	39.6%	+17.4%	−1485	17,716	17,686	−30	+139
Primary Products	6.0%	5.9%	−0.1%	−116	16,415	15,803	−612	−37
Parts & Components	40.3%	28.5%	−11.8%	−876	25,974	30,257	+4283	+1163
Total				−2955				+1794

Source Kumagai & Kuroiwa (2020, Table 4a).

from primary commodities to parts and capital goods. At the same time, the EXPY within each stage has also increased significantly, except for "parts."

On the other hand, from 2000 to 2015, Malaysia's EXPY decreased by $2955 between stages and increased by $1794 within stages. Sophistication within stages continues to progress, with "parts" contributing particularly highly. Meanwhile, the contribution of sophistication between stages has become significantly negative; in particular, the fact that the export share of "processed goods," which has a relatively low EXPY by stage, has increased dramatically since 2000, while the share of "capital goods" and "parts" with high EXPY has decreased. This change has become a significant factor in lowering EXPY.

This analysis seems to represent the reality of industrial upgrading in Malaysia, which relies on multinational corporations in the manufacturing sector. That is, the multinational corporations at the center of Malaysia's manufactured goods exports are constantly striving to improve productivity, which corresponds to the continuous increase in EXPY within production stages such as "consumer goods" and "parts" over the past 25 years.

As a consequence of relying on multinational corporations to export manufactured goods, Malaysia's role in GVCs becomes fixed, making it difficult for structural industrial upgrading to occur across stages, such as from consumer goods to parts or from parts to capital goods. Conversely, in resource-rich Malaysia, the export of "processed goods" such as palm oil and petroleum products with low EXPY has grown due to the primary commodity boom in the 2000s, indicating that the industrial structure has been "downgraded." Looking at the changes in EXPY for Malaysia's primary commodities and processed goods in Table 5.1, while processed goods are slightly higher as of 2015, both are low compared to other stages, showing that even if primary commodities are exported as processed goods, the contribution to industrial upgrading is limited.

5.1.3 Analysis Based on the Flying Geese Paradigm

An analysis applying the flying geese paradigm is helpful to see whether industrial upgrading is progressing smoothly in each country. The economic development of East Asian countries is characterized by each country "taking off" into high growth with a time lag, often called the flying geese pattern of economic development. Japan is the "lead goose" in East Asia's economic development, followed by the "Asian NIEs" of Singapore, South Korea, Taiwan, and Hong Kong, then the advanced ASEAN4 countries, and finally China and the later ASEAN CLMV countries.

While this flying geese paradigm is often used to describe how countries within a region develop in sequence with time lags, it also applies well to cases where different industries within a country develop with time lags. In fact, this version is the original flying geese paradigm, although this is not widely known. In the original flying geese paradigm, a country's exports typically start with consumer goods, followed by more sophisticated goods such as capital goods.15 The proponent, Kaname Akamatsu, explained the basic pattern of the flying geese paradigm in four stages:

Stage 1: Import of consumer goods manufactured overseas begins.

Stage 2: Domestic industries start producing consumer goods that were previously imported, and capital goods to manufacture these consumer goods are imported.

Stage 3: Domestic industries begin exporting the consumer goods they manufacture.

Stage 4: The consumer goods industry catches up with similar industries in advanced countries. Exports of consumer goods begin to decline, and capital goods used in the production of consumer goods are exported.

Here, we use the net export ratio to represent the flying geese paradigm based on the data in the figures. The net export ratio = (exports - imports)/(exports + imports), where if a country exports a specific good while not importing it at all, the net export ratio is 1; if it imports a specific good while not exporting it at all, the net export ratio is -1; and if exports and imports are balanced, the net export ratio is 0. The higher the net export ratio, the higher the international competitiveness of that good for a country can be understood to be.

The change in trade structure along Akamatsu's four-stage flying geese paradigm can be illustrated using net export ratios as follows (Fig. 5.4). The vertical axis represents the net export ratio, with consumer goods shown by a solid line and capital goods by a dotted line. By using the net export ratios of two types of goods, the four stages of the flying geese paradigm can be visually represented. In Stage 1, as consumer goods are mainly imported, the net export ratio for consumer goods is significantly negative. In Stage 2, as domestic import substitution production of consumer goods begins, the net export ratio improves. Meanwhile, as almost all capital goods used in the domestic production of consumer goods are imported, the net export ratio for capital goods approaches −1. In Stage 3, exports of domestically produced consumer goods begin, and the net export ratio for consumer goods rises into positive territory. At the same time, domestic import substitution production of capital goods also begins, improving the net export ratio for capital goods. In Stage 4, as the international competitiveness of the consumer goods industry peaks and imports from other countries increase again, the net export ratio for consumer goods begins to decline. Meanwhile, as capital goods gain competitiveness and exports start, the net export ratio for capital goods rises into positive territory, eventually surpassing that of consumer goods.

Figures 5.5 and 5.6 show the trends in net export ratios for South Korea and Malaysia from the 1960s to 2010, broken down into the five stages mentioned earlier

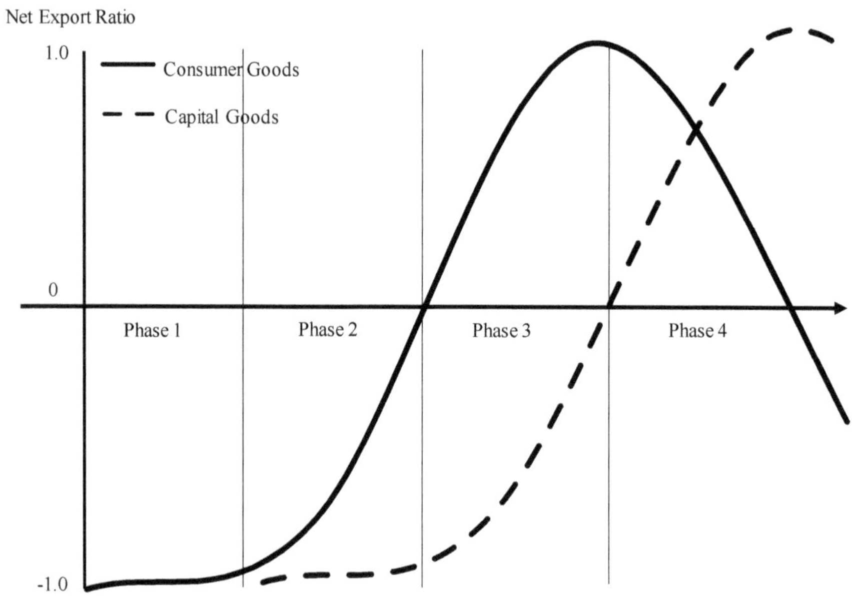

Fig. 5.4 Flying geese model and net export ratios. *Source* Author's compilation

(capital goods, parts, processed goods, consumer goods, primary commodities). Figure 5.5 shows the changes in South Korea's net export ratios by stage. South Korea has always been a net exporter of consumer goods, but its peak was in the 1970s and 1980s. The net export ratios for capital goods and parts were significantly negative until the 1970s but turned positive for both goods from the 1990s onwards. Until the 1970s, South Korea was in Stages 1 to 2 of the flying geese paradigm, producing export consumer goods through the assembly of imported parts and the use of imported capital goods. Since the 1990s, it has successfully progressed to Stages 3 to 4 of the flying geese paradigm export structure, upgrading to export more sophisticated goods such as parts and capital goods instead of consumer goods.

Figure 5.6 shows the changes in Malaysia's net export ratios. In the 1960s, Malaysia was a net exporter of primary commodities and processed goods while being a net importer of capital goods and parts. Malaysia's export structure in the 1960s was that of a typical primary commodity exporting country. In the 1970s, while the structure of net export ratios did not change much, only the net export ratio for parts rose significantly. This corresponds to the initial success of the Free Trade Zone in Penang, where mainly American semiconductor manufacturers began exporting assembled semiconductors to the United States from the Free Trade Zone.

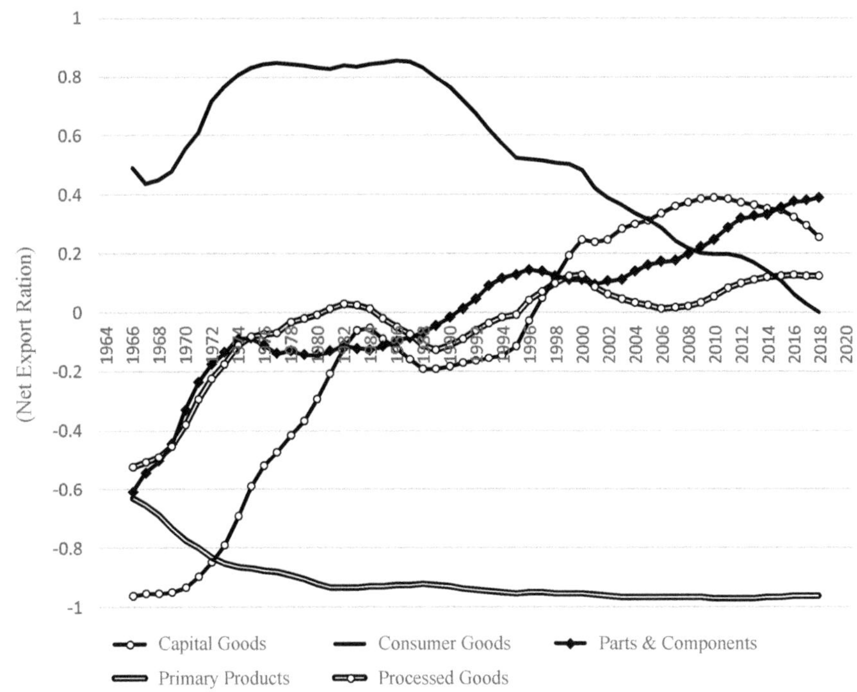

Fig. 5.5 Trends in net export ratio by product category in South Korea (1966–2018). *Source* Created by the author

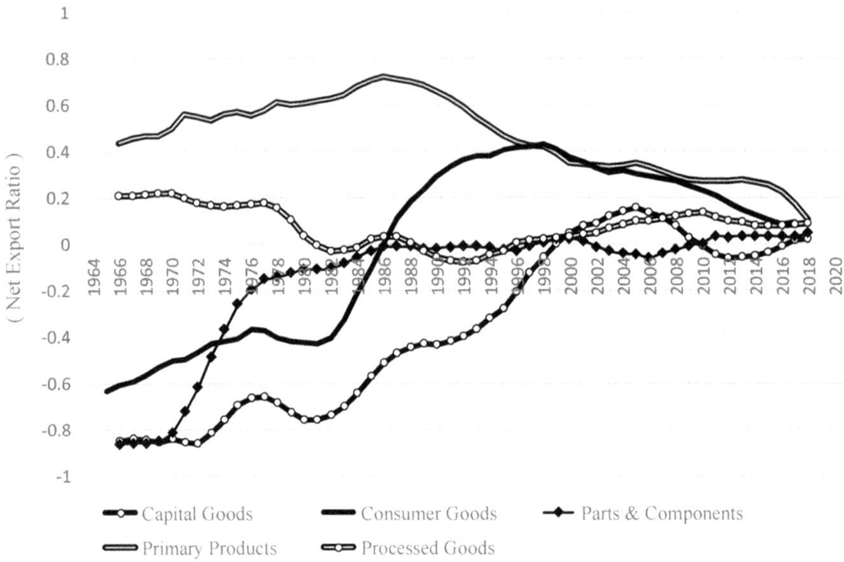

Fig. 5.6 Trends in net export ratio by product category in Malaysia (1964–2018). *Source* Created by the author

In the 1980s, Malaysia's export structure changed dramatically in just ten years. The net export ratio for consumer goods turned positive due to increased exports of home appliances and AV equipment, and the net export ratio for capital goods also began to increase due to the import substitution of commercial vehicles and increased exports of industrial electrical products. In the 1990s, the net export ratio for consumer goods increased, and the net export ratio for capital goods approached a balanced state of exports and imports by the end of the 1990s. In terms of the flying geese paradigm, this corresponds to Stages 2–3.

While Malaysia's export structure rapidly upgraded until the 1990s, this upgrading process has stagnated since the 2000s. The net export ratio for consumer goods peaked in the late 1990s, but for both capital goods and parts, the net export ratios have remained near zero, not improving from the balanced state of exports and imports. While it cannot be said that Malaysia has failed in upgrading its export structure since capital goods and parts are not in a state of one-sided import surplus, it is clear that at least since entering the 2000s, the movement towards upgrading has stagnated. Unlike South Korea, Malaysia has not reached Stage 4 of the flying geese paradigm.

5.2 Challenges for Industrial Upgrading

5.2.1 The Resource Curse

One reason why Malaysia's industrial upgrading lags behind South Korea's is, as mentioned in Chapter 4, the "resource curse." Figure 5.7 shows the correlation of net export ratios for four types of goods (capital goods and parts combined) based on data from 198 countries worldwide from 1960 to 2000. The net export ratios for capital goods/parts, consumer goods, and processed goods have positive correlations. As capital goods/parts are more sophisticated than consumer goods, it is thought that industrial upgrading through backward linkages from consumer goods to capital goods/parts is likely to occur as economic development progresses.

On the other hand, the correlations between the net export ratios of primary commodities and consumer goods, and primary commodities and capital goods/parts, are both negative. This indicates that it is rare to be a net exporter of both primary commodities and consumer goods, or both primary commodities and capital goods/parts. Net exporters of primary commodities are less likely to become net exporters of consumer goods, making it challenging to advance industrialization using backward linkages from consumer goods to capital goods. Industrialization in primary commodity exporting countries often progresses only to the stage of producing and exporting processed goods through forward linkages, using primary commodities as raw materials. However, it rarely advances beyond this stage.

Thus, Malaysia, which started as a primary commodity exporting country, faced more difficulties in subsequent industrialization than South Korea, which was not blessed with natural resources. However, from the perspective of export stability, Malaysia's export structure for both manufactured goods and primary commodities/processed goods is not necessarily negative. By the late 2010s, Malaysia had achieved a relatively rare trade structure where exports and imports were almost balanced for

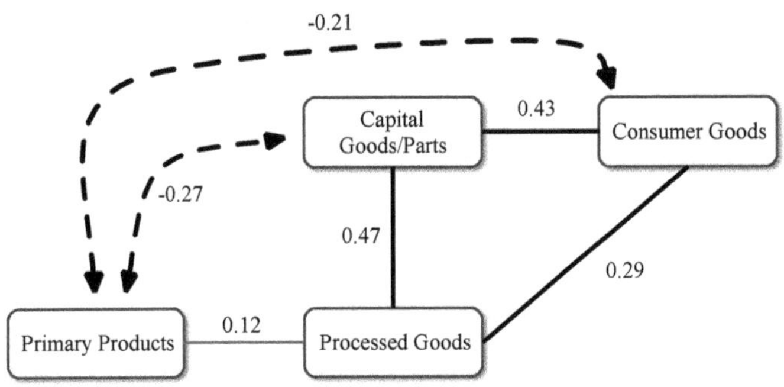

Fig. 5.7 Correlation of net export ratios by product category. *Source* Author's compilation based on Kumagai (2015)

all four types of goods, stabilizing exports against fluctuations in the world economy. This point regarding export stability will be discussed further in Chapter 6.

5.2.2 *Dependence on Multinational Corporations*

Another factor thought to be impeding Malaysia's industrial upgrading is the lack of domestically originated multinational corporations in the manufacturing sector. This is evident when compared to Japan, South Korea, and China, which have multiple domestically originated multinational corporations in various manufacturing sectors such as the automotive, electronics, electrical, steel, and shipbuilding industries. While Malaysia has domestically originated multinational corporations and has recently been investing overseas, these are mainly in service industries such as finance and telecommunications or primary commodity-related industries. In the 2018 Fortune Global 500 ranking of the world's largest multinational corporations by country, Japan had 52 companies (27 in manufacturing), South Korea had 16 (9), and China had 119 (44). In contrast, Malaysia had only one company (Petronas) in the ranking, and none in manufacturing.

Why are domestically originated multinational corporations, especially those in manufacturing sectors, important for a country's industrial upgrading? The reason lies in the difference between consumer goods and parts/capital goods. Production networks between companies are essential for the export of capital goods and parts. When a manufacturing company that procures parts and materials domestically invests overseas and starts production locally, it is expected to procure parts and capital goods from the home country, especially in the early stages of overseas operations. Therefore, foreign direct investment (FDI) by a country's manufacturing multinational corporations makes that country an exporter of parts and capital goods. On the other hand, to export consumer goods, the presence of domestic retailers in overseas markets is not necessarily essential.

Of course, it is not easy to have overseas retailers handle products, but this problem can be solved by attracting multinational corporations with established global brands. On the other hand, relying on multinational corporations makes it more challenging to become an exporter of parts and capital goods later.

Another approach is exemplified by Taiwan. Taiwan's electronics and electrical industry overcame this problem by engaging in OEM/ODM (Original Equipment Manufacturing/Original Design Manufacturing) for multinational corporations, using the partner's brand to sell in the global market and thus enhancing its competitiveness.16

In the early 1980s, the Mahathir administration established Proton as a national car manufacturer to foster a domestic automobile company with its own technology. This was the same strategy as the South Korean automotive industry, which nurtured domestic companies. However, unlike South Korea, which established the automotive industry as an export industry, Proton succeeded in gaining a significant share in the Malaysian domestic market but unfortunately failed in the export market.

If successful, policies to foster domestic companies with their own technology, like Taiwan's electronics and electrical industry or South Korea's automotive industry, can achieve long-term international competitiveness in that industry. However, such policies do not always succeed, and once they fail, the country becomes isolated from the GVCs of multinational corporations, making the price of failure very high.

The reason for Proton's failure is its lack of market competitiveness. Proton gained market share from other domestic companies through tax incentives and "concession," enabling it to sell at prices about 30% lower than those of competitors. This situation vastly differed from Taiwanese electronics and electrical companies or Korean automotive companies that exported their products to overseas markets and competed successfully against multinational corporations from other countries.

Another strategy for developing countries to develop industries is to attract export-oriented FDI. This seems to be a lower-risk choice for many developing countries than nurturing domestic companies. FDI brings capital, advanced technology, and access to overseas markets to developing countries, enabling participation in GVCs.17 Thailand's automotive industry did not implement a domestic car project like Malaysia's. By opening its domestic market to foreign capital in the early 1990s, Thailand succeeded in becoming a regional production base for multinational automotive companies and now plays a part in the global automotive industry's GVC.

While attracting export-oriented FDI may seem like a shortcut for developing countries to industrialize, it comes at the cost of dependence on foreign companies and foreign technology. For overseas multinational corporations, the developing country they invest in is just one of many investment destinations, so their contribution to industrial upgrading from assembly to production and export of parts and capital goods is limited. Thailand is also just one of many countries constituting the GVCs of multinational corporations. While it exports many completed vehicles, it has not become a significant net exporter of automotive parts.

Therefore, the choice between "deep" industrialization by domestic companies with their technology and "shallow" industrialization through FDI attraction is critical in determining the path of industrialization and economic sophistication for developing countries. Which of the two strategies is more suitable differs by country, and governments need to make appropriate choices knowing the merits and demerits of each approach.18

5.2.3 Aging and Hereditary Succession Stand Out in Large Local Private Companies

Ethnic Chinese companies have maintained a dominant position in Malaysia's large local private companies, except for a brief period from the late 1980s (when large Bumiputera companies were created through the privatization policy of government-linked companies) until the late 1990s when they were re-nationalized. The Malaysian business magazine "Malaysian Business" annually publishes "Malaysia's

40 Richest" based on stock prices and shareholder composition data of companies listed on the Kuala Lumpur Stock Exchange. Looking at the 2015 edition, out of 40 people, 30 are Chinese, 8 are Bumiputera, and two are Indian, showing that Chinese companies are still at the center of Malaysia's local private companies. Also, in the 2003 edition, the ethnic composition of the 40 people was exactly the same as that of the 2015 edition, indicating that this trend has continued for a long time.

From the perspective of industrial upgrading, Malaysia's local private companies, especially large companies, have several structural problems. First, many are non-manufacturing conglomerates centered on real estate, plantations, hotels, and casinos. Among the companies owned by "Malaysia's 40 Richest" in 2015, only a few can be considered manufacturing-centered companies, such as the DRB-HICOM Group19 (which is also a shareholder of Proton and manufactures automobiles) and Top Glove, the world's largest rubber glove manufacturer. The Sapura Group now focuses on the oil and gas business, and the IOI Group, a plantation company, handles resource-related manufacturing to some extent. The fact that few companies are engaged in manufacturing—where there is great potential for productivity improvement through technological progress—is a significant weakness of Malaysia's large local private companies from the perspective of industrial upgrading.

The second problem is the aging of management. In 2003, 26 out of "Malaysia's 40 Richest" were in their 50s or younger, with an average age of 55.7 years. By 2015, the number of those in their 50s or younger had decreased to 16 out of 40, with the average age rising to 64.8 years. Generally, as management ages, it becomes more difficult to innovate based on new technologies.

The third problem is the decrease in founder-owners and the increase in second and third generations who have inherited the companies. Comparing managers under 60 years old: in 2003, 18 out of 30 (about two-thirds) were from the founding generation. By 2015, among the 16 managers under 60 years old, the number from the founding generation had decreased to 6, with about two-thirds being second generation or later who had inherited the business from the founding generation.

As of 2015, the founding generation under 60 years old included: Tony Fernandes and Kamarudin Meranun, who founded the low-cost carrier (LCC) AirAsia; Mokhzani Mahathir of the oil and gas company Sapura Kencana, who is the second son of former Prime Minister Mahathir; Lim Wee Chai of Top Glove, the world's largest rubber glove company; Lee Oi Hian of the real estate company Masin Group; and Lim Siu Choon of Pavilion REIT, which operates real estate REITs. Service and resource-related companies are prominent.

However, by 2020, changes in these trends began to appear. The 2020 edition of "Malaysia's 40 Richest"20 newly included founders of five manufacturing-related companies: Greatech Technology (factory automation equipment), Vitrox Corp (semiconductor automatic inspection equipment), UWC (metal precision processing), D&O Green Technology (LED production for automobiles), and Mi Technovation (semiconductor manufacturing equipment). Many of these managers are young, in their 40s and 50s. In particular, four of the five companies are from Penang State, the hub of the electronics and electrical industry, indicating that a new generation of local high-tech companies is emerging.

Also, while Grab, which operates a ride-hailing app, is not included in the ranking because it has now moved its headquarters to Singapore, the company was initially founded in Malaysia in 2012 as "myTeksi." Grab has grown into a multinational company expanding across ASEAN countries and is the most successful new-generation local high-tech company.

5.2.4 Brain Drain Cannot be Ignored

When considering Malaysia's industrial upgrading, brain drain is a problem that cannot be ignored. Malaysia originally had very few higher education institutions (see Chapter 3) and consequently had a very high number of students studying abroad. While there were about 27,000 students enrolled in domestic universities in 1985,[21] the number of students studying abroad exceeded 40,000 at the same time. The main destinations for study abroad were Australia and the United Kingdom.[22] Many of these international students did not return to Malaysia but found employment overseas.

Furthermore, it is not uncommon for Malaysians to leave the country to seek employment opportunities abroad, even after they received their education domestically. When highly educated human resources find employment overseas, it works to lower the average quality of human resources remaining in Malaysia. The World Bank estimates that as of 2010, about 1 million people of Malaysian origin were living abroad, with 30% of them defined as "brain drain"—skilled workers aged 25 and above with tertiary education.[23]

As of the second quarter of 2021, looking at Malaysia's employment by skill level, 24.7% is skilled labor, 62% is semi-skilled labor, and 13.1% is unskilled labor. In contrast, in Singapore, skilled labor accounts for 54.7%.[24] Considering that Malaysians make up a significant portion of Singapore's skilled labor, brain drain is a significant problem for the advancement of the Malaysian economy.

5.2.5 The New Economic Model (NEM) as the Finishing Touch to Governance Reform

Since the currency crisis, the Malaysian government has been promoting governance reform, particularly for government-linked companies, and has achieved some success. This movement towards governance reform is not limited to government-linked companies. For example, Bank Negara, Malaysia's central bank, had been operating based on the 1958 Central Bank of Malaysia Act. However, with the 2009 Central Bank of Malaysia Act (CBA2009), the central bank law was redefined for the first time in about 50 years, increasing the independence of the central bank's personnel decisions and decision-making from the government.[25]

In this context, the "New Economic Model (NEM)" was announced shortly after Prime Minister Najib Razak took office in 2010 and suggested a reform of the New Economic Policy. NEM was positioned as showing the reforms necessary for the last ten years to achieve the goal of becoming a developed country by 2020, as proposed in "Vision 2020" under the Mahathir administration in 1991. NEM set three goals: achieving "high income" along with "inclusiveness" and "sustainability."26

The NEM offered the following in-depth criticism of the New Economic Policy:

The NEP has reduced poverty and substantially addressed inter-ethnic economic imbalances. However, its implementation has also increasingly and inadvertently raised the cost of doing business due to rent-seeking, patronage and opaque government procurement. This has engendered pervasive corruption, which needs to be addressed earnestly.27

The NEM proposed reforming the New Economic Policy in a more market-compatible direction, such as providing support targeted at the bottom 40% income group (B40) regardless of ethnicity. As will be discussed later, the NEM was too radical in its proposed reforms of the Bumiputera policy and was not politically accepted. Conversely, after the 13th general election in 2013, the Bumiputera policy was reinforced as a reward and punishment for the Chinese community's departure from the ruling coalition (discussed later). However, the three goals set out in the NEM have significantly impacted Malaysian government policies since the 2010s. The 12th Malaysia Plan (2021–2025) sets its goal as "A Prosperous, Inclusive, Sustainable Malaysia," exactly the three goals set out in the NEM.

5.3 The Impact of the Political System on Industrial Upgrading

5.3.1 Democratic Political Institutions are Necessary for Sustained Economic Growth

The issue of whether a country can achieve industrial upgrading is not purely an economic issue but also a political one. Even if the policies necessary to shift from factor input-driven growth to productivity-driven growth are known, the government may not implement such policies. If we focus on the problem that policies should be taken are known but not implemented, it can even be said that politics is the key to escaping the middle-income trap.

To promote productivity improvement, an environment is needed that allows companies to invest confidently, enables those with good ideas to start businesses, and allows workers to receive training to improve their skills. Such an environment is only possible with economic institutions such as property rights protection, a fair legal system, and quality public services. Acemoglu and Robinson call these institutions that allow everyone to freely and confidently engage in economic activities "inclusive economic institutions" and argue that they are supported by "inclusive political institutions."28 Their inclusive political institutions mean a stable state and democratic political system. They argue that only with a mechanism to decide policies through a democratic political process and having a high-quality government steadily implement policies can sustainable economic growth based on innovation be possible. Conversely, under "extractive political institutions," dictatorial political systems, extractive economic institutions where elites in power monopolize business opportunities, are likely to form. They argue that economic development cannot be expected in such an environment.

At first glance, the high achievers in East Asia who grew without falling into the middle-income trap, namely South Korea and Taiwan, do not seem to fit this theory. South Korea's high economic growth began under the Park Chung-hee regime, which came to power through a coup, and Taiwan developed under the one-party rule of the Kuomintang. In fact, from the 1960s to the 1980s, which corresponded to the high-growth periods of South Korea and Taiwan, the view that hasty democratization would hinder economic growth was influential.29 It was thought that a rapid expansion of political participation would harm political order. If so, policies necessary for economic development could not be implemented either. It was also said that a system where the state maintains autonomy from society and can make and implement rational policies without being bound by vested interests is more advantageous for economic development.30 Furthermore, the suppression of labor movements and wage restraint were seen as factors in South Korea's success, and it was even said that an authoritarian political system was indispensable for low-income countries to achieve economic development in a short period.31

However, if we are looking for ways to avoid the middle-income trap, we should pay attention to the fact that both South Korea and Taiwan achieved democratization at the middle-income stage and continued to grow steadily thereafter.

Acemoglu and Robinson, as mentioned earlier, state that while extractive political institutions may bring about temporary economic growth, they cannot produce sustained economic growth. This is because innovation, the driving force of sustained growth, has an aspect of "creative destruction" that promotes the replacement of successful individuals in society. If there are industries that newly prosper due to technological innovation, there are also industries that decline because of it. While new economic elites emerge, old elites who cannot adapt to change fall.

Under dictatorial political systems, such creative destruction is less likely to occur. This is because those who hold power are incentivized to regulate economic activities to protect their position, even if it means shrinking the overall pie. Therefore, it is thought that it will be difficult to shift to an innovation-driven economy unless there is a shift to institutions that allow for the replacement of political winners. While China, which has been advancing industrial upgrading under Communist Party rule, seemed to be an exception, in recent years, the government has been strengthening control over corporate activities, such as interfering with the activities of the Alibaba Group, the largest e-commerce company, and Didi, the largest ride-hailing app company, and pressuring online game operators and cram schools.

According to Dollar, who analyzed the relationship between economic growth and civil liberties in 146 countries from 1990 to 2010, countries with lower levels of civil rights, that is, more authoritarian countries, recorded higher economic growth rates at lower income levels. Still, this relationship reversed when per capita GDP exceeded $8000 (a quarter of the U.S. level), and countries with higher levels of civil liberties achieved higher economic growth.32 $8000 corresponds to the level of upper-middle-income countries. What this research suggests is that under authoritarian political systems, factor input-driven development strategies are easier to pursue, and economic growth is promoted at the low-income stage, but democratization is necessary to shift to innovation-driven growth and achieve high-income status.

5.3.2 *Malaysia's Competitive Authoritarianism*

In Malaysia's case, just as its economic development has been slow but steady, politically, it has also been moving gradually towards a more democratic system, with advances and retreats. Figure 5.8 shows the changes in the POLITY score, an indicator of the degree of democracy in political systems, for Malaysia, South Korea, and Taiwan. This indicator ranges from the most democratic system at 10 to the most repressive system at -10, and a score of 6 or above is often considered a democracy.

Malaysia was initially a democracy after independence (with a POLITY score of 7), but after the 1969 riots, parliament was temporarily closed, and subsequently, controls on speech, restrictions on assembly, and regulations on associations were strengthened. Therefore, the political system from the 1969 riots until the change of government in 2018 cannot be called a democracy. However, as shown in Fig. 5.8, the degree of repression was lower compared to South Korea and Taiwan before democratization, and competitive elections were regularly held. Such a political system is called "competitive authoritarianism," and Malaysia is considered a typical example.33

In elections from the 1970s to the mid-2000s, Barisan Nasional (BN, or National Front), a ruling coalition centered on the United Malays National Organisation (UMNO), showed overwhelming strength, consistently securing more than two-thirds of the seats in the lower house of the federal parliament. This allowed the government to amend the constitution without the cooperation of the opposition.

The ruling party's electoral dominance was largely due to a significant imbalance in voting power. Rural areas, home to many Bumiputera residents, were overrepresented in seat allocation. In contrast, urban constituencies, where Chinese and Indian voters were concentrated and the opposition Democratic Action Party (DAP) held sway, remained underrepresented. Furthermore, the opposition was fragmented, with Malay and non-Malay parties often taking extreme and conflicting stances. This resulted in a 'dominant party system' where one party held overwhelming power. Consequently, a change in government seemed highly unlikely, leading the opposition to focus on merely securing at least one-third of the lower house seats to prevent unilateral constitutional amendments by the ruling party.

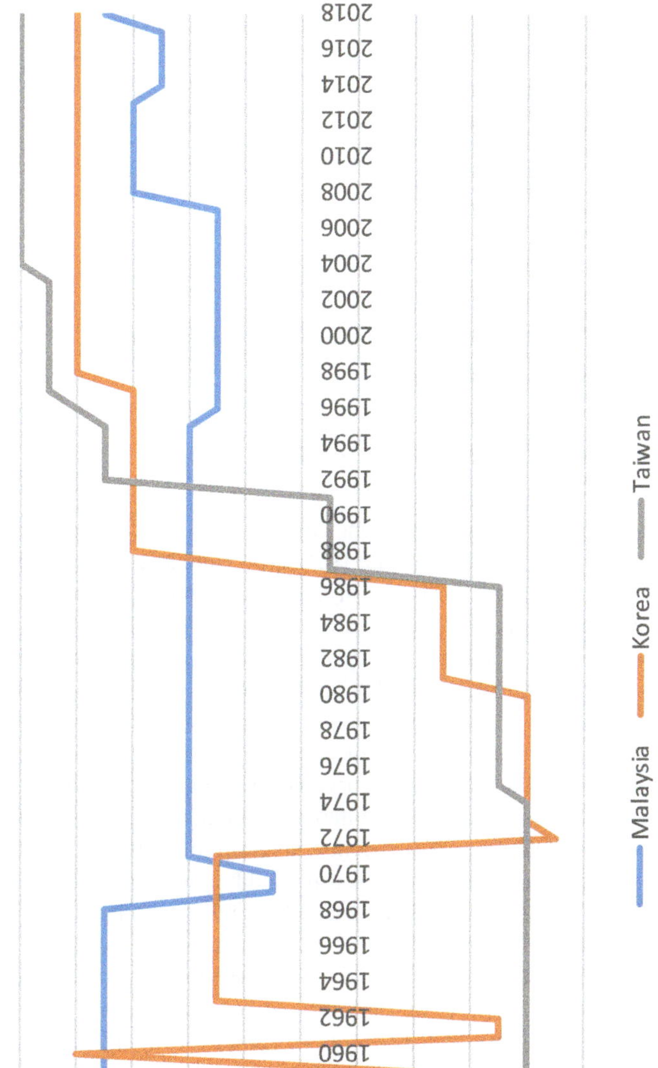

Fig. 5.8 Evolution of POLITY5 scores for Malaysia, South Korea, and Taiwan. *Source* Created by the author based on POLITY5 dataset (Marshall and Gurr 2020)

However, even though there was little chance of a change in government, securing more seats in elections was always an essential task for the government leaders and the ruling party. Losing seats would generate dissatisfaction within the party and lead to the rise of rivals. Therefore, while the government sometimes suppressed societal demands, it also implemented policies that responded to them to a certain extent. This political system was also described as a "repressive-responsive regime."34 In Malaysia, too, elections were an excellent opportunity for citizens to communicate their demands to the government, and the government formulated and implemented policies with elections in mind.

5.4 The Shift in Development Policy Brought About by the Opposition's Advance

5.4.1 *Elections and Development Policy*

So, how did elections influence the government's development policy? Looking back briefly decade by decade, the elections of the 1970s worked to strengthen the Bumiputera policy. As seen in Chapter 2, the rise of non-Malay opposition parties in the 1969 election led to ethnic riots immediately afterward, which triggered the government to implement the New Economic Policy. Subsequently, competition with the Pan-Malaysian Islamic Party (PAS), a Malay opposition party, for Malay votes led to rural-biased policies such as the introduction of rice price subsidies in 1980.

In the 1980s, as seen in Chapter 3, the successor policy to the New Economic Policy, which was scheduled to end in 1990, became an important issue. While non-Malay ruling parties such as the Malaysian Chinese Association (MCA) called for the reduction or termination of the Bumiputera policy, voices from UMNO demanded its continuation and strengthening, making consensus-building within the ruling coalition difficult. Although the ruling coalition managed to navigate the 1986 election by using tactics to postpone policy decisions, the DAP, which demanded the abolition of the Bumiputera policy, gained support, and the Chinese ruling parties struggled. After the election, there was a fierce war of words between UMNO and non-Malay parties over development policy after 1990. This was compounded by a controversy over the management of Chinese-language primary schools, and by 1987, social tensions had risen to the point where there were fears of riots recurring. The government arrested political figures from both the ruling and opposition parties en masse to calm the situation, but this action drew strong criticism from both domestic and international sources.

Subsequently, even in the National Economic Consultative Council (NECC) organized to discuss new development policies, agreement could not be reached between Malay members who demanded the continuation of the ethnic quota system, which allocates a certain percentage of corporate shares and university admission slots to Bumiputeras, and non-Malay members who demanded a shift to meritocracy. The government called a snap general election in October 1990, leaving this issue unresolved, and managed to maintain two-thirds of the seats in the lower house despite facing significant challenges.

After weathering the election, Prime Minister Mahathir announced "Vision 2020" in February 1991, setting a new national goal of becoming a developed country by 2020. Under this policy, the deregulation affecting foreign and Chinese companies that had begun as a recession countermeasure in the mid-1980s accelerated. With the further advancement of foreign companies, especially Japanese manufacturing companies, Malaysia experienced high economic growth for 10 years from 1987 onwards. In the 1995 election held during this period, BN recorded its highest-ever vote share and won a complete victory. This provided a boost to the government and led to educational system reforms that opened the door to higher education for non-Malay children.

5.4.2 Shift Towards Meritocracy and Emphasis on Governance

While elections from the 1970s to the 1990s had issues related to ethnic interests (such as the pros and cons of the Bumiputera policy) as the main points of contention, in the elections of the 2000s and 2010s, issues related to governance also came to be recognized as important, and the overall electoral discourse became more diverse. This shift was triggered by the Asian Financial Crisis that occurred in 1997 and the subsequent political strife.

During the Asian Financial Crisis, Bumiputera entrepreneurs who had benefited from privatization fell into crisis, prompting the government to inject public funds to rescue them. This action was seen as cronyism and was criticized not only by foreign media and experts but also by some within the ruling UMNO. As seen in Chapter 4, the conflict within the government over the response to the currency crisis developed into a power struggle, leading to the dismissal and arrest of Deputy Prime Minister Anwar Ibrahim. The Malay population was deeply shocked by the imprisonment of Anwar, who was popular among them, and by reports of his assault during interrogation. In the 1999 election, the opposition, which criticized the authoritarian nature of the Mahathir administration and called for political reform, gained support from Malay voters and increased its strength.

In the 11th general election held in March 2004, four months after Prime Minister Mahathir's retirement, support for the ruling party recovered due to expectations for the new Prime Minister Abdullah, who had advocated political reform, and BN won 90% of the seats in the lower house. As seen in Chapter 4, Abdullah acknowledged the collusion between UMNO and Malay entrepreneurs and aimed to break away from "rent-seeking addiction," initiating GLC reform.

However, Abdullah's reforms remained half-hearted, as evidenced by his introduction of a new Malay preferential policy that allocated 60% of government procurement to Bumiputera companies. Voters' expectations turned to disappointment, and in the 12th general election in 2008, the opposition made significant gains, with BN's seats falling below two-thirds of the lower house for the first time (the reasons for the opposition's advance will be discussed in the next chapter). After the election, Prime Minister Abdullah lost support within the party and was forced to resign.

The policies of Najib Razak, who became Prime Minister replacing Abdullah, were completely different before and after the 13th election in 2013. The first Najib cabinet advocated a radical reform program, the NEM (mentioned earlier), and was, at least outwardly, an incomparably more liberal administration than previous ones. During this period, the government reviewed the traditional Bumiputera policy, adopted meritocracy in industrial policy, and indicated a policy of targeting groups such as low-income groups, urban middle class, students, and the elderly regardless of ethnicity in social policy. It also promoted political liberalization by abolishing the Internal Security Act, known as a draconian law, and enacting the Peaceful Assembly Act to legalize street demonstrations. The government proactively implemented the opposition's demands to regain support from urban residents lost in the 2008 election.

However, when urban areas further departed from the ruling party in the 2013 election, the Najib administration's policies shifted significantly towards Malay nationalism and authoritarianism. Regarding the Bumiputera policy, it announced a policy of re-strengthening by releasing the "Bumiputera Economic Empowerment Agenda" in September of the same year. It also reversed its policy of abolishing the Sedition Act and abused it, arresting opposition leaders, intellectuals, and journalists one after another. As the MCA and other non-Malay ruling parties suffered a crushing defeat in the 2013 election, the composition of the second Najib cabinet became almost entirely Bumiputera. It appears that as the 2013 election made it clear that it would be difficult for BN to regain votes from the urban middle class, especially Chinese voters, Prime Minister Najib took a defensive stance, shifting towards reinforcing the Bumiputera policy and tightening speech controls to solidify his party base and rural votes.35

However, Najib subsequently lost both intra-party support and rural votes, leading to his loss of power in the 14th general election in 2018. The primary causes were the mismanagement of 1Malaysia Development Berhad (1MDB), a government-linked fund Najib established on his own initiative in 2009, and suspicions of corruption against Najib himself. Subsequent investigations revealed that over $4.5 billion was improperly diverted from 1MDB. The 1MDB scandal became widely known when former Prime Minister Mahathir Mohamad exposed it in September 2014. In July 2015, it was revealed that nearly $700 million had been transferred to Najib's personal account, raising suspicions that Najib had acquired part of the funds improperly diverted from 1MDB—effectively from the national treasury.

Najib temporarily evaded accountability by expelling former Prime Minister Mahathir, Deputy Prime Minister Muhyiddin Yassin, and Rural and Regional Development Minister Shafie Apdal from the ruling party for pursuing the suspicions. Ultimately, however, this measure backfired. As Mahathir and Muhyiddin formed the new Parti Pribumi Bersatu Malaysia (PPBM, or Malaysian United Indigenous Party) and Shafie formed Parti Warisan (Heritage Party) in Sabah, BN lost both urban and rural votes in the 2018 election, resulting in a change of government.

As described above, although Malaysia's political system has long failed to meet the criteria for democracy, elections have strongly influenced government policies. The elections of the 1970s served to strengthen the Bumiputera policy, while the elections of the late 1980s, a period of adjustment in development policy, sparked debate over the successor policy to the New Economic Policy. The elections of the 1990s supported the policy of accelerating economic growth through deregulation, while the elections following the currency crisis promoted reflection on cronyism, emphasis on meritocracy, welfare policies regardless of ethnicity, and expansion of civil liberties and political rights. While the 2013 election triggered the Najib administration's return to Malay nationalism and authoritarianism, the 14th general election in 2018 resulted in a change of government and a complete renewal of the cabinet. Despite various setbacks and reversals, Malaysia's elections can be said to have gradually promoted a shift from policies based on ethnic quotas that tend to breed cronyism toward more efficient policies based on meritocracy.

While the pace of productivity improvement and industrial upgrading in Malaysia is indeed inferior to that of the "high achiever" South Korea, it is not completely stagnant. Despite issues such as the resource curse, dependence on multinational corporations, the absence of domestic manufacturing companies, and brain drain, local high-tech companies have begun to emerge in recent years. Behind this is the gradual transition of the once repressive political system to a more inclusive one. Under a political system where elections strongly influence the direction of development policies, policies emphasizing governance and meritocracy have been formulated and implemented, albeit with twists and turns.

Notes

1. Krugman (1994).
2. Acemoglu and Robinson (2012).
3. Easterly and Levine (2001).
4. Bulman, Eden, and Nguyen (2017).
5. Aiyar et al. (2013).
6. World Bank (2016).
7. Malaysia (2015: 2–15).
8. Malaysia (2021: 48).
9. However, measuring TFP accurately is not easy. For example, during recessions, TFP appears to decrease significantly because capacity utilization falls while capital stock remains the same; and during recovery periods, TFP temporarily increases. Such trends can be observed in Figure 5.1.
10. Following the Solow growth model, industrial upgrading includes both increasing per capita capital stock (capital deepening) and raising technological levels through innovation and imitation (technological upgrading).
11. Kohli, Sharma, and Sood eds. (2011).
12. This represents the total of STIC1–4 excluding primary products.

13. Kumagai and Kuroiwa (2020).
14. Because calculations are based on 1999–2001 PRODY values for the upper section and 2009–2011 PRODY values for the lower section, the figures for year 2000 differ between sections.
15. Akamatsu (1935); Akamatsu (1962).
16. Kawakami (2012).
17. Since the 1990s, developments in information and communication technology and logistics networks have integrated developing countries into Global Value Chains (GVCs) a phenomenon referred to as the "second unbundling." Malaysia has also benefited from this integration. For future perspectives on GVCs, please refer to Baldwin (2016).
18. The industrial policies that are suitable and feasible for developing countries have changed significantly over time. For a discussion on appropriate industrial policy frameworks for developing countries in the 21st century, please refer to Aiginger and Rodrik (2020).
19. The DRB-HICOM Group, which took control of the privatized HICOM and Proton, was one of the few Bumiputera conglomerates to survive the Asian Financial Crisis. However, it had to divest from Proton in the process.
20. "Five new tech company owners in the top 40," The Star, February 20, 2021.
21. Malaysia (1986: 234).
22. Tanaka (2018).
23. World Bank (2011).
24. "In need of more high-skilled jobs," The Star, January 5, 2022.
25. CBA2009 established: (1) the Monetary Policy Committee (MPC) for monetary policy decisions, (2) strengthened authority for financial system stabilization, (3) enhanced Islamic finance supervision, and (4) strengthened Bank Negara governance. The governance-strengthening measures became particularly significant in the 2010s as tensions grew between Bank Negara and the Najib administration over the 1MDB issue.
26. The "High income" target was initially defined as raising per capita national income from $15,000 to $20,000 by 2020 but was later changed to achieving "high-income country status" according to World Bank criteria. The "Inclusiveness" target was defined as all communities being able to benefit sufficiently from national wealth. The "Sustainability" target was defined as meeting current needs without sacrificing future generations.
27. NEAC (2010: 61).
28. Acemoglu and Robinson (2012).
29. Huntington (1968).
30. Evans (1995).
31. Watanabe (1989).
32. Dollar (2016: 169–172).
33. Levitsky and Way (2010).
34. Crouch (1996).
35. Suzuki (2018).

References

Acemoglu D, Robinson JA (2012) Why nations fail: the origins of power, prosperity, and poverty. Crown Business, New York

Aiginger K, Rodrik D (2020) Rebirth of industrial policy and an agenda for the twenty-first century. J Ind Compet Trade 20:189–207

Aiyar S, Duval R, Puy D et al. (2013) Growth slowdowns and the middle-income trap. IMF Working Paper WP/13/71, International Monetary Fund

Akamatsu K (1935) Trade trends in Japanese wool industry products (Wagakuni Yōmō Kōgyōhin no Bōeki Sūsei). Shōgyō Keizai Ronshū 13(1):129–212

Akamatsu K (1962) Historical pattern of economic growth in developing countries. Dev Econ 1:3–25
Baldwin R (2016) The great convergence: information technology and the new globalization. Harvard University Press, Cambridge
Bulman D, Eden M, Nguyen H (2017) Transitioning from low-income growth to high-income growth: is there a middle-income trap? J Asia Pac Econ 22(1):5–28
Crouch H (1996) Government and society in Malaysia. Cornell University Press, Ithaca
Dollar D (2016) Institutional quality and growth traps. In: Hutchinson FE, Das SB (eds) Asia and the middle-income trap. Routledge, Abingdon, pp 161–178
Easterly W, Levine R (2001) It's not factor accumulation: stylized facts and growth models. World Bank Econ Rev 15(2):177–219
Evans P (1995) Embedded autonomy: states and industrial transformation. Princeton University Press, Princeton
Huntington SP (1968) Political order in changing societies. Yale University Press, New Haven
Kawakami M (2012) Compressed industrial development: growth mechanism of Taiwan notebook PC companies (Asshuku Sareta Sangyō Hatten). Nagoya University Press, Nagoya
Kohli HS, Sharma A, Sood A (eds) (2011) Asia 2050: realizing the Asian century. SAGE Publications India
Krugman P (1994) The myth of Asia's miracle. Foreign Aff 73(6):62–78
Kumagai S (2015) The Middle-income Trap from the Viewpoint of Trade Structures: Are the Geese Trapped or Still Flying? J Int Commer Econ Policy, 6(03): 1550017
Kumagai S, Kuroiwa I (2020) Export structure upgrading in East Asia: implications for the middle-income trap (Higashi Asia ni okeru Yushutsu Kōzō no Kōdoka). Asian Econ (Ajia Keizai) 61(2):2–35
Levitsky S, Way LA (2010) Competitive authoritarianism: hybrid regimes after the cold war. Cambridge University Press, New York
Malaysia (1986) Fifth Malaysia Plan 1986–1990. National Printing Department, Kuala Lumpur
Malaysia (2015) Eleventh Malaysia Plan 2016–2020. Percetakan Nasional Malaysia Berhad, Putrajaya
Malaysia (2021) Twelfth Malaysia Plan 2021–2025. Percetakan Nasional Malaysia Berhad, Putrajaya
Marshall MG, Gurr TR (2020) Polity5: political regime characteristics and transitions, 1800–2018. Center for Systemic Peace
National Economic Advisory Council (NEAC) (2010) New economic mechanism for Malaysia. Percetakan Nasional Malaysia Berhad, Kuala Lumpur
Suzuki A (2018) Political liberalization and leader survival: analysis of legal reform centered on the 2015 sedition act amendment bill (Seiji no Jiyūka to Rīdā no Seizon). In: Nakamura M, Kumagai S (eds) Malaysia in the post-Mahathir era (Post-Mahathir Jidai no Malaysia). Institute of Developing Economies, Tokyo, pp 139–171
Tanaka R (2018) Ethnicity-based policies as the main factor of Malaysian brain drain?: Re-examining the distribution of opportunities for education and employment. In: Tyson A (ed) The political economy of brain drain and talent capture. Routledge, London, pp 81–105
Watanabe T (1989) Political economy of the Western Pacific era: new industrializing Asian states (Nishitaiheiyō no Jidai). Bungeishunju, Tokyo
World Bank (2011) Malaysia economic monitor: brain drain. World Bank
World Bank (2016) Malaysia economic monitor: the quest for productivity growth

Newspapers and Online Media

The Star

Chapter 6
From External to Domestic Demand

Private Consumption Driving the Economy (2000s–2010s)

Many East Asian countries have achieved rapid economic development through export-oriented industrialization, a strategy that offers several advantages for developing countries.[1] First, because developing countries have low incomes, their domestic demand is small, with exceptions like China and India due to their large populations. By seeking markets overseas, countries can engage in mass production without being constrained by their domestic market size. In many cases, competition in overseas markets is more intense than in domestic markets, and if successful in entering these markets, it helps a country continuously enhance its industrial competitiveness.

However, when many countries simultaneously adopt export-oriented industrialization, problems can arise. If a situation called a "race to the bottom" emerges—where countries compete to attract multinational corporations by lowering labor standards and environmental regulations—social and economic conditions may deteriorate.

Furthermore, East Asian countries have primarily relied on exports to the United States as the main driver of their growth. However, it is difficult to sustain a structure where East Asian countries accumulate large trade surpluses with the United States over a long period, creating global financial imbalances. Specifically, from the early 2000s to the 2008 Global Financial Crisis, excessive consumption in the United States led to high household debt levels, which were financed by capital inflows from East Asian countries and oil-producing nations. Moreover, as seen in the past Japan-U.S. trade friction and the recent U.S.-China trade war, extreme trade imbalances can lead to political conflicts.

Therefore, for middle-income countries to continue stable growth towards high-income status, they need to expand domestic demand to some extent rather than relying solely on external demand. This requires a shift away from policies that maintain export price competitiveness by suppressing wage increases or devaluing exchange rates. It is also essential to increase the income share of middle and low-income groups, which typically have higher consumption propensities.

S. Kumagai and M. Nakamura, *Economic Development Strategies*, Emerging-Economy State and International Policy Studies, https://doi.org/10.1007/978-981-95-6899-4_6

East Asian countries have historically achieved high growth by prioritizing external demand over domestic demand and investment over consumption. Transitioning from this export-led high-growth system to a stable growth system emphasizing domestic demand and consumption is difficult. For example, Japan attempted to shift towards emphasizing domestic demand and consumption by advocating a "lifestyle superpower" in the 1990s.[2] However, disposable income has remained almost flat over the past 30 years, and even now, the transition cannot be considered successful. China has also recently attempted to shift from Deng Xiaoping's "let some people get rich first" policy to "common prosperity" under Xi Jinping's administration, aiming for widespread affluence among the people. However, the success of this approach remains uncertain.

With its relatively small population, Malaysia inevitably relied on external demand from the early stages of its economic development. Now that Malaysia has reached a level approaching high-income status, has it been able to get on track for continued stable growth by increasing the weight of domestic demand and consumption?

6.1 The Driver of Economic Development Shifts from Exports to Domestic Demand

6.1.1 Contribution of Demand Components to Economic Growth

Malaysia has been an exporter of primary commodities since the British colonial era. After independence, it transformed from a primary commodity exporter to an industrial product exporter, but exports have consistently played a significant role in economic growth.

Export-led economic growth was particularly prominent from the late 1980s until the 1997–98 Asian Financial Crisis. Following the Plaza Accord in 1985 and the subsequent yen appreciation and dollar depreciation, export-oriented multinational corporations, especially Japanese companies, entered Malaysia and contributed to export expansion. Malaysia's export dependence (exports/GDP) increased from 47.1% in 1981 to 77.5% in 1997, reaching 106.0% immediately after the currency crisis in 1999. Since 2005, export growth has been slowing, and by 2020, export dependence had decreased to 55.0%, the same level as in the late 1980s.

Analysis of demand component contributions helps identify the factors that have driven a country's economic growth. By showing the contributions of consumption, investment, and exports to the economic growth rate, we can understand the factors that have driven Malaysia's economic growth. However, especially for small countries like Malaysia, which have high export dependence, calculating contributions in the usual way often deviates from intuitive recognition. In Malaysia's case, the contribution of net exports (exports minus imports) from 1981 to 2019 was only

0.2%, suggesting that external demand contributed minimally to economic growth in numerical terms.[3]

The reason why the usual analysis of demand component contributions does not match intuitive recognition lies in the calculation method of net exports. Net exports represent the total export value minus the total import value, but calculating contributions this way assumes that only exports induce imports. If all imported goods were used solely as inputs for export production, net exports would correctly measure the contribution of exports (external demand) to growth. However, in reality, consumption and investment also induce imports. Therefore, to calculate how much consumption and investment have increased domestic value-added, it is necessary to subtract the imports they each induce. To correctly apportion import values to consumption, investment, and exports, we need to know how much imports each induces. In this analysis, we have calculated import inducement coefficients by demand component using input-output tables and adjusted the contributions accordingly.

Figure 6.1 shows the contributions by demand component modified this way.

6.1.2 Structural Change from the 2000s

Looking at the modified demand component contributions, exports showed the largest contribution in many years during the 1980s. Entering the 1990s, the contribution of investment also became significant, backed by "mega-projects" such as the construction of the Kuala Lumpur International Airport and the Petronas Twin Towers. The average modified contributions from the 1980s to before the Asian Financial Crisis were 4.9% for exports, 1.1% for private consumption, 0.8% for investment, and 0.5% for government consumption (Table 6.1).

During the Asian Financial Crisis period (1998–2004), the contribution of investment generally remained negative. Starting with a negative 5.0% contribution in 1998, investment's contribution remained negative except in 2000, which showed a rebound from the decline during the currency crisis. Investment contribution turned positive in 2006, indicating that the impact of the currency crisis persisted until the mid-2000s. This generally coincides with Malaysia's progress in resolving non-performing loans. The average modified contributions during the currency crisis period were 2.9% for exports, 1.2% for private consumption, 0.5% for government consumption, and -0.8% for investment.

From 2005 onwards, the contribution of exports rapidly declined while the contribution of private consumption increased. Investment also escaped the impact of the Asian Financial Crisis, and its contribution remained positive. The average modified contributions from 2005 to 2019 were 2.3% for private consumption, 1.7% for exports, 0.5% for investment, and 0.5% for government consumption, with private consumption overtaking exports.

Thus, analysis using modified demand component contributions shows that the Malaysian economy's engine of growth has changed over time. Before the currency

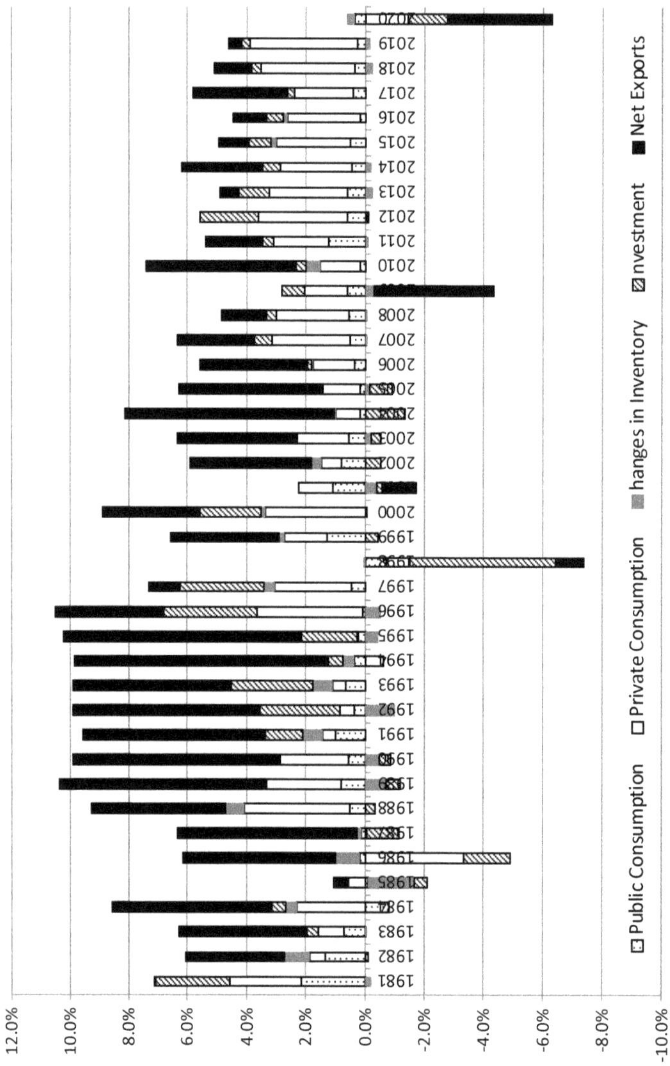

Fig. 6.1 Contribution of demand components to Malaysia's economic growth (1981–2020). *Source* Created by the author based on Fig. 6.4 in Nakamura and Kumagai (2018)

Table 6.1 Modified average contribution of demand components by period (1981–2019).

Period	Government Consumption	Private Consumption	Inventory	Investment	Net Exports	Real GDP Growth Rate
1981–2019	0.5	1.6	0.0	0.4	3.3	5.7
1981–1997	0.5	1.1	0.0	0.8	4.9	7.3
1998–2004	0.5	1.2	0.0	−0.8	2.9	3.7
2005–2019	0.5	2.3	0.0	0.5	1.7	4.9

Source Created by the author based on Table 6.3 in Nakamura and Kumagai (2018)

crisis, exports drove the economy, and in the 1990s, investment emerged as an additional engine of growth. From 2005 onwards, the economic structure gradually shifted to one where private consumption drives growth.

6.2 Policies to Expand External Demand

While the analysis so far has shown that Malaysia has shifted to domestic demand-led economic growth since the mid-2000s, this does not mean that external demand has become unimportant. Malaysia's export dependence (exports/GDP) as of 2020 was 55.0%, ranking fourth highest in ASEAN after Singapore (121.1%), Vietnam (104.2%), and Cambodia (71.8%).[4]

6.2.1 Evolution of Foreign Investment Attraction Policies

Since the 1960s, Malaysia has been attracting foreign investment mainly in import substitution sectors through the enactment of the Pioneer Industries Ordinance. Panasonic, which now has a significant presence among Japanese companies in Malaysia, initially entered the country in the mid-1960s not as an export base but to produce dry batteries and black-and-white televisions for the Malaysian domestic market, aligning with the import substitution policy. However, for many of these companies, development was hindered by Malaysia's small market size, with a population of less than 10 million at the time.

As the limitations of import-substitution industrialization became apparent, the Malaysian government enacted the Investment Incentives Act in 1968, thereby shifting its industrialization strategy towards export orientation. Subsequently, with the development of several related legal frameworks, the entry of export-related companies into Malaysia accelerated in the 1970s.

The symbolic development of this shift was Malaysia's first Free Trade Zone (FTZ) established in Bayan Lepas, Penang. After losing its duty-exempt free port status in 1969, Penang Island faced an unemployment rate of 15%. The Penang state government began promoting industrialization by establishing an FTZ to increase employment. In response, the Malaysian government enacted the Free Trade Zone Act in 1971, allowing companies operating within FTZs to import intermediate goods duty-free, provided they exported the finished products.

American semiconductor manufacturers primarily entered the Bayan Lepas FTZ, spearheading the rapid development of the semiconductor industry. Intel, HP, National Semiconductor, AMD, Hitachi Semiconductor, Robert Bosch, and others were among the early entrants, and these companies continue to drive the development of Malaysia's semiconductor industry to this day. Manufacturing and testing ICs (integrated circuits) was labor-intensive and unsuitable for high-wage America, so American companies sought investment destinations in low-wage Asia. Additionally, the U.S. system that allowed American semiconductor manufacturers to bring back products manufactured overseas duty-free also encouraged investment in FTZs.[5] The factors that led semiconductor companies, primarily American ones, to choose Malaysia as a location in the early 1970s reportedly included: (1) an abundant and high-quality English-speaking labor force, (2) investment incentives from the Malaysian government, (3) excellent infrastructure such as industrial parks, and (4) political stability.[6]

Around the time of Mahathir's appointment as Prime Minister in 1981, Malaysia's industrialization strategy entered a phase known as "Second Import Substitution Industrialization" or "Dual-Track Industrialization." This strategy aimed to continue emphasizing export-oriented industries, particularly the semiconductor industry, while promoting heavy industries like automobiles, steel, and cement through import substitution policies. Specifically, as mentioned in Chapter 4, the Heavy Industries Corporation of Malaysia was established, under which various heavy industry companies were formed. However, the recession in the mid-1980s caused these industries to encounter difficulties before their viability could be fully tested, and a combination of factors ultimately prevented them from achieving success.

Meanwhile, following the "Plaza Accord" in September 1985, a strong global trend toward U.S. dollar depreciation emerged. For example, the yen appreciated against the U.S. dollar from 260 yen per dollar at the beginning of 1985 to 120 yen per dollar by the end of 1988. Many Japanese companies—especially those in the electronics and electrical industries that had the United States as their primary export destination—began to explore overseas expansion to reduce costs.

Malaysia, where the heavy industrialization policy was reaching an impasse, sought to attract foreign direct investment using this opportunity. In 1986, the Promotion of Investments Act was enacted, allowing for income tax exemptions and other incentives under specific conditions. Additionally, guidelines announced by Prime Minister Mahathir in September of the same year relaxed export ratio requirements for the entry of wholly foreign-owned companies.

6.2.2 Promotion of Economic Integration

In addition to attracting foreign companies, promoting economic integration serves as another policy to expand external demand. Economic integration encompasses both *de facto* integration, where regional economic relations intensify through private company investments, and *de jure* integration through formal international institutions such as Free Trade Agreements (FTAs) and Regional Trade Agreements (RTAs).

While Malaysia was proactive in *de facto* integration through the establishment of FTZs, it was equally active in *de jure* integration. Within ASEAN, Malaysia has been one of the leading member countries actively promoting economic integration. During the Mahathir era in 1990, Malaysia proposed the East Asian Economic Group (EAEG, later renamed East Asian Economic Caucus [EAEC]), which expanded ASEAN to include China, Japan, and South Korea. Additionally, Malaysia has emphasized South-South cooperation among developing countries and strengthened diplomatic ties with Muslim-majority countries in Central Asia and the Middle East. In the 2010s, it joined the negotiations for the Trans-Pacific Partnership (TPP) and participated in the Regional Comprehensive Economic Partnership (RCEP).[7]

6.2.3 Diversification of Export Items and Export Destinations

Since the beginning of the U.S.-China trade war in 2018, Malaysia has managed to maintain good trade relations with both countries. As of 2020, China is Malaysia's largest export destination, and the United States is the third-largest export destination after Singapore. Despite exports being significantly affected by the COVID-19 pandemic in the first half of 2020, for the full year, exports to China and the United States increased by 13% compared to the previous year.

Figure 6.2 shows Malaysia's exports to the U.S. and China divided into five categories: "capital goods," "parts," "consumer goods," "processed goods," and "primary commodities," as shown in Chapter 5. In exports to the United States, consumer goods account for 31.6%, followed by parts (31.5%) and capital goods (25.4%), with manufactured goods dominating. On the other hand, for exports to China, processed goods account for 48.3%, and together with primary commodities (13.9%), they make up over 60% of exports.

In the composition of total exports, capital goods, parts, and consumer goods have almost equal shares, together constituting 57.1%, while primary commodities and processed goods collectively account for 42.9%. As noted in Chapter 5, the increased share of primary commodities and processed goods since the 2000s has delayed the upgrading of Malaysia's trade structure. However, the diversification of exports provides stability against fluctuations in the global economy. In fact, by exporting different items to the United States and China—the world's first and second

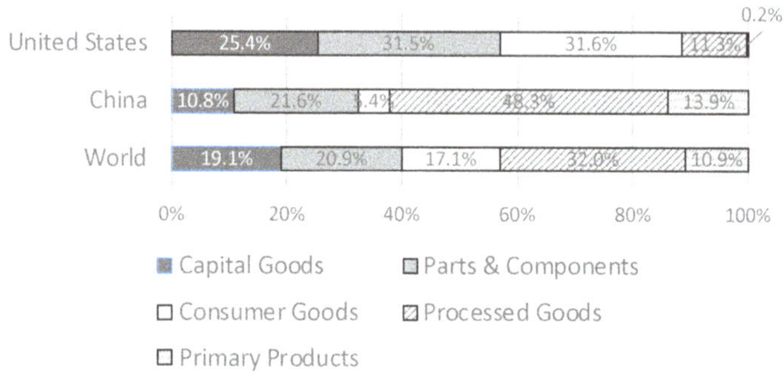

Fig. 6.2 Share of Malaysia's exports to the US and China by product category (2020). *Source* Created by the author based on UN COMTRADE data

largest economies—Malaysia has succeeded in increasing exports to both countries even during the U.S.-China trade war and the COVID-19 pandemic.

6.3 Policies to Expand Domestic Demand

6.3.1 Policy Shift After Mahathir's Retirement

One factor that has driven Malaysia's economy through domestic demand since the mid-2000s, while maintaining its fundamentally export-driven open nature, is the shift in government policy from emphasizing growth to emphasizing distribution. Malaysia's economic policy has traditionally balanced growth and distribution, though the emphasis between these two objectives has shifted over time. From the 1980s until the Asian Financial Crisis, during Mahathir's tenure as Prime Minister, economic growth was prioritized, with inequality addressed through the Bumiputera policy based on the premise that the economic pie would expand.

The policy direction shifted when Mahathir retired in 2003 and the Abdullah administration assumed office. The Ninth Malaysia Plan (2006–2010), announced by the Abdullah administration in 2006, aimed to "address persistent socio-economic inequalities constructively and productively."[8] This plan emphasized the need to address not only inter-ethnic disparities but also intra-ethnic inequalities and urban-rural divides. Additionally, the Ninth Plan proposed developing the Iskandar region in Johor state and strengthening regional core cities to address geographical economic inequality.[9]

When the Najib administration took office in 2009, the New Economic Model (NEM) announced the following year established three goals for economic growth[10]: "High Growth," "Sustainability," and "Inclusiveness"—the latter specifically aimed at reducing income disparities. Specifically, strengthening support for the bottom

40% income group (B40) was proposed as a "market-compatible affirmative action" and subsequently incorporated into the Tenth Malaysia Plan (2011–2015).[11]

The Eleventh Malaysia Plan (2016–2020), subtitled "Anchoring Growth on People," made the distribution-oriented policy direction more explicit. In the preface, Prime Minister Najib declared that the Eleventh Plan was "disproportionately focused on the Rakyat (people)."[12] Although income redistribution and social welfare had been essential themes in previous 5-year plans, the chapter structure of the Eleventh Plan clearly indicates that the Malaysian government had shifted its stance to prioritize distribution over economic growth. For example, 5-year plans typically begin with an analysis of the macroeconomic situation and goal setting; however, the first chapter of the Eleventh Plan is titled "Anchoring Growth on People" and focuses on improving people's lives.

The distribution focus in the Eleventh Plan covers both income levels and geographical aspects. The Eleventh Plan established two notable numerical targets for the bottom 40% income group (B40). These were: first, to double the average income of B40 households from 2537 ringgit per month in 2014 to 5270 ringgit per month by 2020; and second, to increase the labor income share (the proportion of national income allocated to labor rather than capital) from 33.6% in 2013 to 40% by 2020.

The Eleventh Plan also addresses geographical development, proposing "Rural transformation to enhance the well-being of rural communities" and "Accelerating regional growth for better geographic balance." The first initiative aims to develop essential infrastructure—electricity, water, roads, and internet—in underserved rural areas. Meanwhile, the second initiative focuses on accelerating the development of five previously established economic corridors. The development of four key cities—Kuala Lumpur, Johor Bahru, Kuching, and Kota Kinabalu—was incorporated as part of "Re-engineering economic growth for greater prosperity." The Eleventh Plan's approach to regional development is more comprehensive and multi-layered than in previous plans.

This distribution-oriented policy stance of the Malaysian government materialized in the 2010s through two specific initiatives. These were: first, the introduction of a long-debated minimum wage system; and second, the implementation of income-based cash transfers to households. The Minimum Wages Order was implemented in January 2013 (July 1, 2013, for companies with five or fewer employees), setting the minimum wage at 900 ringgit per month for Peninsular Malaysia and 800 ringgit per month for Sabah, Sarawak, and Labuan. The minimum wage was subsequently revised in July 2016, increasing to 1000 ringgit per month for Peninsular Malaysia and 920 ringgit per month for Sabah, Sarawak, and Labuan. The minimum wage has continued to increase, and from 2020, it became 1200 ringgit per month for 56 municipalities and 1100 ringgit per month for other areas. Furthermore, effective May 1, 2022, the minimum wage was significantly increased to 1500 ringgit per month across all regions, with limited exceptions.

The household cash transfer program, BR1M (Bantuan Rakyat 1 Malaysia), was introduced in 2012, providing an annual payment of 500 ringgit to households with monthly incomes below 3000 ringgit. According to official figures, 3.4 million households, representing 53% of all households nationwide, were eligible for this benefit. BR1M has been expanded annually, and despite name changes following administrative transitions, the cash transfer program has continued uninterrupted. In 2022, the program operates as BKM (Bantuan Keluarga Malaysia), providing up to 2500 ringgit for households with monthly incomes of 2500 ringgit or less and up to 1300 ringgit for households with monthly incomes of 5000 ringgit or less, with the exact amount determined by the number of children and elderly dependents in each household.

6.3.2 Demographic Dividend Period Continuing Until 2045

The Malaysian government's emphasis on stimulating domestic demand is clearly reflected in the strong private consumption figures. This contrasts with neighboring Thailand. A quarterly comparison of private consumption growth rates between Malaysia and Thailand over the past 15 years (Fig. 6.3) clearly shows that Malaysia consistently maintains levels 3–4 percentage points higher than Thailand. This differential closely corresponds to the GDP growth rate gap between the two countries in the 2010s and represents a major factor in Malaysia's ability to maintain "medium growth" of 4%–6% even as external demand plateaued during this period (Fig. 6.4).

Another factor driving Malaysia's strong private consumption in the 2010s is the country's entry into its "demographic dividend" period. The demographic dividend period refers to the time when the working-age population (15–64 years old) exceeds twice the combined population of dependents—children (0–14 years old) and the elderly (65 years and older)—a condition considered favorable for economic growth.

Figure 6.5 illustrates the 5-year progression of this ratio for Malaysia, Japan, China, and Thailand based on United Nations statistical data. For each country, the demographic dividend period is defined as the timespan when this ratio exceeds 2. Among these countries, Japan was the first to enter its demographic dividend period, which lasted from 1965 to 2000. This period closely coincides with Japan's era of sustained economic growth. China and Thailand exhibit similar patterns in the graph, both entering their demographic dividend periods in 1995, with projected

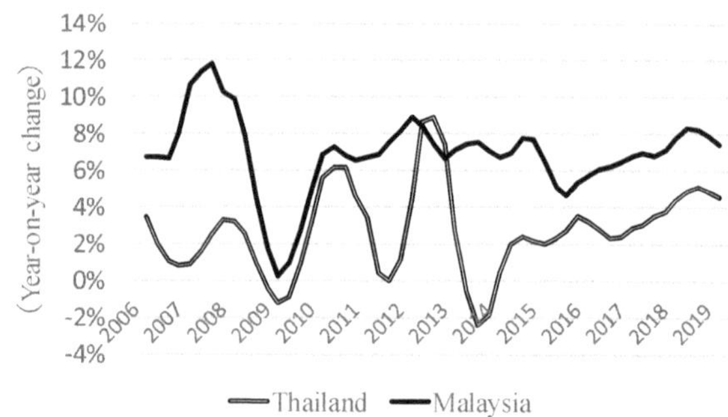

Fig. 6.3 Private consumption growth in Malaysia and Thailand (2006–2020). *Source* Created by the author based on NESDB, Thailand and DOS, Malaysia data

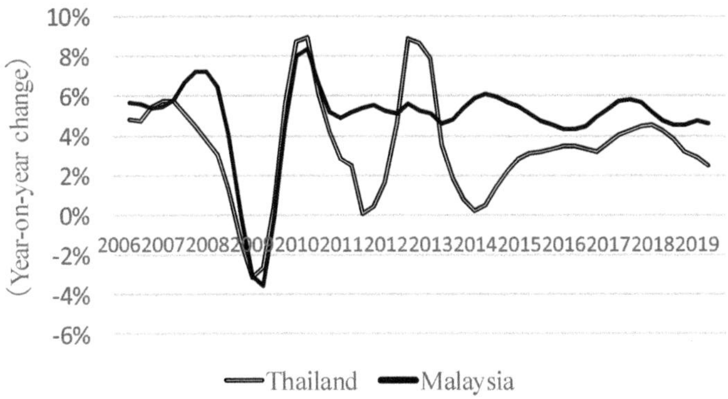

Fig. 6.4 GDP growth in Malaysia and Thailand (2006–2020). *Source* Created by the author based on NESDB, Thailand and DOS, Malaysia data

conclusions in 2030 for China and 2025 for Thailand. For Thailand, there is concern that sustaining economic growth may become challenging after 2025 due to the relatively early end of its demographic dividend period while still at a comparatively low-income level.

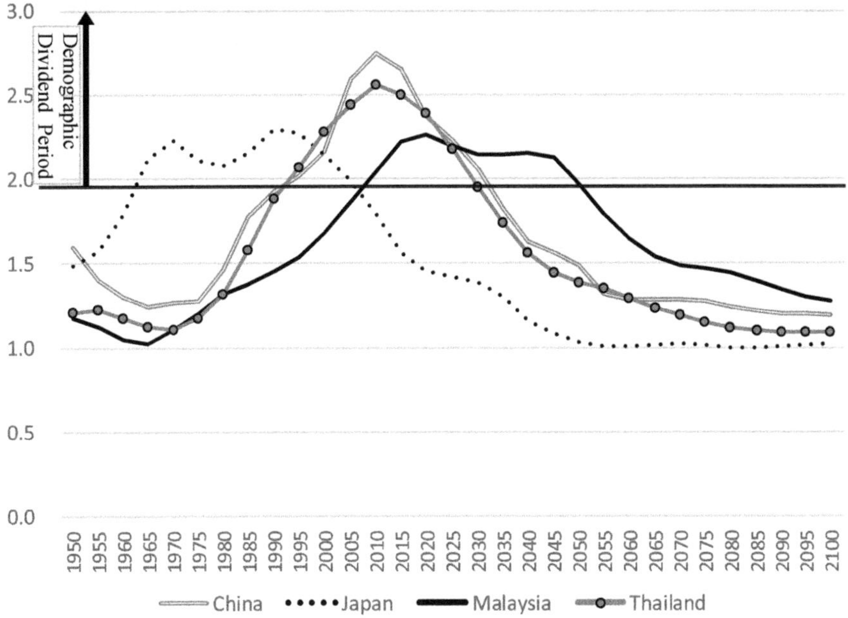

Fig. 6.5 Demographic dividend period in selected Asian countries. *Source* Created by the author based on United Nations population division projections (https://population.un.org/wpp/) Accessed on 30 Sep 2022.

In contrast, Malaysia entered its demographic dividend period relatively late, beginning only in 2010. Malaysia's demographic dividend period begins significantly later than the other countries examined and is projected to extend until 2045. This suggests that the strength of Malaysia's domestic demand could be sustained until approximately the mid-21st century.

6.4 The Declining Exchange Rate of the Malaysian Ringgit

6.4.1 Currently more Undervalued than During the Currency Crisis

When analyzing the balance between domestic and external demand in Malaysia, it is important to recognize that the Malaysian ringgit has experienced long-term depreciation. A persistently weak ringgit benefits exports by enhancing price competitiveness but simultaneously undermines consumers' purchasing power and hampers domestic demand.

Figure 6.6 illustrates the movement of nominal exchange rates for the Malaysian ringgit and Singapore dollar against the U.S. dollar from 1970 to 2020. The Malaysian ringgit and Singapore dollar maintained a fixed 1:1 exchange ratio until mid-1973. Afterward, although they began to fluctuate independently, both currencies exhibited similar patterns throughout the 1970s, gradually appreciating against the U.S. dollar.

However, from the 1980s onwards, the currencies diverged: while the Singapore dollar steadily appreciated against the U.S. dollar, the Malaysian ringgit gradually

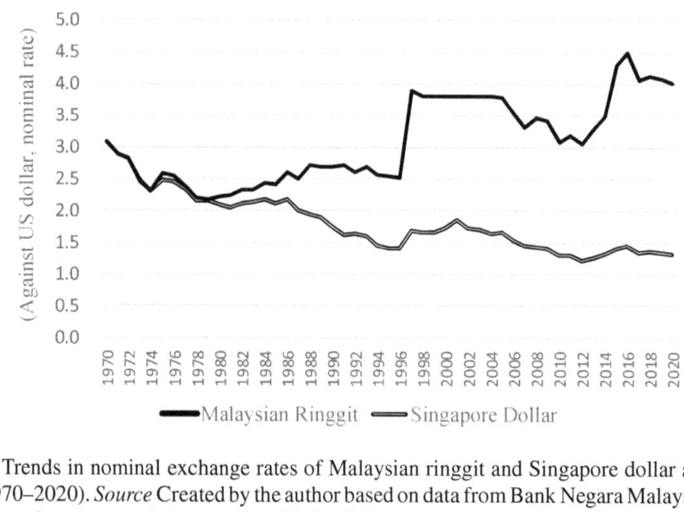

Fig. 6.6 Trends in nominal exchange rates of Malaysian ringgit and Singapore dollar against US dollar (1970–2020). *Source* Created by the author based on data from Bank Negara Malaysia website (https://www.bnm.gov.my/) Accessed on 30 Sep 2022.

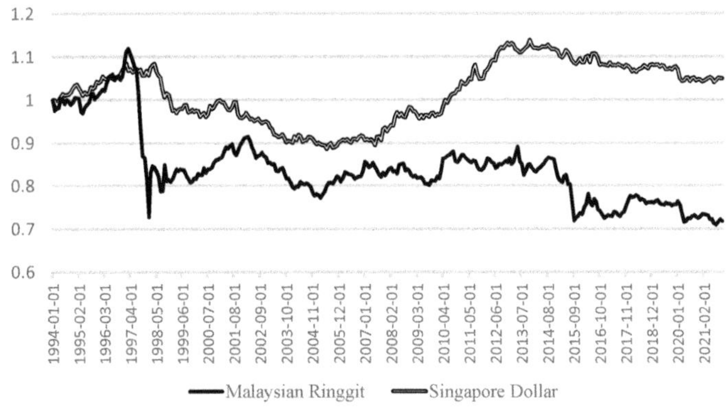

Fig. 6.7 Trends in real effective exchange rates of Malaysian ringgit and Singapore dollar (1970–2020). *Source* Created by the author based on data from Federal Reserve Bank of St. Louis website (https://www.stlouisfed.org/) Accessed on 30 Sep 2022.

depreciated, then plummeted during the 1997–98 Asian Financial Crisis, and experienced another significant decline amid the 1MDB scandal in the mid-2010s. As a result, by 2020, the nominal value differential between the Malaysian ringgit and the Singapore dollar had widened to approximately 1:3.

For a more accurate evaluation of currency value, economists use the real effective exchange rate, which accounts for inflation differentials between a country and its trading partners. Figure 6.7 tracks the real effective exchange rates of the Malaysian ringgit and Singapore dollar, using January 1994 as the base period (1.0). The Singapore dollar has experienced fluctuations but has generally maintained a relatively strong position since the 2010s. In contrast, the Malaysian ringgit plummeted during the Asian Financial Crisis, temporarily recovered, and then weakened significantly again during the 1MDB scandal in the mid-2010s. As of November 2021, the ringgit was more undervalued than during the Asian Financial Crisis and approximately 30% weaker than its 1994 level.

6.4.2 *Need for Exchange Rate Normalization*

Maintaining an undervalued exchange rate can stimulate economic growth. Research suggests that a 20% currency depreciation can boost annual economic growth rates by 0.4 percentage points. However, this effect diminishes as a country develops and vanishes entirely when per capita income approaches approximately $20,000.[13]

In Malaysia's case, the currency weakness stems largely from the aftereffects of the Asian Financial Crisis and the 1MDB scandal, rather than from intentional policy to maintain a weak currency. While the weak currency may have temporarily boosted economic growth, given Malaysia's current income level, the ringgit appears significantly undervalued. According to the Big Mac Index (July 2019), which measures currency valuation based on purchasing power parity and the law of one price, the Malaysian ringgit was undervalued by 62.8%—ranking as the second most undervalued currency globally, behind only the Russian ruble among the 56 countries tracked by the index.

The continuous depreciation of the Malaysian ringgit against the U.S. dollar is a key factor delaying Malaysia's transition to high-income country status according to World Bank criteria. The ringgit's undervaluation also exacerbates brain drain to countries like Singapore by widening the effective wage gap between the countries. Therefore, exchange rate normalization represents a crucial challenge for Malaysia's advancement to high-income country status.

6.5 Restructuring of Redistribution Policies Under the Two-Coalition System

6.5.1 Demands for Non-Ethnic-Based Inequality Correction

As previously discussed, the government's policy shift from growth prioritization to distribution emphasis during the mid-2000s through the 2010s drove the expansion of domestic demand. This policy reorientation was largely driven by pressure from an increasingly influential opposition during the same period. Parti Keadilan Rakyat (PKR, or People's Justice Party), led by former Deputy Prime Minister Anwar, made significant electoral gains in 2008 by promising a transition to non-ethnic-based inequality correction.

Expanding domestic demand requires addressing inequalities and elevating the income levels of middle and low-income groups, which typically have higher consumption propensities. Since the 1970s, the government has attempted to address inequalities through the implementation of the Bumiputera policy. However, as we saw in Chapter 3, the narrowing of inter-ethnic disparities contributed to reducing overall societal inequalities only until the late 1980s. Subsequently, despite continued narrowing of inter-ethnic disparities, overall inequality remained persistently high. This occurred because intra-ethnic inequality reduction failed to materialize. While the entry of Malays into commercial and industrial sectors raised their overall income levels, significant disparities emerged between those who successfully leveraged Bumiputera policy benefits and those who could not.

Those with connections to the government and ruling party disproportionately benefited from the Bumiputera policy. The problem of cronyism gained widespread recognition in Malay society following controversies over corporate bailouts during the currency crisis, eventually evolving into a significant political issue. As discussed in Chapter 4, Abdullah, who succeeded Mahathir as Prime Minister in 2003, acknowledged this problem and called for eliminating "rent-seeking addiction," but his reform efforts proved inadequate.

In contrast, PKR, representing the opposition, explicitly called for abolishing the Bumiputera policy during the 2008 election campaign, garnering significant attention by pledging to implement needs-based policies instead.

PKR had proclaimed itself as a non-communal party since its foundation. However, in both the 1999 and 2004 elections, the party failed to secure Chinese voter support and consequently won only a minimal number of seats. Following former Deputy Prime Minister Anwar's release from prison and his resumption of political activities as party advisor in 2004, PKR's political influence began to steadily grow. In 2006, Anwar spearheaded street demonstrations protesting against fuel and electricity price hikes. In November of the same year, the three main opposition parties, namely PKR, Parti Islam Se-Malaysia (PAS), and the Democratic Action Party (DAP), established the Coalition for Clean and Fair Elections (Bersih) in collaboration with various NGOs to advocate for electoral reform. The following year, Bersih organized a major street demonstration in downtown Kuala Lumpur, successfully mobilizing approximately 10,000 participants.

Meanwhile, PAS and DAP, which had been antagonistic toward each other in the early 2000s, also modified their positions following their devastating defeat in the 2004 election. Following its significant gains in the 1999 election, PAS intensified its Islamic stance as the influence of ulama (religious leaders) grew within the party. As a consequence, the opposition coalition Alternative Front (see Chapter 4) collapsed, leading to PAS losing numerous seats in the 2004 election. After the election, non-ulama executives rose to prominence within the party leadership. At the 2006 party conference, PAS adopted a policy to field non-Muslim candidates in the next election, signaling a strategic shift toward a more moderate position.

Similarly, DAP amended its party constitution at its 40th-anniversary conference in 2006, abandoning the "Malaysian Malaysia" slogan that had served as its foundational motto. As explained in Chapter 2, this slogan—originally advocated by Lee Kuan Yew when Singapore was part of Malaysia—conveyed the controversial message that Malaysia was not exclusively a "Malay country." Lim Guan Eng, the Secretary-General who orchestrated the constitutional amendment in 2006, declared that the revision aimed to reposition the party as a centrist political force.

In preparation for the 2008 election, the main opposition parties—PKR, PAS, and DAP—actively explored avenues for cooperation. Although they did not establish a formal coalition or develop a unified manifesto before the election, they strategically coordinated candidate nominations in virtually all constituencies to avoid splitting the opposition vote. In this election, voters shifted decisively toward the opposition, resulting in the Barisan Nasional (BN) losing its two-thirds majority in the lower house of the federal parliament for the first time in the country's history.

PKR, which had campaigned on non-ethnic-based inequality correction policies, achieved remarkable electoral success. The party, having secured only a single seat in the 2004 election, won 31 seats in 2008, catapulting it to become the largest opposition party.

A significant factor contributing to the opposition's breakthrough in the 2008 election was the widespread adoption of the Internet. Malaysia's traditional media—newspapers and television—were tightly controlled through government licensing and capital ownership by ruling party associates, severely restricting the opposition's ability to disseminate their message. However, with the widespread proliferation of the Internet from the late 1990s onward, the opposition gained the ability to broadly disseminate their policies through websites and YouTube channels. In addition, independent online news outlets and individual political blogs proliferated rapidly, significantly expanding public access to government-critical perspectives.

This media environment had already begun developing by the 2004 election; however, at that juncture, deep disagreements between PAS and DAP over religious policies prevented the formation of the cooperative framework necessary to challenge the entrenched ruling party dominance. Consequently, in the 2008 election campaign, all three major opposition parties strategically set aside ethnicity-related issues and instead focused their manifestos on addressing economic concerns, combating corruption, and promoting democratic reforms. Pre-election opinion poll analysis revealed that voters who primarily consumed online news demonstrated significantly greater interest in these specific issues.[14]

6.5.2 *Elections Promoting the Transformation of Redistribution Policies*

Shortly after the 2008 election, the three parties formalized their cooperation by establishing the "Pakatan Rakyat" (PR, or People's Alliance) coalition. The immediate impetus for this formalization was to secure control of state governments. In the concurrent state assembly elections held in 12 states, BN lost its majority in five states: Kelantan, Kedah, Penang, Perak, and Selangor. In Kelantan, where PAS had governed since 1990, the party secured an outright majority. In Kedah, a PAS-PKR coalition could form a majority; in Penang, a DAP-PKR coalition could achieve the same; while in both Perak and Selangor, all three opposition parties together could secure majority control. The three parties immediately initiated coalition negotiations following the election and successfully established governments in all five states.

The electoral gains of PKR, DAP, and PAS in the 2008 election and their subsequent formation of PR marked a fundamental transformation in Malaysia's party system—from BN's long-standing one-party dominance to a competitive two-party configuration. However, since both BN and PR were coalitions rather than single parties, a more precise characterization would be a transition from "one-coalition dominance" to a "competitive two-coalition system."

Prior to the 2004 election, as major parties primarily represented the interests of specific ethnic groups, voters predominantly viewed ethnicity and religion as the primary dimensions of political competition. Figure. 6.8 provides a simplified illustration of party relationships after PAS departed from BN in 1977.

Figure 6.9 illustrates how party relationships transformed following the 2008 election and the subsequent formation of PR.

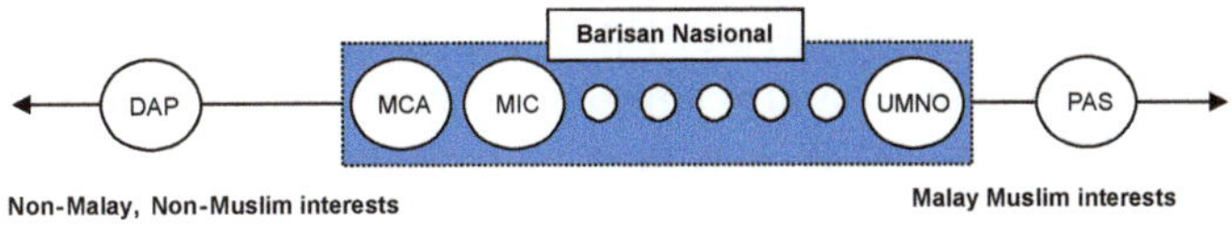

Fig. 6.8 Inter-party relations from 1977 to the 2004 general election. *Source* Created by the author

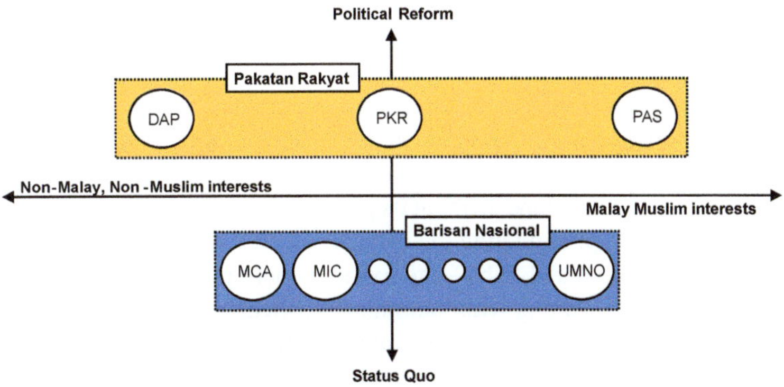

Fig. 6.9 Inter-party relations after the 2008 general election through 2015. *Source* Created by the author

While ethnic and religious positioning remained an important dimension of political competition, a new axis of conflict emerged that highlighted policy differences between the two coalitions. The most salient issue on this new dimension was political reform. PR convened its inaugural conference in December 2009, where it unveiled a comprehensive common policy platform. This platform articulated specific measures organized under four key pillars: (1) transparent and genuine democracy, (2) driving a high-performance, sustainable, and equitable economy, (3) social justice and human development, and (4) federal-state relationship and foreign policy. Political reform initiatives were prominently positioned as the cornerstone of this platform. In the policy document "Buku Jingga" (Orange Book) adopted at the subsequent year's conference, transparent government administration was designated as the highest priority for implementing the common policy platform.

Within this new political dynamic between ruling coalition and opposition, as discussed in the previous chapter, the first Najib cabinet (formed in 2009) initiated political liberalization measures, including legalizing street demonstrations. This strategic move aimed to recapture support from urban middle-class voters, particularly Chinese voters who had defected in the 2008 election, by preemptively adopting key elements of the opposition's platform. Driven by the same electoral strategy, the Najib administration promoted the "1Malaysia" slogan and implemented needs-based inequality reduction measures targeting the bottom 40% of households irrespective of ethnic background. A centerpiece of these initiatives was the BR1M cash transfer program discussed earlier.

As analyzed in the previous chapter, following the ruling coalition's further erosion of support in urban areas during the 2013 election, the Najib administration pivoted sharply toward Malay nationalist rhetoric and increasingly authoritarian governance. On the opposition side, PAS simultaneously reverted to a more rigid Islamic stance, advancing legislation to implement hudud punishments. Hudud punishments refer to "Islamic criminal law penalties explicitly prescribed in the Quran or Hadith that cannot be altered,"[15] including severe measures such as stoning for adultery committed by married persons and amputation of limbs for theft. DAP vehemently opposed the implementation of hudud punishments, which intensified the conflict between the two parties. In June 2015, at its party conference, PAS formally decided to sever ties with DAP, precipitating the collapse of PR.

Subsequently, Mohammad Sabu—the former deputy president of PAS who was considered progressive—along with like-minded colleagues, left the party to establish Parti Amanah Negara (Amanah, or National Trust Party). This new party then formed the "Pakatan Harapan" (PH, or Alliance of Hope) coalition with DAP and PKR. Concurrently, within the ruling coalition, the conflict between Prime Minister Najib and former Prime Minister Mahathir escalated dramatically. This led Mahathir and his supporters to establish Parti Pribumi Bersatu Malaysia (PPBM, or Malaysian United Indigenous Party) in August 2016. The following year, PPBM joined the PH coalition, reconfiguring the political landscape prior to the 2018 election as illustrated in Fig. 6.10. In the 2018 election, PH secured victory, thwarting Najib's strategy to maintain power through intensified Bumiputera policies and systematic suppression of government critics.

As with the growing emphasis on meritocracy discussed in the previous chapter, electoral competition drove the transition from ethnic quota systems toward needs-based redistribution policies. During the 1970s and 1980s, the Bumiputera policy

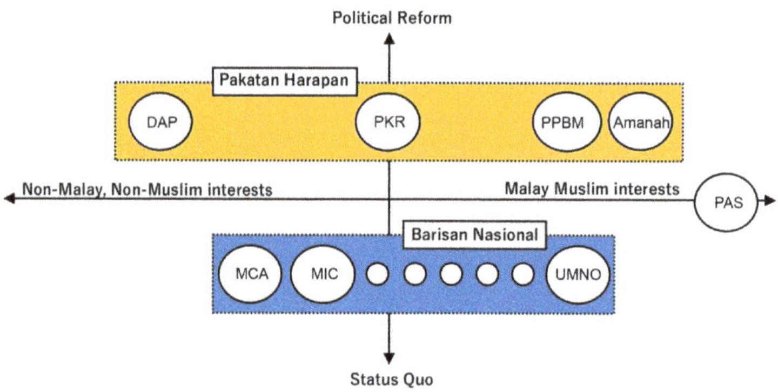

Fig. 6.10 Inter-party relations during the 2018 general election. *Source* Created by the author

successfully reduced disparities and enhanced economic inclusiveness; however, its effectiveness began to wane in the 1990s. The opposition recognized this policy exhaustion and advocated for a transition to needs-based redistribution policies, garnering substantial voter support. Consequently, the government strategically adopted elements of the opposition's platform in an attempt to recapture lost electoral support. When these concessions failed to win back voters in the subsequent election and the government reverted to reinforcing Bumiputera policies, voters ultimately opted for regime change in the following election, enabling a fundamental policy reorientation. In Malaysia, electoral competition has repeatedly served as a catalyst for policy evolution that better aligns with emerging societal needs.

Notes

1. Urata (2001).
2. Economic Planning Agency, Japan (1992).
3. Kumagai (2018).
4. Malaysia's exports increased by more than 50% over 2 years, growing 26.1% in 2021 and 25.0% in 2022 due to the global economic recovery after COVID-19 and rising export prices including resources. As a result, export dependence rose again to 86.8% in 2022.
5. Among the earliest companies to enter Penang, Intel has invested over RM22 billion in Malaysia over nearly half a century, employing over 12,000 people, including thousands of engineers participating in advanced microprocessor design. In 2021, Intel announced plans to invest more than RM30 billion over the next decade in its factories in Penang State and neighboring Kedah State. Thanks to contributions from multinational corporations like Intel, Penang has become one of Asia's semiconductor industry hubs.
6. Torii (1990, pp. 247–248).
7. Malaysia ratified and implemented CPTPP on November 29, 2022, and RCEP on March 18, 2022, after completing domestic procedures.
8. Malaysia (2006, p. 16).
9. Umezaki and Nakamura (2007, p. 343).
10. NEAC (2010, p. 35).
11. Malaysia (2010, pp. 149–162).
12. Malaysia (2015, p. i).
13. Rodrik (2008).
14. Nakamura (2015, pp. 228–232).
15. Mori (2002).

References

Economic Planning Agency (1992) Five-year plan for living nation: aiming for coexistence with global society (Seikatsu Taikoku 5-Kanen Keikaku). Ministry of Finance Printing Bureau, Tokyo

Kumagai S (2018) Economic overview of the post-Mahathir period: structural reform delayed despite approaching high-income status (Post-Mahathir Ki no Keizai Gaikan). In: Nakamura M, Kumagai S (eds) Malaysia in the post-Mahathir era (Post-Mahathir Jidai no Malaysia). Institute of Developing Economies, Tokyo, pp 225–259

Malaysia (2006) Ninth Malaysia Plan 2006–2010. Percetakan Nasional Malaysia Berhad, Putrajaya

Malaysia (2010) Tenth Malaysia Plan 2011–2015. Percetakan Nasional Malaysia Berhad, Putrajaya
Malaysia (2015) Eleventh Malaysia Plan 2016–2020. Percetakan Nasional Malaysia Berhad, Putrajaya
Mori N (2002) Hadd punishment (Haddo Kei). In: Otsuka K, Kosugi Y, Komatsu H et al (eds) Iwanami dictionary of Islam (Iwanami Islam Jiten). Iwanami Shoten, Tokyo, pp 764–765
Nakamura M (2015) Power sharing: the experience of multi-ethnic state Malaysia (Power Shearingu). University of Tokyo Press, Tokyo
Nakamura M, Kumagai S (eds) (2018) Malaysia in the post-Mahathir era: how politics and economy have changed (Post-Mahathir Jidai no Malaysia). Institute of Developing Economies, Tokyo
National Economic Advisory Council (NEAC) (2010) New economic mechanism for Malaysia. Percetakan Nasional Malaysia Berhad, Kuala Lumpur
Rodrik D (2008) The real exchange rate and economic growth. Brook Pap Econ Act 2008(2):365–412
Torii T (1990) Electronics industry: IC and TV production base (Denshi Sangyō). In: Horii K (ed) Industrialization in Malaysia (Malaysia no Kōgyōka). Institute of Developing Economies, Tokyo, pp 242–272
Umezaki S, Nakamura M (2007) Malaysia in 2006: complete set of long-term development policies (2006 nen no Malaysia). In: Institute of Developing Economies (ed) Yearbook of Asian Affairs 2006 (Ajia Dōkō Nenpō 2006). Institute of Developing Economies, Tokyo, pp 333–364
Urata S (2001) Emergence of an FDI-trade nexus and economic growth in East Asia. In: Stiglitz JE, Yusuf S (eds) Rethinking the East Asian miracle. World Bank, Washington, pp 409–459

Chapter 7
Hints for Escaping the "Middle-Income Trap" and Future Challenges

7.1 Balancing Industrialization and Rural Development

In the early stages of economic development, the Malaysian government focused on both industrialization and rural development simultaneously. Unlike many other countries, Malaysia pursued industrialization without neglecting or exploiting rural areas, aiming for balanced development between urban and rural areas. The Malaysian government's serious approach to rural issues was because the majority of the population, or voters, were Malays, most of whom lived in rural areas and engaged in agriculture.

A unique challenge for Malaysia was the ethnic division of the labor market, with Malays predominantly in rural areas and Chinese in urban areas. This hindered the natural movement of labor from rural to urban areas and from agriculture to commerce and industry. Unlike in many developing countries, urbanization in Malaysia did not naturally occur despite wage disparities between urban and rural areas. Consequently, the Malaysian government had to provide policy-driven support for the movement of labor and capital between agriculture and commerce/industry.

The New Economic Policy, initiated in 1971 in response to the 1969 ethnic riots, was also known as the "Bumiputera Policy" due to its preferential treatment of Bumiputeras. However, it was also an urbanization and industrialization policy that supported farmers, predominantly Bumiputera, and assisted their migration to cities and employment in commerce and industry. Furthermore, the government prioritized rural development, where Bumiputeras were the majority, alongside industrialization, which helped reduce the gap between urban and rural areas.

What can be learned from Malaysia's policies during this period is the simultaneous advancement of industrialization, urbanization, and rural development. In many countries, industrialization is pursued at the expense of rural development, or vice versa, often creating an either-or situation. Rural areas serve as a source of labor and economic surplus for commerce and industry. However, this does not

S. Kumagai and M. Nakamura, *Economic Development Strategies*, Emerging-Economy State and International Policy Studies, https://doi.org/10.1007/978-981-95-6899-4_7

justify treating rural areas as objects of exploitation for industrial gain or creating conditions that force workers to "escape" from rural to urban areas.

Enriching rural areas does not necessarily halt population movement to cities or trigger a reverse flow from urban to rural areas as long as industrialization and urbanization policies are simultaneously pursued. As mentioned earlier, "disguised unemployment" is common in rural areas of developing countries; therefore, rural development does not immediately lead to increased wages for agricultural workers. Moreover, agriculture is constrained by the availability of land, so enriched rural areas do not absorb urban workers.

Enriching rural areas and providing primary education to rural youth to enable future employment in commerce and industry support long-term economic development. Furthermore, reducing the income gap between urban and rural areas through rural development can prevent serious political conflicts between urban and rural voters later on.

In Malaysia's case, the rural areas were not neglected or exploited politically because the majority ethnic group, the Malays, resided in rural areas. The overrepresentation of rural areas in electoral districting also contributed to the political emphasis on rural areas. While the ethnic issue may not be applicable to other countries, there may be some merit in adjusting electoral districting to slightly overrepresent rural areas until a specific stage of economic development is reached.

On the other hand, Malaysia serves as a cautionary example of how strong government policy intervention creates considerable politically distributed benefits (rents) that become vested interests, making policy changes difficult later on. Specifically, the lack of a clear phase-out plan for the New Economic Policy resulted in various forms of Bumiputera preferential policies continuing beyond the initial plan's final year of 1990, thereby creating problems that hindered economic development.

7.2 Addressing Urbanization, Income Disparity, and Expansion of Education

From the 1970s to the 1980s, the Malaysian government implemented the New Economic Policy to guide Malays, who had remained in the traditional rural sector, into urban and modern sectors. This policy supported the industrialization and urbanization of the Malaysian economy. While the New Economic Policy is often criticized for its preferential treatment of Bumiputeras and perceived as hindering Malaysian economic development, at least during the initial planned period of 1971–1990, its implementation was necessary. Without this policy, Malays would have remained in rural areas with low incomes, and it would have been impossible to meet the increased labor demand in the commerce and industry sectors that supported economic development during this period.

Typically, urbanization in developing countries occurs naturally as workers flow into cities due to significant wage disparities between rural and urban areas. In such cases, many workers flow into slums, forming an urban informal sector. However, in pre-New Economic Policy Malaysia, urbanization was impeded by ethnic barriers. As urbanization was policy-driven and government-led in Malaysia, there was no disorderly influx of labor into cities, thereby preventing the expansion of the informal sector in metropolitan areas. However, as the surplus rural labor force was depleted early on, Malaysia had to introduce a large number of foreign workers in the 1990s, leading to the expansion of the informal sector where foreigners were employed to alleviate labor shortages.

The characteristics of Malaysia's foreign worker issue include not only the large number of foreign workers but also the high proportion of undocumented migrants. These numerous foreign workers mainly engage in 3D (Dangerous, Dirty, and Demanding) jobs that Malaysians are reluctant to perform, thus complementing the domestic workforce. On the other hand, employing many foreign workers in the manufacturing sector, which has great potential for productivity improvement, may encourage business managers to rely on cheap labor and reduce incentives for mechanization, automation, and higher value-added production. Furthermore, the size of the informal sector where foreign workers are employed has led to criticism from developed countries over human rights, resulting in exclusion from government procurement.[1] Additionally, the poor living conditions have become a breeding ground for COVID-19 infections.[2]

Income inequality often emerges as a significant problem in developing countries once they have achieved a certain level of economic development. The gap widens between citizens who benefit from industrialization and urbanization and those who are left behind. It is significant that the ethnic riots in Malaysia occurred in 1969, at the end of the 1960s, when economic development was progressing smoothly through import substitution industrialization.

The uniqueness of the income inequality issue in Malaysia lies in the fact that those experiencing poverty were the politically dominant Malays. Furthermore, the linkage between income class and ethnicity led to the 1969 riots, placing income inequality resolution at the top of the political agenda thereafter. With strong government intervention through the New Economic Policy that began in 1971 and steady economic growth, poverty rates declined rapidly across all ethnic groups, and absolute poverty is no longer a significant issue in present-day Malaysia. Income disparities between ethnic groups and between urban and rural areas narrowed until the 1980s.

However, from the 1990s onwards, the urban-rural gap widened again, and income disparities within the same ethnic groups began to attract attention. In particular, even among the Bumiputeras, who constitute the majority of the population, the gap between those who benefited from the New Economic Policy and those who did not widened, becoming a political issue.

For developing countries to achieve economic growth through industrialization, it is necessary to facilitate migration from rural to urban areas and enhance the quality of the workforce by developing the education system. As a multi-ethnic nation, Malaysia recognized schools using the national language, Malay, as the primary medium of instruction, while also designating English, Chinese, and Tamil schools as public primary schools. The government has fully funded their operating costs since 1961.

The net enrollment rate for primary education in 1970, shortly after Malaysia entered the lower-middle-income category, exceeded 87%, reaching a level comparable to that of developed countries at the time.

However, when the New Economic Policy was implemented, the government prioritized raising the relative status of Malays over expanding secondary and higher education by converting English schools to Malay schools, introducing ethnic quotas for university admissions, and rejecting the establishment of private universities demanded by the Chinese community. As a result, the gross enrollment rate for higher education in 1985 remained at a mere 5.7%, far behind not only OECD member countries (32.7%) but also the Philippines (27.8%) and Thailand (20.7%).

This situation changed dramatically in the mid-1990s. When the Mahathir administration, which had set a new national goal of becoming a developed country by 2020, prioritized human resource development and began liberalizing higher education, Chinese voters who welcomed these changes increased their support for the government, leading to a landslide victory for the ruling party in the 1995 election. This coincided with the time when Malaysia entered the upper-middle-income category. Subsequently, the liberalization of higher education progressed further, including the approval of private university establishments, and the higher education enrollment rate rose rapidly.

What can be learned from Malaysia's policies during this period is the government's active support for the movement of labor from rural to urban areas and the strategic expansion of urban centers. In Malaysia, due to the unique circumstance of the labor market being ethnically segregated between urban and rural areas, urbanization would have been significantly delayed without government intervention. Furthermore, without policy support for labor movement from rural to urban areas, extensive slums might have formed in metropolitan areas centered on the capital, leading to the proliferation of the informal economy.

In many countries, urbanization occurs naturally through wage disparities between rural and urban areas. As a result, controlling the pace of urbanization becomes difficult, and urban infrastructure development and housing provision often lag behind, leading to the formation of vast slums and the growth of the informal economy. In this respect, it may be challenging for other countries to emulate Malaysia's example, where ethnic barriers hindered natural urbanization. Nevertheless, other countries could learn from Malaysia's proactive approach in anticipating urban growth needs and actively engaging in infrastructure and housing development.

The expansion of the education system also contributed significantly to Malaysia's economic development. The focus on spreading primary education in the early stages of independence, achieving enrollment rates comparable to those of developed countries, facilitated the transition from low-income to middle-income country status. When the New Economic Policy began, the emphasis on Malay preferential treatment impeded the expansion of higher education. However, around the time Malaysia entered the upper-middle-income category, a policy shift occurred, and subsequently, the enrollment rate in higher education rose rapidly.

On the other hand, Malaysia serves as a cautionary example regarding its approach to managing foreign labor. Introducing foreign workers on a certain scale to address labor shortages is a viable policy option for any country. However, the proportion of foreign workers in Malaysia's domestic labor force is exceptionally high. Furthermore, the employment of foreign workers in the manufacturing sector was deregulated at a relatively early stage of economic development, undeniably hampering industrial upgrading by reducing incentives for business managers to adopt mechanization and shift towards higher value-added production.

7.3 Appropriate Management of the "Tripod Structure"

In developing countries, local private enterprises are commonly underdeveloped, and foreign-affiliated companies and government-linked companies tend to play significant roles as drivers of economic development. Economic development in developing countries varies depending on how these three entities (the "tripod structure" supporting the developing country's economy) share economic activities.

Before the New Economic Policy, British companies from the former colonial power and Chinese enterprises had a significant presence in Malaysia as drivers of economic development. However, with the New Economic Policy setting a target of 30% capital ownership by Bumiputeras by 1990, British companies and some Chinese enterprises became acquisition targets for state-owned investment funds, and newly established government-linked companies expanded their presence in the Malaysian economy.

From the 1980s until the currency crisis of 1997–1998, these government-linked companies were privatized and sold to Bumiputera entrepreneurs with close government ties. Such corporate groups achieved a certain level of success riding the wave of the economic boom in the 1990s, but their excessively expansionary management stance backfired, and their management deteriorated when triggered by the Asian Financial Crisis, leading to many being re-nationalized. For these corporate groups, significant governance reforms were implemented through the GLC Reform Program launched in the mid-2000s.

The Malaysian government also implemented proactive policies to attract foreign investment. While free trade zones were established in the 1970s to attract export-oriented foreign investment, the enactment of the Promotion of Investments Act in 1986 and the relaxation of guidelines allowing 100% foreign-owned companies led to a large influx of export-oriented foreign investment. This influx, which took advantage of the yen appreciation following the Plaza Accord in 1985, became the driving force for subsequent economic development and industrialization. However, the Malaysian government did not accept foreign investment unconditionally. The Malaysian government actively encouraged foreign investment primarily in the manufacturing sector. In contrast, the presence of foreign companies was restricted in primary commodity sectors and the financial sector, where local private companies and government-linked companies maintained a significant presence.

In Malaysia's case, the ethnic capital ownership ratio target of the New Economic Policy acted as a constraint, complicating the implementation of industrial policy.

As a result, although the management structure of Malaysian government-linked companies changed several times, after the 2000s, they developed into multinational companies expanding overseas operations, primarily in ASEAN countries, through the GLC Reform. Chinese enterprises, which were not particularly favored under the New Economic Policy, continued to grow and maintain their significant presence in the Malaysian economy. Regarding foreign companies, which are generally considered to relocate easily, they have continued to invest in Malaysia for half a century, particularly in Penang, with gradual upgrading of their corporate activities.

While it is indisputable that the New Economic Policy significantly impacted the nature of government-linked companies, foreign companies, and local private companies—and, at times, constrained development—Malaysia managed to prevent these constraints from becoming fatal to economic development by repeatedly making appropriate policy shifts according to changing circumstances.

What can be learned from Malaysia's policies during this period is, first, the strong emphasis on governance reform in government-linked companies. In developing countries, government-linked companies often have a substantial presence; therefore, their proper management has a significant impact on economic development. In Malaysia, partly due to the shock of the Asian Financial Crisis, the government was able to implement remarkably bold governance reforms of government-linked companies through the subsequent GLC Transformation Program. Ironically, in the 2010s, a massive corruption scandal involving a government-linked fund, the 1MDB issue, was uncovered under the Najib administration. However, this actually demonstrates that the governance of many large government-linked companies had been strengthened by the GLC Reform, limiting the funds that even the Prime Minister could freely manipulate. If the GLC Reform had not progressed, government-linked companies with even greater financial power (such as Khazanah Nasional or Petronas) might have become vehicles for corruption, potentially leading to national fiscal insolvency.

Second, Malaysia's approach to attracting foreign investment has varied according to industry. Malaysia's foreign investment strategy focused on the manufacturing sector. Numerous incentives were offered to export-oriented foreign manufacturing companies to actively attract them. On the other hand, Malaysia did not rush to liberalize foreign investment in primary commodity sectors and services, and instead promoted the Malaysianization of these sectors by acquiring British companies in the 1970s. This contrasts with countries in South America, for example, where major multinational grain companies maintain a significant presence in the primary commodity sector. The policy of maintaining limited foreign capital dependence in the primary and tertiary sectors, where the domestic value-added ratio is high, likely contributed positively to Malaysia's economic growth by preventing the outflow of value-added abroad.

7.4 Beware of the "Resource Curse." Multinational Corporations are a Double-Edged Sword

The "middle-income trap" can be simply described as a "failure of industrial upgrading." Malaysia's industrial upgrading progressed smoothly until the 2000s but has since stagnated. One reason is a phenomenon known as the "resource curse," where management resources shift from the production of sophisticated goods (such as consumer goods, capital goods, and parts) to the production of lower-grade goods (such as primary commodities and processed goods), resulting in an overall "downgrading" of the industrial structure.

The multinational corporations, government-linked companies, and local private companies that support the Malaysian economy each face distinct challenges in transforming into entities befitting a high-income country. Malaysia achieved industrialization by attracting export-oriented multinational corporations and integrating into global value chains (GVCs). However, the Malaysian subsidiaries of these multinational corporations often lack decision-making authority regarding which segments of the GVC they will manage, resulting in corporate activities being confined to low value-added operations. For government-linked companies, while the GLC Reform Program in the 2000s successfully improved governance, since the 13th General Election in 2013, political resistance to such governance reforms has intensified, and demands for compliance with the Bumiputera policy have also strengthened. There have been signs of regression in GLC reforms, exemplified by increasing pressure from the ruling party to appoint politicians to the management positions of government-linked companies. For local private companies, challenges include the concentration of activities in primary commodity-related and real estate sectors, and the retirement of the founding generation without a successive generation of managers emerging.

What can be learned from Malaysia's policies during this period is that despite the stagnation in industrial upgrading in overall exports since the 2000s, data analysis indicates that productivity improvement efforts were widely implemented at the company level. This can be attributed to a stable business environment and the availability of adequately skilled human resources necessary for productivity improvement. This is also evidenced by the fact that multinational corporations, exemplified by Intel, have continued to invest in Malaysia for 50 years, with progressive upgrading of their corporate activities.

Furthermore, while Malaysia appears to have been affected by a mild "resource curse" since the 2000s, the main reason this has not significantly hindered economic growth is the effective management of the national oil company, Petronas. While government interference in the management of national oil companies is almost unavoidable in many developing countries, Petronas's operational independence from the government and exceptional management capability are particularly noteworthy.

On the other hand, the structural industrial upgrading experienced by Japan and South Korea, such as the transition from exporting consumer goods to manufacturing sophisticated parts and capital goods, did not materialize in Malaysia. Instead, the export share of primary commodities and processed goods increased substantially due to the global primary commodity boom. This phenomenon should be recognized as a challenge specific to resource-rich countries. While it is natural for companies to gravitate toward industries with rising commodity prices, primary commodities and processed goods offer limited potential for productivity improvement and innovation compared to other manufacturing industries, creating a risk of falling into the "resource curse."

Furthermore, while foreign companies have been a significant force in promoting industrialization, they represent a double-edged sword for Malaysia's economic development as a host country. They facilitated integration into GVCs but simultaneously had the adverse effect of constraining Malaysia's role within these value chains. Currently, Malaysian companies cannot deeply engage in the R&D activities of multinational corporations, and they are typically relegated to supplying specified parts or handling low-value-added tasks such as assembly. Some multinational corporations have experienced "intra-firm upgrading," with Malaysian subsidiaries managing the entire process from R&D to production for specific product lines. However, this progress is considerably slower than what might be achieved if these companies were Malaysian-owned. Managing relationships with foreign companies represents a significant challenge for contemporary developing countries.

7.5 Emphasizing Domestic Demand in Addition to External Demand

For developing countries, export-oriented industrialization policies offer advantages over import substitution industrialization policies, such as overcoming the limitations of small domestic markets. Indeed, numerous East Asian countries have achieved substantial economic development through export-oriented industrialization strategies. However, export-oriented industrialization frequently generates international trade and financial imbalances as well as trade friction. Therefore, to sustain stable economic growth over an extended period, it is essential to expand domestic demand rather than relying exclusively on exports. However, transitioning from an export-led economy to a domestic demand-driven economy presents significant challenges. For example, suppressing workers' wages may maintain export competitiveness, but domestic demand cannot expand without increasing workers' incomes.

In Malaysia's case, similar to other Asian economies, economic growth was initially achieved through export-oriented industrialization. However, in the mid-2000s, there was a strategic shift in policy from growth-oriented to distribution-oriented approaches. Simultaneously, as Malaysia entered its demographic dividend period, a transition to a domestic demand-driven economy has been progressing since the 2010s. Compared to neighboring Thailand, Malaysia's economic growth rate has consistently been 1–2 percentage points higher in the 2010s, largely because

Malaysia's private consumption growth rate has consistently outperformed Thailand's by 2–3 percentage points. The transition to a domestic demand-led economy has bolstered the Malaysian economy even as exports have not expanded as rapidly as before, facilitating stable economic growth of 4%–6% annually.

Concurrently, Malaysia has vigorously pursued policies to attract foreign investment, especially since the mid-1980s, and has also been actively engaged in free trade agreements to expand exports. Until around 1980, Malaysia's exports were dominated by primary commodities, which accounted for 70% of total exports. However, by the time of the currency crisis in 1997, non-primary manufactured goods had risen to account for 80%. In the 2000s, the export share of primary commodities increased again due to the sharp rise in primary commodity prices. However, with primary commodity prices having stabilized, Malaysia's exports are now more balanced between industrial products and primary commodities and processed goods.

A key lesson from Malaysia's policies during this period is the importance of expanding domestic demand. Although Malaysia's exports have not grown as robustly as before in the 2010s, the strong growth of private consumption has maintained the economic growth rate at an impressive level for an upper-middle-income country. To expand domestic demand, policies addressing income inequalities are necessary. In Malaysia, cash transfer programs targeting the bottom 40% of income earners and minimum wage systems were introduced in the 2010s, contributing to the reduction of income disparities.

Simultaneously, the Malaysian government has not neglected export promotion. The Malaysian government has actively participated in regional trade agreements such as the ASEAN Economic Community, RCEP, and CPTPP. The growth in exports of primary commodities and processed goods, despite its negative implications for industrial upgrading, has contributed to the diversification of export products and destinations, leading to greater economic stability. Even amid the US-China trade tensions and the COVID-19 pandemic, Malaysia has increased its exports to both the United States and China, the world's two largest economies.

Malaysia serves as a cautionary example regarding the management of currency depreciation. While the Malaysian ringgit has not been intentionally guided toward depreciation by the government, it has continuously lost value over an extended period, initially triggered by the Asian Financial Crisis and later exacerbated by the 1MDB scandal. This persistent depreciation has become a significant factor in lowering Malaysia's dollar-denominated income and delaying its entry into high-income country status. Research suggests that maintaining a moderately undervalued rather than overvalued currency is more beneficial for economic growth. However, such effects diminish as income levels rise, and once Malaysia achieves high-income country status, efforts to maintain appropriate currency valuation will be necessary to ensure consistency with domestic demand expansion.

7.6 It's Too Late After Falling into the Middle-Income Trap

Examining Malaysia's development process reveals the phenomenon of "path dependency" in the economy, whereby the effects of policies implemented at one income stage often manifest at subsequent stages. In other words, by the time a country has fallen into the middle-income trap, it may be too late to implement effective escape strategies.

In Malaysia's case, focusing on rural development in parallel with industrialization during the early stages of economic development helped mitigate income disparities between rural and urban areas. This approach prevented a scenario where rural and urban residents became politically polarized, which would have made it impossible to implement effective economic development policies. Furthermore, the government's strategic involvement in urbanization limited the growth of the urban informal sector, which subsequently facilitated the enhancement of worker education.

The robustness of private consumption underpinning the economic growth rate at the upper-middle-income country stage can also be attributed to the consistent focus on reducing economic disparities since the early stages of development. This approach prevented the fragmentation of society along income lines. This social cohesion made it politically feasible to introduce supportive policies for lower-income groups, such as the minimum wage system and cash transfers to the bottom 40% (B40) of households.

Of course, as discussed later, Malaysia also exhibits negative path dependencies, whereby effective policies implemented at one income level manifest as adverse effects at subsequent stages. In such cases, it becomes imperative to rapidly adjust policies and implement new strategies appropriate for the changed economic circumstances. However, such policy shifts are often challenging to implement due to various political factors, including resistance from vested interests and societal divisions. While political factors hindering policy shifts certainly exist in Malaysia's case, the country has nonetheless successfully implemented bold policy transitions when necessary. What factors, then, enabled these successful policy transitions in Malaysia?

7.7 Elections are Necessary for Appropriate Policy Changes

As economic development advances, policy adjustments become essential to facilitate continued progress. In Malaysia's case, three major policy transitions have been implemented: (1) from laissez-faire to the New Economic Policy (from the 1970s to the early 1980s), (2) from prioritizing Malay support measures to emphasizing economic growth (from the late 1980s to the 1990s), and (3) from prioritizing economic growth to emphasizing equitable distribution (from the late 2000s). All of these transitions can be considered essential strategies to advance economic development during their respective periods.

These three shifts in economic policy were prompted by significant political developments. The ethnic riots following the 1969 election catalyzed the shift from laissez-faire to the New Economic Policy. Subsequently, competition for Malay votes in elections intensified Malay support measures, such as the implementation of rice price subsidies.

The transition from prioritizing Malay support measures to emphasizing economic growth was precipitated by the economic recession in the mid-1980s. After extensive debates between the ruling and opposition parties and within the ruling coalition, the policy crystallized into the national vision of becoming a developed country by 2020. This growth-oriented approach was solidified and accelerated by the ruling party's landslide victory in the 1995 election.

After the currency crisis and subsequent political turmoil, urban voters' interests shifted toward governance issues and intra-ethnic disparities. Consequently, the opposition made significant gains in the 2008 election by promising political reforms and implementation of inequality correction measures not based on ethnicity. To recapture the support of the urban middle class that it had lost, the government proactively implemented political liberalization measures, relaxed the Bumiputera policy, and introduced redistributive policies targeting the bottom 40% of households regardless of ethnicity. When this policy shift failed to restore public support, the government temporarily reverted to Malay nationalism and authoritarian tendencies. However, it ultimately lost public confidence due to corruption allegations against Prime Minister Najib and internal divisions within the ruling party, culminating in a historic change of government in the 2018 election.

The fundamental element that shaped these political developments and policy shifts was the functioning of elections. Although a change of government did not occur until the 2018 election, electoral voting patterns significantly influenced the direction of subsequent policies.

However, it should be noted that the first policy transition was precipitated by a dysfunctional electoral outcome. The 1969 election did not facilitate a peaceful policy transition but instead became a catalyst for violent expression of dissatisfaction with inter-ethnic disparities that had remained unaddressed under the laissez-faire economic policy. Subsequently, restrictions on civil liberties, particularly freedom of speech, were intensified, and Malaysia's political system evolved into a form that could no longer be classified as a full democracy.

Nevertheless, the maintenance of highly competitive elections enhanced the government's responsiveness to societal demands. Within this framework of competitive authoritarianism, while the government occasionally suppressed societal demands, it also remained attuned to public sentiment and implemented measures to secure political support.

Through this political dynamic, economic policies were adjusted in response to changing circumstances. Since the 2000s, as public interest in governance intensified, the political system has gradually evolved toward greater democratization, albeit through a non-linear process. This democratization process culminated in the historic change of government following the 2018 election. At the time of this election, institutional structures favorable to Barisan Nasional (BN), which had long dominated Malaysian politics, remained entrenched. Nevertheless, Pakatan Harapan (PH) led by Mahathir overcame these systemic disadvantages to achieve a remarkable victory. With this change of government, Malaysia can be considered to have achieved "democratization through elections."

7.8 Remaining Challenge 1: Negative Legacy of the New Economic Policy

The trajectory of Malaysia's economic development thus far and the diverse policies implemented to facilitate this development can be considered largely successful. Although not matching the extraordinary growth rates of Northeast Asian economies, Malaysia's achievement in steadily elevating its income level, even if gradually, to position itself on the threshold of high-income country status is commendable. Many of the diverse policies implemented to achieve this progress were strategically timed and have significantly contributed to the realization of sustainable economic development.

However, policies designed to address challenges at a specific stage of economic development can become impediments to further advancement at subsequent stages. In Malaysia's case, the implementation of the comprehensive New Economic Policy achieved remarkable success in industrialization, urbanization, poverty eradication, and narrowing of inter-ethnic disparities, but it simultaneously generated four significant structural problems. These are: (1) expansion of the public sector, (2) over-reliance on labor-intensive industries, (3) dependence of manufacturing on foreign capital, and (4) excessive preferential treatment of Bumiputeras, as illustrated in Fig. 7.1.

These four structural problems are deeply interrelated; when efforts are made to address one issue, another often intensifies, resulting in their persistence to the present day. For example, in response to the "expansion of the public sector," the Mahathir administration implemented privatization policies in the mid-1980s. However, this privatization initiative evolved into a mechanism for fostering Bumiputera entrepreneurs in the 1990s, thereby reinforcing the "preferential treatment of Bumiputeras." Subsequently, precipitated by the Asian Financial Crisis, the financial performance of privatized companies deteriorated significantly, forcing many to be re-nationalized and essentially returning the issue of public sector expansion to its starting point.

Regarding the "over-reliance on labor-intensive industries," the Mahathir administration established the Heavy Industries Corporation of Malaysia (HICOM) in the early 1980s to promote capital-intensive heavy industries. However, this initiative contributed to the "expansion of the public sector." Additionally, the selection of predominantly Japanese companies as technological partners inadvertently reinforced the "dependence of manufacturing on foreign capital."

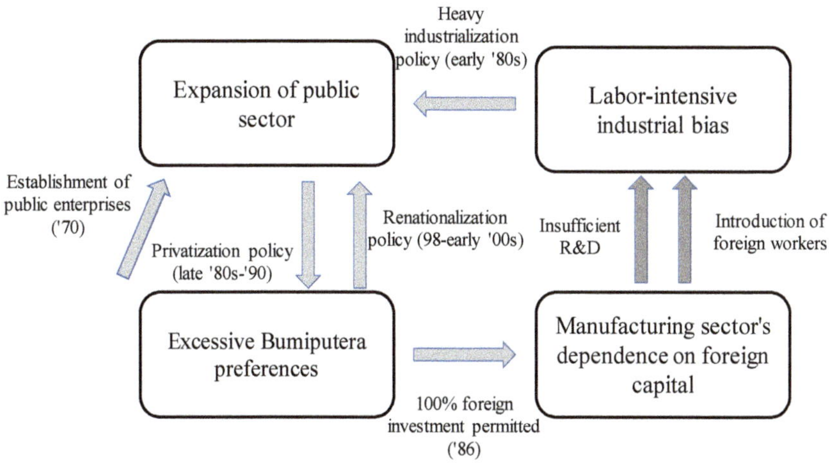

Fig. 7.1 Structural problems in the Malaysian economy generated by the new economic policy. *Source* Author's compilation

Furthermore, to overcome the economic recession in the mid-1980s, the Mahathir administration permitted 100% foreign ownership for export-oriented companies under specific conditions through the 1986 Promotion of Investments Act and relaxation of investment guidelines. This policy adjustment moderated the "preferential treatment of Bumiputeras" but significantly intensified the "dependence of manufacturing on foreign capital." Moreover, when labor shortages became evident in the 1990s, the large-scale admission of foreign workers contributed to the perpetuation of "over-reliance on labor-intensive industries." This trend was reinforced by persistent demands from foreign companies seeking access to less expensive labor resources.

The "dependence of manufacturing on foreign capital" facilitated Malaysia's integration into Global Value Chains (GVCs) but diminished its decision-making autonomy regarding which segments of these chains it would manage. Consequently, Malaysia often found itself restricted to low value-added segments within these global networks. As a result, despite the Malaysian government's implementation of various policies promoting industrial value enhancement, the economic structure characterized by "over-reliance on labor-intensive industries" persists, which is incongruous for a country with per capita national income exceeding $10,000.

These four structural challenges will likely persist as significant impediments to Malaysia's continued economic advancement even after it attains high-income country status. The Malaysian government attempted to address public sector expansion and reduce excessive preferential treatment of Bumiputeras through the GLC Reform Program initiated in the mid-2000s. However, this reform trajectory shifted following the 13th General Election in May 2013. The Malaysian government pivoted toward reinforcing preferential policies for Bumiputeras, who constituted the ruling party's core support base. In September 2013, Prime Minister Najib announced the

"Bumiputera Economic Empowerment Agenda," signaling a renewed commitment to expanding support measures for Bumiputeras. Under the Najib administration, pressure on GLCs intensified to comply with Bumiputera policies in employment and procurement, as well as to participate in infrastructure investments—partly in response to growing fiscal constraints.

Regarding Malaysia's GLCs, the government is likely to retain substantial ownership stakes for the foreseeable future. Reforms toward "re-privatization" that would significantly reduce government shareholdings appear improbable. The primary rationale for this continued government ownership is that Bumiputera policy implementation through GLC-centered approaches has proven commercially viable compared to alternative methods attempted thus far. However, the GLC Transportation Program concluded in 2015, and no successor initiative has been announced since then. Moreover, with regard to GLCs, persistent political pressure to appoint politicians to management positions has continued unabated, even following the governmental transitions of 2018 and 2020. If a significant number of politicians are appointed to GLC management positions, the operational efficiency achieved through previous GLC reforms could be seriously compromised. In 2021, under the Muhyiddin administration, a reform initiative for government-linked investment companies (GLICs) titled "Perkukuh Pelaburan Rakyat" was launched.[3] This policy prioritizes reforming GLICs, which function as shareholders, rather than focusing on individual GLCs. Notably, these GLICs include the Minister of Finance Incorporated (MoF Inc.), which was previously excluded from the GLC reform plan initiated in 2004. The effectiveness and scope of this reform initiative remain to be seen.

Meanwhile, the over-reliance on labor-intensive industries and dependence of manufacturing on foreign capital continue to mutually reinforce each other. However, as the third unbundling progresses in the global economy[4] and the costs of face-to-face communication continue to decline, opportunities for middle-income countries to attract global R&D centers of multinational corporations are expanding. Not all R&D activities conducted by multinational corporations are cutting-edge or require large numbers of elite researchers. There exists what might be termed "moderate" R&D that is more cost-effective to conduct in middle-income countries. Examples include design modifications to existing products or the development of derivative products. Such activities can provide employment opportunities for Malaysia's higher education graduates and could represent a critical first step for the country to ascend the global R&D value chain.

While dependence on foreign multinational corporations can contribute to the middle-income trap, paradoxically, these same entities may also hold the key to escaping it. Accumulating the knowledge and capabilities necessary to produce increasingly sophisticated products is essential for a country's continued economic growth.[5] Malaysia needs to formulate effective strategies for further industrial upgrading, carefully balancing both the advantages and limitations of its reliance on foreign multinational corporations.

7.9 Remaining Challenge 2: Consolidation of Democracy and Leadership

From a political perspective, Malaysia is currently confronting the fundamental challenge of how to ensure the sustainability of its democratic system.

Following the change of government in the 2018 election, significant institutional reforms aimed at revitalizing democratic governance were implemented in Malaysia. Specifically, these reforms included lowering the voting age (from 21 to 18), transforming the voter registration system (from voluntary to automatic registration), and implementing parliamentary system reforms (establishing departmental select committees to monitor each ministry). A proposal to limit the Prime Minister's tenure to two terms or a maximum of 10 years is also under consideration. Moreover, the suppression of speech through the Sedition Act, which was prevalent during the Second Najib Cabinet, has almost ceased. Additionally, the Anti-Fake News Act, which many feared could be misused as a tool for information control, has been abolished, strengthening the protection of civil liberties. In an era when "democratic recession" has become a global concern, Malaysia represents a relatively rare case of evolution from competitive authoritarianism toward a more robust democratic system.

However, significant challenges to political stability have emerged since the 2018 election. The Pakatan Harapan (PH) government led by Prime Minister Mahathir collapsed in less than 2 years after taking office. In February 2020, the dissenting factions of the Parti Pribumi Bersatu Malaysia (PPBM, or Malaysian United Indigenous Party) and Parti Keadilan Rakyat (PKR, or People's Justice Party) announced their withdrawal from the PH coalition. They subsequently formed a new coalition government with the former opposition Barisan Nasional (BN), Parti Islam Se-Malaysia (PAS, or Pan-Malaysian Islamic Party), and regional parties from Sarawak. This substantial reconfiguration of political alliances effectively constituted a change of government, as the composition of the ruling coalition changed fundamentally. This political realignment was spearheaded by Muhyiddin Yassin of PPBM, who subsequently became the new Prime Minister, and Azmin Ali, then the deputy president of PKR.

However, the new government led by Muhyiddin proved equally short-lived, and he was compelled to resign in August 2021. He failed to maintain parliamentary majority support following the defection of Ahmad Zahid Hamidi, the president of the United Malays National Organisation (UMNO), and other coalition partners. Following Muhyiddin's resignation, Ismail Sabri Yaakob, the UMNO vice-president, was appointed Prime Minister, but his administration also proved ephemeral, lasting only approximately 1 year. Under intense pressure from party president Zahid and others demanding an early general election, Prime Minister Ismail dissolved parliament in October 2022. This precipitated the 15th general election in November, which resulted in BN suffering significant electoral losses. In this pivotal election, no political coalition managed to secure an outright majority in the lower house of parliament. After intensive post-election coalition negotiations, an unprecedented alliance was formed between BN and PH—political entities that had been fierce adversaries as ruling and opposition parties until immediately before the election. Consequently, Anwar Ibrahim, the president of PKR and leader of PH, was appointed as Malaysia's 10th Prime Minister.[6]

Democratic governance cannot function effectively in an environment characterized by such political instability and extremely short-lived administrations. Fulfilling electoral commitments requires substantial time and institutional continuity. When an administration survives for merely a year, it cannot effectively implement even the budgetary initiatives it has formulated. This political volatility renders it impossible for governments to fulfill their accountability obligations adequately or to formulate and implement coherent policies responsive to long-term societal needs. To ensure Malaysia's democracy functions effectively and sustainably in the future, it is imperative to address three critical challenges: (1) the excessive fluidity of inter-party relations, (2) the deterioration of institutional governance, and (3) the deepening of social and political polarization.

The first challenge, the excessive fluidity of inter-party relations, constitutes the most significant factor contributing to governmental instability. Following the 2018 election, the fragmentation and realignment of political parties occurred repeatedly, precipitating multiple changes of Prime Ministers within a remarkably short timeframe. Fig. 7.2 illustrates the evolution of inter-party relations since the period preceding the 2018 election. BN, which held power until the 2018 election, was a complex coalition comprising 13 distinct political parties. After the electoral defeat, nine constituent parties, including regional parties from Sabah and Sarawak, abandoned the BN coalition, transforming Malaysia's political landscape from a relatively stable two-coalition system to a fragmented multi-party configuration. The four Sarawak-based parties that departed from BN subsequently established a new regional coalition called "Gabungan Parti Sarawak" (GPS, or Sarawak Parties Alliance). In February 2020, as mentioned earlier, PPBM left PH, led by Muhyiddin and others who aimed to seize power through coalition reshuffling, further advancing the multi-party system. Following this political realignment, PPBM, PAS, and Parti Gerakan Rakyat Malaysia (Gerakan, or Malaysian People's Movement Party) established a new political alliance called "Perikatan Nasional" (PN, or National Alliance). Concurrently in Sabah, PPBM and other regional parties in the state formed "Gabungan Rakyat Sabah" (GRS, or Sabah People's Coalition).

Within this fragmented multi-party environment, no single political coalition could secure an independent majority in the lower house, inevitably leading to increasingly fluid and opportunistic inter-party relations. As opportunities emerged for any party to potentially join a ruling coalition depending on various permutations of alliances, party leaders strategically maneuvered to align themselves with whichever faction offered the most advantageous position for acquiring and maintaining political power.

The most conspicuous demonstration of this political opportunism was exemplified by UMNO president Ahmad Zahid Hamidi. UMNO returned to power by forming an alliance with PPBM during the February 2020 political realignment; however, party president Zahid was conspicuously excluded from any ministerial

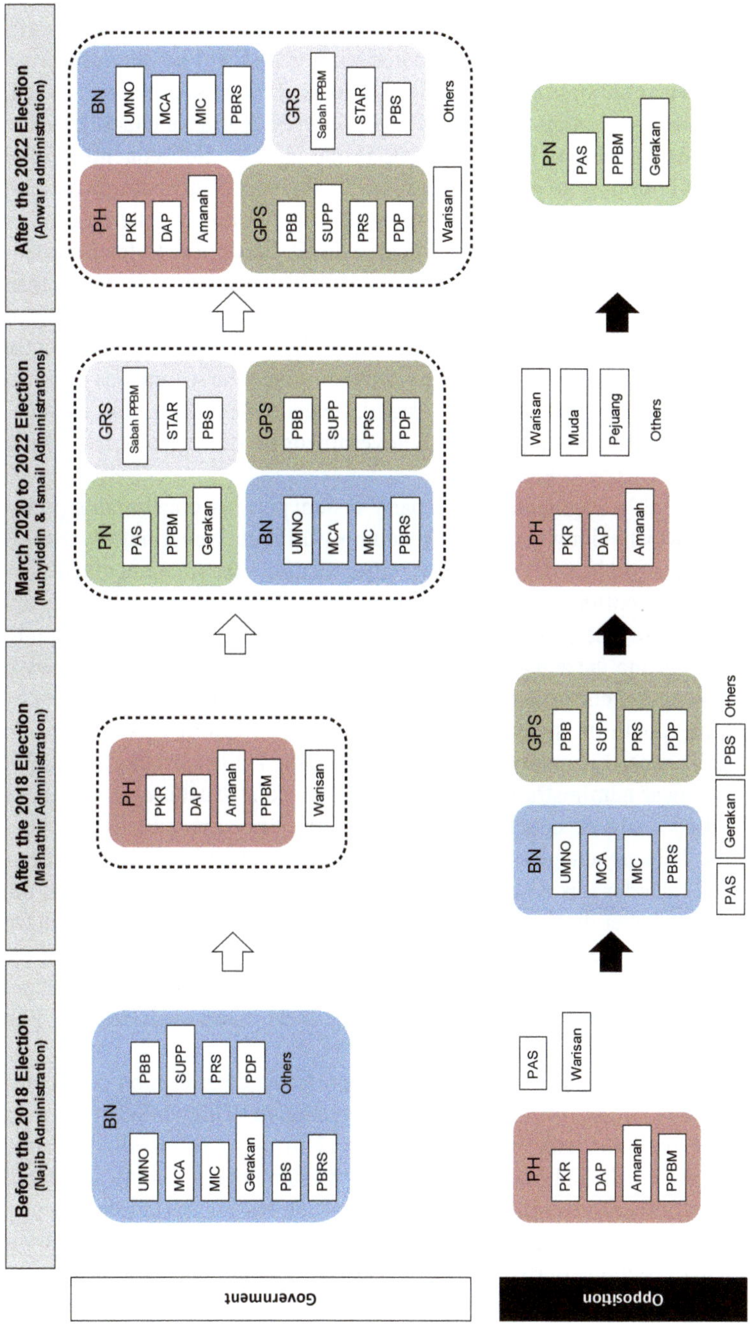

Fig. 7.2 Evolution of inter-party and coalition relationships. *Note* BN, PH, PN, GPS, and GRS represent political coalitions. All other entities are individual political parties. Dotted lines delineate members of the governing coalition. *Source* Compiled by the author

appointment. Zahid, effectively marginalized under the Muhyiddin administration, began negotiations to forge an alliance with opposition leader Anwar Ibrahim merely 6 months after the political realignment. Although this initiative failed to garner sufficient support within UMNO and did not materialize, Zahid and his faction subsequently expressed no confidence in Muhyiddin in August 2021, as previously noted. This strategic maneuver ultimately forced Muhyiddin's resignation and facilitated the appointment of UMNO's Ismail Sabri Yaakob as Prime Minister. Subsequently, Zahid and his supporters continued to publicly criticize PN, their nominal coalition partner, creating ongoing tensions within the governing alliance. Following the November 2022 general election, in a remarkable political reversal, they opted to form a coalition with PH—a political entity they had long regarded as an adversary—rather than renewing their alliance with PN. Anwar Ibrahim, the PKR president who ascended to the Prime Ministership through the unprecedented PH-BN coalition, subsequently appointed Zahid as Deputy Prime Minister—a move widely interpreted as political reciprocity. Although UMNO suffered substantial electoral losses in this election, Zahid adroitly secured a pivotal position in government by strategically navigating the fragmented multi-party landscape.

As long as this highly fragmented multi-party system persists, constraining politicians' opportunistic behavior will remain exceedingly difficult. Nevertheless, considering that Malaysia's ethnic and regional diversity constitutes the fundamental reason for the proliferation of political parties, a significant reduction in their number appears improbable. Therefore, the prospect of forming a stable government in the future hinges primarily on the capacity to establish durable and substantive cooperative relationships among the constituent parties of any ruling coalition.

The governing coalition supporting the Anwar administration, established in November 2022, primarily comprises four distinct political alliances: PH, BN, GPS, and GRS. The Anwar administration possesses a significant structural advantage in maintaining ruling coalition cohesion compared to the three preceding ephemeral administrations. This advantage derives from the anti-defection law formally legislated in July 2022. Under this new legal framework, legislators who defect from the party under whose banner they were elected automatically forfeit their parliamentary seats. The defection of the PKR dissident faction constituted a primary catalyst for the "change of government without an election" during the February 2020 political realignment. This significant legal amendment effectively deters such destabilizing political maneuvers.

The second critical challenge concerns the significant deterioration of institutional governance resulting from extensive political maneuvering aimed at forming and maintaining parliamentary majorities. Muhyiddin, who assumed the Prime Ministership following the February 2020 political realignment, promptly appointed himself chairman of the sovereign wealth fund Khazanah Nasional. He subsequently distributed chairmanship positions of numerous government-linked companies—including Tenaga Nasional Berhad (TNB), Prasarana (which operates urban railways), Federal Land Development Authority (FELDA), Majlis Amanah Rakyat (MARA), and UDA Holdings—to parliamentarians and executives from the ruling coalition parties. Takiyuddin Hassan (PAS Secretary-General), who was then serving as Minister in the Prime Minister's Department overseeing Parliamentary Affairs and Law, publicly declared that all backbenchers from the ruling coalition would receive management positions in GLCs. This policy was expeditiously implemented, as evidenced by the fact that all PPBM parliamentarians had secured various political appointments by July 2020.[7]

Following the 2022 election, newly appointed Prime Minister Anwar Ibrahim initiated governance reforms by removing GLC executives who had received political appointments under previous administrations. However, this action did not signify the complete elimination of political appointments to GLC management positions. Instead, BN and PH executives were systematically appointed to chairmanship positions at various GLCs,[8] essentially continuing the practice under different political alignments. Although implemented with greater subtlety than previous administrations, the practice of utilizing GLC executive positions as political resources for consolidating the Prime Minister's support base persists under the Anwar administration.

The Anwar administration also faces a significant challenge regarding Deputy Prime Minister Zahid, who serves as UMNO President. Zahid was a defendant in criminal proceedings involving charges of bribery, breach of trust, money laundering, and related offenses. Prior to the election, PH leadership vehemently criticized Zahid and his associates, labeling them "kleptocrats" and emphatically declaring that their return to power should be prevented. However, following the election, these same leaders formed political alliances with them and ceased their criticism. Although Zahid ultimately avoided legal consequences when a Discharge Not Amounting to an Acquittal (DNAA) was issued, this decision generated considerable public criticism. Consequently, questions about his conduct remain unresolved, and it cannot be definitively stated that the allegations have been cleared.

The third challenge, the intensification of political and social polarization, has manifested periodically as inter-party relationships have become increasingly unpredictable and opportunistic. This polarization became particularly pronounced when UMNO and PAS initiated a strategic alliance after BN lost power in the 2018 election. In response to reports that the incumbent PH administration was considering ratification of the International Convention on the Elimination of All Forms of Racial Discrimination (ICERD), both parties vehemently asserted that ICERD contravened the Malaysian constitution, which explicitly recognizes the "special position" of Bumiputeras. They subsequently mobilized approximately 100,000 demonstrators for a massive protest rally in Kuala Lumpur's city center. As a consequence of both parties deliberately leveraging ethnic sensitivities as a central political issue, the PH administration experienced a significant erosion of Malay support. According to a June 2019 public opinion survey, the administration's approval rating among ethnic Malays plummeted to a mere 32%.

Since that pivotal moment, a persistent pattern has emerged wherein both Prime Ministerial approval ratings and administration support levels demonstrate significant variations along ethnic lines. A May 2020 opinion poll, conducted merely 2 months after the inauguration of the Muhyiddin administration, revealed a stark ethnic divide:

the Prime Minister's approval rating among ethnic Malays reached an extraordinarily high 93%, while among ethnic Chinese, it registered a dramatically lower 26%.

This pattern of ethnically differentiated political support was further reinforced during the 2022 general election. In Peninsular Malaysia, where electoral competition evolved into a three-way contest between PH, PN, and BN, PH overwhelmingly dominated constituencies with lower proportions of Malay voters—specifically those with significant Chinese and Indian populations. Concurrently, PN secured victories in the majority of constituencies where ethnic Malays constitute an overwhelming demographic majority (Fig. 7.3). For the Anwar administration, securing broader political support in the northern and eastern regions of Peninsular Malaysia, where the ethnic Malay population proportion is predominantly high, represents a formidable strategic challenge.

The pivotal question facing Malaysia is whether it can effectively formulate and implement policies conducive to achieving high-income country status while simultaneously addressing these three fundamental political challenges. The ultimate success or failure of this endeavor will depend significantly on the leadership capabilities, political acumen, and consensus-building skills of key political figures, particularly the Prime Minister.

Former Prime Minister Mahathir Mohamad was instrumental in shaping and significantly influenced all three major policy transitions related to economic development analyzed throughout this book. Born in 1925, Mahathir emerged as an influential Malay nationalist youth leader within UMNO during the 1960s and became

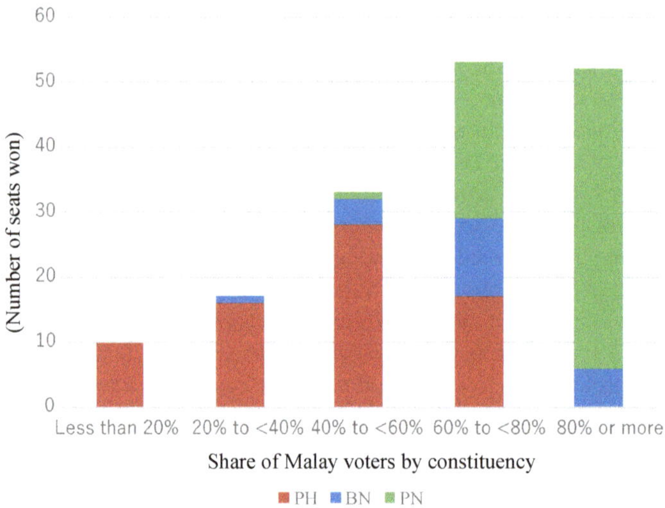

Fig. 7.3 Relationship between Malay population share in constituencies and seat distribution among three major political blocs in peninsular Malaysia (2022 General Election). *Source* Compiled based on Malaysian Government Gazette P.U. (B) 605/2022 to P.U. (B) 620/2022 and various media reports

one of the key architects who catalyzed the momentum toward the implementation of the New Economic Policy—the first significant policy transition.

Subsequently, the second major policy transition—from prioritizing Malay affirmative action to emphasizing broad-based economic growth—was strategically implemented during Mahathir's premiership. Mahathir, who assumed the premiership in 1981, actively pursued policies that attempted to achieve the delicate balance between economic growth imperatives and Malay socioeconomic advancement. In the mid-1980s, he resolutely implemented investment liberalization measures, effectively overcoming significant opposition within his own party. When these reforms demonstrated success and catalyzed substantial foreign investment inflows, generating unprecedented economic growth, he intensified this growth-oriented strategy by establishing the ambitious national vision of transforming Malaysia into a fully developed country by 2020. During the Asian Financial Crisis in the late 1990s, he astonished the international financial community by implementing policy measures that included the introduction of stringent capital controls and the adoption of a fixed exchange rate system. These controversial interventions ultimately facilitated a remarkable V-shaped economic recovery within a remarkably short timeframe.

After relinquishing the premiership at the age of 78 in 2003, Mahathir reasserted his Malay nationalist perspectives, publicly opposing both the Abdullah administration's and the first Najib administration's initiatives regarding political liberalization and modification of Bumiputera preferential policies. However, when substantial corruption allegations emerged against Najib, who had reverted to increasingly authoritarian governance and heightened Malay nationalist rhetoric following the 2013 election, Mahathir vigorously pursued these corruption charges. In a remarkable political realignment, he formed an alliance with his former political adversaries to achieve "democratization through elections." Following this unprecedented political transition, he appointed Lim Guan Eng—the Secretary-General of the predominantly Chinese Democratic Action Party (DAP) whom he had previously imprisoned during his earlier tenure—as Finance Minister. This historic appointment marked the first time in 44 years that an ethnic Chinese Malaysian had been given the crucial position of Finance Minister. The third major policy transition—from prioritizing economic growth to emphasizing equitable distribution of wealth regardless of ethnicity—was not initially championed by Mahathir. Nevertheless, by successfully challenging and ultimately defeating the Najib administration, Mahathir contributed significantly to sustaining and legitimizing this important policy direction.

Reviewing Mahathir's extensive political career reveals how he, as a uniquely pragmatic political figure, both personified and transcended the inherent policy tensions and political contradictions that characterized the longstanding BN governance system. He demonstrated remarkable political dexterity in balancing and advancing the seemingly contradictory policy objectives of maintaining Malay preferential treatment while simultaneously promoting robust economic growth—at times employing authoritative leadership approaches and at other times skillfully leveraging broad-based popular support.

For Malaysia to sustain and enhance its economic development trajectory in the coming decades, replicating the personalized political system characteristic of the Mahathir era may not be optimal or sustainable. To foster a dynamic society that facilitates creative destruction and cultivates sustainable innovation, Malaysia requires a more balanced political ecosystem without any single overwhelmingly dominant political entity. Malaysia now requires a more institutionalized form of leadership capable of maintaining sufficient governmental stability to implement effective economic policies, while simultaneously preserving democratic mechanisms that ensure peaceful political transitions and genuine electoral competitiveness. The next several years represent a critical juncture for Malaysia in determining whether it can successfully develop and consolidate a resilient, transparent, and institutionalized political system commensurate with its aspirations to achieve and sustain high-income country status.

Notes

1. "Canada ends contract with Malaysia's Supermax," Reuters, January 19, 2022.
2. "Malaysia's Top Glove says has resolved overcrowding at staff dormitories," Reuters, February 20, 2021.
3. "PM launches Perkukuh to reform Malaysia's GLICs," The Edge, August 12, 2021.
4. Baldwin (2016).
5. Felipe et al. (2012).
6. Nakamura (2023).
7. "PAS sec-gen: All MPs not holding gov't positions to be made GLC heads," Malaysiakini, April 12, 2020; "Bersatu's Sipitang MP appointed Felcra chair," Malaysiakini, July 29, 2020.
8. "Azeez appointed Keda chair, Syed Ibrahim heads MDEC," Malaysiakini, April 6, 2023.

References

Baldwin R (2016) The great convergence: information technology and the new globalization. Harvard University Press, Cambridge

Felipe J, Abdon A, Kumar U (2012) Tracking the middle-income trap: what is it, who is in it, and why? Working Paper No. 715, Levy Economics Institute of Bard College

Nakamura M (2023) The strange coalition of "reformists" and "thief politicians": 2022 Malaysian general election (Kaikakuha to Dorobō Seijika no Kimyōna Renritsu). IDE Square. http://hdl.handle.net/2344/00053559. Accessed 15 Jan 2023

Newspapers and Online Media

Malaysiakini

The Edge

GPSR Compliance
The European Union's (EU) General Product Safety Regulation (GPSR) is a set of rules that requires consumer products to be safe and our obligations to ensure this.

If you have any concerns about our products, you can contact us on

ProductSafety@springernature.com

In case Publisher is established outside the EU, the EU authorized representative is:

Springer Nature Customer Service Center GmbH
Europaplatz 3
69115 Heidelberg, Germany

www.ingramcontent.com/pod-product-compliance
Ingram Content Group UK Ltd.
Pitfield, Milton Keynes, MK11 3LW, UK
UKHW021614260926
475829UK00010B/57
* 9 7 8 9 8 1 9 5 6 8 9 8 7 *